JUSTICE AND MERCY

When the Holy One, blessed is He,
ascends His throne on the New Year,
He first sits on the Throne of
Judgment. But when Israel, assembled
in the synagogues, sounds the Shofar,
He rises from the Throne of Judgment
and ascends the Throne of Mercy.

Pesikta de Rav Kahana

MAX ARZT

JUSTICE AND MERCY:
COMMENTARY ON
THE LITURGY OF THE NEW YEAR
AND THE DAY OF ATONEMENT

HOLT, RINEHART AND WINSTON
New York · Chicago · San Francisco

Library of Congress Catalog Card Number: 63-11872

Designer: Jack Reich

80529-0223

Printed in the United States of America

FOR ESTHER

"And Esther obtained favor
in the sight of all them
that looked upon her."
Esther 2:15

PREFACE

This book is addressed to men and women who seek to understand the origin, history, and pervasive ideas of the liturgy of the High Holy Days. Because this liturgy includes almost all the standard prayers used throughout the year, the book also offers relevant information on the structure and content of many of the prayers recited on Sabbath, Festivals, and weekdays.

My guiding principle has been to respect the intellectual alertness of the reader. Therefore, I have not hesitated to confront the reader with the sources and source material on which I drew in the writing of this book. As a rule, however, more detailed and technical comments on a text follow a summary of the content of a prayer and an exposition of its contemporary meaning.

To facilitate the use of this book, each prayer and each significant part of a prayer is identified by its Hebrew key word. With the kind permission of the Prayer Book Press, I have used the translation of the *High Holiday Prayer Book*, edited by Morris Silverman, because it is in use in so many congregations. Where the Silverman edition paraphrases or condenses the original, I have given my own rendering, and in doing so, I have benefited greatly by consulting the *High Holyday Prayer Book*, edited by Philip Birnbaum, and the *High Holyday Prayer Book*, edited by Ben Zion Bokser (both published by the Hebrew Publishing Company of New York). While the commentary has been planned with a view to its being used as a companion book to the Silverman, Birnbaum, and Bokser editions of the *Mahzor*, it can serve the same purpose for other editions of the traditional High Holy Day liturgy.

Unless otherwise indicated, I have cited The Jewish Publication Society of America's 1917 translation of the Hebrew Scriptures, since, as of this date, only the Torah has been published of the new translation. I have, however, made use of the new Jewish Publication Society translation in the explanation of the sequence of the reading of the Torah for Yom Kippur morning. The translations of rabbinic texts are my own, unless otherwise indicated. Citations from the Palestinian Talmud are preceded by the mnemonic TP; and the pagination follows the Krotoshin edition. In the transliteration of Hebrew words, I have deviated from the technical rules wherever phonetic considerations necessitated such deviations.

In the preparation of this book I took advantage of my privileged association with scholars on the faculty of The Jewish Theological Seminary of America. I am abidingly grateful to Chancellor Louis Finkelstein who, for over two decades of my service at the Seminary, has consistently encouraged me; and to Professor Mordecai M. Kaplan, from whom I learned so much about methods of reinterpreting ancient texts. My gratitude to Professor Shalom Spiegel and to Professor Saul Lieberman for their patient perusal of the manuscript and for their innumerable insights and suggestions exceeds my power of expression. For the exposition of the fundamental rabbinic ideas which are embedded in the text and structure of the liturgy, I am indebted to Dr. Max Kadushin. However, I accept sole responsibility for whatever errors or shortcomings may be found in this book.

I am indebted to my devoted secretaries, Mrs. Mary Feinstein and Mrs. Dora Levine, who efficiently organized their office tasks to allow for the preparation of the manuscript, while I had to give priority to pressing administrative responsibilities at the Seminary.

Finally, I gratefully record the invaluable assistance given me by Mr. Arthur A. Cohen of Holt, Rinehart and Winston who, with his perspicacity and keen understanding of the task I had undertaken, stimulated me to enlarge the scope of the book, thus enhancing its usefulness.

Max Arzt

Nisan, 5723
April, 1963
The Jewish Theological Seminary of America
New York

CONTENTS

III THE DAY OF ATONEMENT (YOM KIPPUR)

THE LITURGY: AN INTRODUCTION

THE ANCIENT LITURGY
AND CONTEMPORARY MAN

Despite a gratifying increase in synagogue affiliation during recent decades, there seems to be no commensurate intensification of the impact of Judaism's basic religious teachings on the lives of modern Jews. At this moment, synagogue affiliation is primarily a means of satisfying a need for "Jewish togetherness" and of reacting to the current climate of opinion, which regards identification with "a belief" to be a requisite sign of social respectability. We need, however, to advance from affiliation to affirmation, from external compliance to inner conviction. Solomon Schechter, the great Anglo-American theologian, called our attention to the truism that one cannot love God with his father's heart. The contemporary Jew needs to be convinced that the basic insights of Judaism are, despite their antiquity, not antiquated, that their subject matter deals with his own hopes, with his moral dilemmas, and with his need for significant spiritual resources.

If our efforts for "turning the hearts of the children to their fathers" are to be fruitful, we shall have to bring our people closer to the Prayer Book. On the High Holy Days, the synagogues are filled to capacity, and in many congregations there are overflow services to accommodate the vast numbers for whom no seats would otherwise be available. These multitudes of worshipers hold in their hands a *Mahzor* containing the liturgy of Rosh Hashanah and Yom Kippur.

For many Jews, this is virtually the only Jewish religious book they ever read. Nevertheless, despite translations into elegant English, the *Mahzor* is, to most of these people, a "sealed book," whose grandeur and sublimity are by and large unapprehended. It would be in accord with sound pedagogic practice to make this book a vehicle for a more profound understanding of the basic teachings of Judaism. People would then learn that the Prayer Book, more than a source of nostalgic recollection, speaks to them about matters of importance and abiding significance. They would come to realize that the prayers,

though written in other ages and in the context of different times and circumstances, address themselves to the
perennial concerns of man. The prayers aim to effect in
us a transformation from an egocentric life activated by
the caprice of the moment, to a life inspired by an awareness of God the Father, King, and Judge.

The time is now ripe for the resumption of communication between the Jew and Judaism. Many morally sensitive people have become disillusioned with systems and
ideologies that sought to displace religion. Despite their
all-encompassing claims, the pretenders to religion's role
have failed to satisfy man's search for life's enduring
meaning.

Most audible among these claimants has been "scientism," the wayward offspring of science. Science has been
a great boon to mankind. It has made it plausible for us
to believe more firmly that many utopian objectives
contain within themselves the possibility of realization.
Science has already prolonged human life, subdued ravag-
ing diseases, performed miracles in communication and
transportation, and eased life's physical burdens through
countless labor-saving devices. Its spectacular successes
in nuclear research and in the exploration of outer
space serve to heighten our respect for the mind of man,
whom God has made "just a little lower than the angels."
More important, if not as dazzling, have been the ad-
vances made by scientific research into the "inner space"
of man's soul. Through such research, many of man's
subconscious impediments to genuine maturity have been
identified, and therapeutic treatments have been evolved.
But "scientism" drew unwarranted conclusions from what
had been so painstakingly accomplished by science. From
science's empire of facts, "scientism" deduced a law of
necessity which, though validated in the realm of the
physical, is irrelevant to the realm of the spirit. It is not
empirically true that an inexorable law of causality governs the inner life of man. When a human being exercises
his volition, he becomes a person capable of overcoming
circumstances that would otherwise make of him a mere
thing. A person is not a preconditioned, predetermined,
and prefabricated product of his biological and environmental antecedents. The quality of a person's character
is determined by his response to what happens, by his

ability to transcend and overcome "conditioning" circumstances. "Scientism" has tended to ignore the Divine
Being behind the physical fact and to deny the moral
autonomy and initiative which our awareness of that
Being confers upon us.

The first pretender to the role of religion, and the an-
cestor of modern scientism, was naturalism. It intrigued
men with its cheering dogma of inevitable progress and
with its deification of nature as the infallible guarantor
of human goodness. Blinded by man's capacity for progress, naturalism virtually ignored that which the Rabbis
had identified as the *yetzer hara,* the "evil impulse," and
which, they knew, needed to be sublimated, controlled,
and redirected. Such romantic optimism is now less prev-
alent. But the latter-day claimants to modern man's absolute loyalty were socialism and its imperialist derivative,
communism. These political movements attracted many,
for they were outlets for the expression of indignation
at the economic and social degradation of the masses.
Having magnified a partial truth into a scheme of human
salvation, they became, however, enemies of religion. Out
of the Marxist ideology of economic determinism was
forged an irreligious substitute for religious belief. The
opportunist and ruthless policies of the Communists,
their perverse pact with the Nazis, and their blatant repudiation of moral scruples resulted in a crushing disillu-
sionment with communism. Among the disillusioned
were many who had abandoned Judaism for communism, without realizing that their own passion for justice
was an essential attribute of the religion they had denied.

Each of the contemporary ideological claimants to
man's absolute loyalty and total commitment has had
its Jewish counterpart. Modern Jewish nationalism, for
one, served as a strong deterrent to assimilation, providing a temporary spiritual refuge for many whose religious
belief had been shaken in its collision with modernism.
It inspired the organization of the Zionist movement and
the transformation of Hebrew into a living language. It
was a prime factor in the historic miracle of the creation
of the State of Israel. But unless it strengthens its connection with its religious antecedents, Jewish nationalism
will not satisfy our personal need for spiritual truth, nor
will it supply a valid rationale for our continued per-

sistence as Jews in the Diaspora. The introduction into
the Israeli educational system of courses designed to instruct and deepen "Jewish consciousness" is an initial
attempt to infuse secular nationalism with sacred associations. Thus, even in Israel, where Jewish nationalism
has a natural habitat, there is need for a deeper understanding of the basic religious insights of Judaism, so
that these insights may become for us what they were for
our forebears, "a lamp for our feet and a light for our
path."

When, in the midst of the night, an angel attacked
Jacob and injured him, the patriarch would not release
his assailant until he had elicited a blessing from him.
The skeptical scrutiny to which Judaism has been subjected with the tools of scientific research has had its
salutary effects, despite the blows administered to traditional belief and behavior by such a testing.

This very spirit of free inquiry conferred a lasting
benediction upon the traditions it questioned. It liberated people from bigoted and imperialistic attitudes
toward other faiths, and taught them that religious plu-
ralism is not a lamentable pact of convenience, but a
glorious principle of the civilized community. Evidence
of this can be seen in the increasing willingness of people
of different religious traditions to co-operate with one
another, without demanding the dilution or submergence
of religious differences.

For an understanding of Judaism, the labors of the
school of *Jüdische Wissenschaft* (Science of Judaism) have
been particularly enlightening. Modern Jewish scholar-
ship has provided us with critical editions of classic Jewish texts and has traced the history and development of
the fundamental religious concepts which these texts
communicate. Because of these labors, we can, by a study
of the Jewish Prayer Book, hear more clearly the enduring truth in the archaic expression. Insights of great
profundity, which are to be found in the liturgy, can be
made to speak beyond the boundaries of their time and
the limitations of their pristine form.

There is an additional, equally compelling reason for
focusing more attention on the ideas inhering in the
Jewish liturgy. The liturgy is an indispensable source for

a true understanding of the essence of Judaism. The beliefs of Judaism have never been formulated into officially adopted propositions. Nor can these beliefs be sharply delineated amidst the diversity of views expressed in the talmudic literature. The Talmud embraces, as Max Kadushin has so convincingly proved, an organic system of value-concepts, "categories of significance," which are, by their very nature, not defined with precision. The creedal definitions offered by Saadyah, Maimonides, Albo, and other Jewish philosophers of the Middle Ages were ambitious endeavors to explain Jewish beliefs in Greek and Arabic philosophical categories. As such, they served their purpose in reaching and teaching the perplexed of their times. But these creedal formulations were never accepted as obligatory, because Judaism finds its truest expression in the continuing tradition of a living people, rather than in the logical formulations of the theologians.

The fact that Judaism is not subject to creedal formulation prompted Moses Mendelssohn and others to assert that Judaism is a religion with revealed laws but without dogmas. Solomon Schechter applied the scalpel to this definition by pointing out that according to it, the only dogma that Judaism teaches is that it has no dogmas. While its *halakhic* structure is Judaism's unique process and possession, this does not justify the glib opinion, often heard, that Judaism is a religion of deed and not of creed. Here again Schechter helps us when he says that while it is true that a person does not have to carry his backbone in front of him, he nevertheless must have a backbone. The system of sacred duties which makes of Judaism a "portable religion" is buttressed and sustained by certain convictions which transform the *Halakhah* into a sacred access to God. These convictions are embedded and expressed in our liturgy. In this special sense, Judaism can be said to be a "liturgical religion," for its fundamental beliefs are most clearly reflected in its liturgy. In his prayers, the Jew gave voice to his yearning for God, to his deep sense of moral accountability, to his ecstatic love for the Torah, and to his invincible faith in his people's rehabilitation in a peaceful world. It was the liturgy in word (prayer) and in act (*mitzvah*) which gave our forebears high hope in the face of despair, and perseverance in the midst of persecution.

An examination of the *Siddur* (Prayer Book) enables us to identify those beliefs which were primary in the religious life of our ancestors and to see in true perspective other beliefs which, though firmly held, were not the core of their spiritual life. Thus, the liturgy makes recurrent reference to God as King of the Universe and to the hope that His sovereignty would be accepted by all men. Every blessing uttered in the synagogue, and indeed on all occasions, refers to the idea of *Malkhut Shamayim* ("The Kingship of God"). It is this concept which is the dominating motif of the Rosh Hashanah liturgy. On the other hand, the belief in a hereafter, while just as firmly held (witness the blessing *Mehayyeh Hametim,* "He who revives the dead," in the *Amidah*), is otherwise infrequently mentioned in the liturgy—even the *Kaddish* fails to refer to the afterlife. It would be entirely wrong, however, to say that Judaism does not cling tenaciously to this belief. The affirmation of the dignity of the person and of God's justice evokes the belief in personal immortality. But this belief did not cause our forebears to defer their hopes to the consummation of the afterlife. It is indeed astonishing that a religion, for whose adherents the path through life was perilous, did not lapse into quietism and into a repudiation of this world. It is here on earth that Judaism envisions the realization of its hopes for Israel and for all humanity. In their prayers, our forebears found the courage to embrace life, to surmount its trials, and to persist in hoping for the day when all peoples "will form one band to perform God's will with a perfect heart." Because the Prayer Book reflects the beliefs about God, man, and the universe which are distinctive of historic Judaism, it is the most authentic source book for an understanding of the faith which animates it and the people that poured its spirit into it.

FORM AND FERVOR
IN JEWISH WORSHIP

We have said that Judaism is a liturgical religion in that its fundamental beliefs are embedded in its liturgy. It is a liturgical religion in still another sense. Its form of worship calls for the recitation of a fixed order of prayers at set times of the day.

In theory, Jewish law offers the individual considerable latitude for the insertion of personal petitions into the body of the *Shemoneh Esreh*—the eighteen blessings recited on weekdays. Rabbi Jonah Gerondi (d. Toledo, Spain, 1263) outlines the conditions which govern such interpolations: (1) The content of the interpolated prayer must be of the same theme as that of the blessing into which it is inserted. Thus, a personal prayer for health should be interpolated into the blessing *Refaenu* ("Heal us"), and one for sustenance into *Barekh Alenu* ("Prosper this year for us"). However, no limitation is placed on the nature and content of personal prayers inserted in the blessing *Shema Kolenu* ("Hear our prayer"). (2) The personal petition may be introduced by the reader, during the repetition of the *Amidah,* into the very text of a particular blessing, providing that it is worded in the first person plural, thereby constituting a prayer on behalf of the entire household of Israel. (3) The worshiper may, during the silent *Amidah,* word his petition in the first person singular, but he must first recite the entire standard text of the particular blessing and insert his petition just before the *Barukh Attah* ("Blessed art Thou") conclusion of the blessing (R. Jonah on Alfasi Ber. 22b).

The scholars of the Palestinian academies were more lenient than their Babylonian colleagues. They even encouraged variations in the wording of the text of the *Amidah* prayers, and insisted only on retaining the wording of the closing *Barukh Attah* blessing (TP Ber. 8a). Among the Genizah manuscripts discovered by Solomon Schechter were Palestinian versions of the *Shemoneh Esreh* dating from the ninth century, with many deviations from the standard text. In the section entitled "Poetry and *Piyyut,*" we shall see how the greater receptivity of the Palestinian authorities to textual interpolation encouraged gifted liturgical poets to compose their hymns and to introduce them into the body of the service.

In practice, however, the text of the liturgy was standardized for historic and doctrinal reasons. Already in talmudic times, the need for protecting the liturgy against the intrusion of doctrinal elements alien to the spirit of

Judaism placed restrictions on the introduction of textual improvisations. Later, in the times of the Geonim, the rise of Karaism, with its denial of the authority of the Talmud, necessitated the further consolidation of the liturgy. Written texts of the prayers were first used in the eighth century. Prior to that the prayers were recited from memory. When Amram Gaon (*ca.* 850 C.E.) and Saadyah Gaon (*ca.* 925 C.E.) wrote their respective liturgical works to define and protect the authenticity of the liturgy, they delineated and delimited the area of permissiveness. Amram Gaon, whose *Seder Rabbi Amram* is an important source for the study of the text and history of the liturgy, warns against any deviation from the text of the prayers as prescribed in the Babylonian Talmud, and even suggests that a reader who takes such liberties should be deposed. The tendency toward standardization was advanced among Palestinian Jews under the influence of Babylonian scholars who had emigrated to Palestine. Despite the latitude that seems to be reflected in the existence of over fifty different Jewish liturgical rites, the standard prayers in these versions are substantially the same, with only minor textual differences.

A standardized liturgy has the merit and advantage of establishing and maintaining among the worshipers a community of spirit and a sense of historic continuity. Jewish worship is essentially and deliberately communal in content and in spirit. Samuel, the Babylonian scholar of the third century, laid down the rule that when one prays for himself one should include the entire community (the *kelal*) in wording his prayer (Ber. 49b). There are only a few prayers in the standard liturgy which address God as "My God and the God of my fathers," rather than as "Our God and the God of our fathers." Of twelve prayers recorded in the Talmud as having been offered by their authors at the conclusion of the *Amidah,* only three are worded as purely individual prayers. One of them, *Elohai Netzor Leshoni Mera* ("O my God guard my tongue from evil"), is recited in our liturgy after each *Amidah.* All the others are worded in the first person plural. A preference for prayers that are corporate in spirit was explicitly expressed by Abaye, a Babylonian scholar of the fourth century. It had been suggested that at the start of a journey, one should pray as follows:

"May it be Thy will O Lord my God, to lead me in safety and to protect me from all danger." Abaye, reiterating the rule that one must always associate himself with the community, insisted on the plural wording: "May it be Thy will O Lord our God, to lead us in safety and to protect us from all danger" (Ber. 29b).

The corporate, community consciousness that pervades the standard Jewish liturgy intensified in the individual a feeling of identity with the destiny and hopes of his people. Yet, far from being thereby submerged, his self-awareness was deepened, his self-respect broadened, and his sense of accountability for his moral conduct was sharpened. Whether it was a prayer of gratitude, or the confession of sins, or a petition for relief from distress, the sense of community expressed in the tenor of the prayer was a help and not a hindrance to the individual. Viewing the present in the perspective of bygone centuries and in the light of Israel's hopes for future redemption, the Jew found in the prescribed prayers a homeland of the spirit and a perennial inspiration for purposeful living.

Abraham Joshua Heschel describes the community spirit of Jewish worship in these words:

Judaism is not only the adherence to particular doctrines and observances, but primarily living in the spiritual order of the Jewish people, the living *in* the Jews of the past and *with* the Jews of the present. Judaism is not only a certain quality in the souls of the individuals, but primarily the existence of the community of Israel. . . . What we do as individuals is a trivial episode; what we attain as Israel causes us to become a part of eternity.

The Jew does not stand alone before God; it is as a member of the community that he stands before God. Our relationship to Him is not as an I to a Thou, but as a We to a Thou.*

Judaism's predilection for a fixed order of worship necessitated a confrontation with the problem of *kavanah*—proper devotion on the part of the individual worshiper. Routine prayers tend to be recited by rote, and such worship can descend to the level of *keva*—a fixed and formal task performed without feeling. The cultivation and achievement of genuine devotion were

* Abraham Joshua Heschel, *Man's Quest for God* (New York: Charles Scribner's Sons, 1954), p. 45.

therefore a subject of frequent concern among the Rabbis. Prominent among the exhortations to a proper concentration in prayer is the advice given on his deathbed by Rabbi Eliezer ben Hyrcanus, to his students: "When you pray, know before Whom you stand" (Ber. 28b). In many synagogues these words are inscribed above the lectern to remind the reader of the indispensability of true inwardness in worship.

The Rabbis laid down rules for the cultivation and achievement of proper intention and intensity in prayers. The preferred place for prayer is the synagogue; and the proper hour, even for one who is confined to his home, is the time when the congregation is at worship (Ber. 8a). Wherever they find themselves, worshipers should face toward Jerusalem, in the direction of the site of the Temple and toward the place of the Holy of Holies (*Tosefta Ber.*, 3:16). Prayer should be offered only when one is in a proper frame of mind. The *Tosefta* (Ber. 3:21) states that one should not recite his prayers when in a mood of sadness, indolence, levity, or hilarity; nor should one engage in prayer immediately after an idle conversation or when possessed by a feeling of frivolity. One should recite his prayers only in a mood of *Simhah Shel Mitzvah* (literally: the joy of performing a religiously prescribed duty). Commenting on this quotation from the *Tosefta*, Rashi says that the psalms recited before the *Tefillah* serve to generate a feeling of exhilaration at the performance of a *mitzvah* (Ber. 31a). In earlier times, men of piety would sit in silence for an hour before prayer "that they might direct their heart toward God" (Mishnah Ber. 5:1). The father of Samuel deemed proper concentration in prayer to be so important that when he returned from a tiring journey, he would wait three days before reciting the *Tefillah* (Erub. 65a).

To induce devotion and yet to reduce excessive gesticulation, which might betray an ostentatious type of piety, the worshiper was bidden to bow the head and bend the knee only at the beginning and conclusion of the first blessing of the *Amidah* and at the beginning and conclusion of the blessing of *Modim*. One who bowed at any of the other blessings was to be instructed not to do so (*Tosefta Ber.*, 1:8). During the *Amidah* one must stand in an upright posture with his feet together, as did

the angels in Ezekiel's vision (Ber. 10b). At the conclusion
of the *Amidah,* while one recites *Oseh Shalom Bimero-
mav* ("May He who makes peace in His heavenly regions
bestow peace upon us and upon all Israel"), one recedes
three steps as one takes leave of the Divine Presence with
the salutation *Shalom* (Yoma 53b).

Among other rules of reverential etiquette pertaining
to prayer are these: It is deemed praiseworthy to walk to
the synagogue with a vigorous gait, but one should not
walk fast when leaving the synagogue (Ber. 6b). One
should not greet a friend with *Shalom* before one has
said his morning prayer (Ber. 14a). In the spirit of this
admonition, it was the practice among Provençal Jews
to greet any friend whom they would meet in the morning on their way to the synagogue, with the salutation
Tzafra tava lemar ("Good morning to you, Sir"), rather
than with *Shalom* (*Bet Yosef, Tur Orah Hayyim,* 89).

THE UNIVERSAL EMPHASIS
IN THE HIGH HOLY DAY LITURGY

Some years ago, a prominent Protestant clergyman offered the suggestion that Rosh Hashanah and Yom Kippur could very well be adopted as religious occasions for
people of all faiths. He was intrigued by the predominance of the theme of universalism in the Days of Awe.
Passover, Shavuot, and Sukkot convey their respective
messages of human freedom, of man's duty as a moral
being, and of the thanksgiving man owes to God, in the
context of the historic vicissitudes and experiences of the
ancient Israelites. Rosh Hashanah and Yom Kippur, however, are not related to any particular event in Israel's
past. They are, as Yehezkel Kaufmann characterizes them,
"cosmic holidays" linked with the hopes and the destiny
of mankind. The liturgy of Rosh Hashanah and Yom
Kippur is indeed suffused with a spirit of universalism.
The *Mahzor* characterizes Rosh Hashanah as "the birthday of the world" and continually reiterates the hope
that mankind may unite to perform God's will with a
perfect heart. The prayers declare Rosh Hashanah to be
a Day of Judgment on which the Ruler of the Universe
summons all men before His Tribunal of Justice. In the

heavenly Book of Records, the deeds of each person are inscribed and in that book is "the seal of every person's hand." Making proper allowance for the symbolic language employed, we can acknowledge the indisputable value of a periodic occasion for self-analysis and self-examination.

Although Rosh Hashanah is a Day of Judgment, it is not, however, to be regarded as a day of doom. Its efficacy as an opportunity for moral self-renewal is suggested in many rabbinic passages. The judgment day itself is fixed by man, and the outcome depends on man's initiative. This is the lesson that suggests itself by the following two rabbinic passages which were originally intended to validate the powers of the *Bet Din* (the authoritative court) to fix the calendar:

The angels asked the Holy One, blessed is He, "When is Rosh Hashanah?" Said He, "Ask not me. Let us go down to earth and ask the court on earth" (*Midrash Tehillim,* ed. Buber, p. 368).

How different Israel is! Ordinarily when the judge says, "The trial is today," and the accused says, "The trial is tomorrow," whose order is followed? The judge's of course. But not so is the case with the Holy One, blessed is He. When the *Bet Din* of the people decrees, "Today is Rosh Hashanah," the Holy One blessed is He, says to the ministering angels, "Set up the platform for holding court, summon the attorneys for the prosecution and the defence, for my children have declared that today is Rosh Hashanah." Should the *Bet Din* decide to postpone Rosh Hashanah until the following day, God says, "Set up the platform for holding court, summon the attorneys for the prosecution and the defence, for my children have decided to postpone Rosh Hashanah until tomorrow." Why [does God follow the decisions of the *Bet Din*]? Because, "It is a statute of Israel, an ordinance of the God of Jacob" (Ps. 81:5). Unless it is a statute of Israel, it cannot be a day of judgment by the God of Jacob (TP R. H. 57b).

SIDDUR AND *MAHZOR:*
THE UNITY AND VARIETY
OF THE LITURGY

The Prayer Book is designated by two words: *Siddur,* a word telescoping *Seder Tefillot* ("Order of prayers"), and

Mahzor, the literal meaning of which is "cycle." The former connotes a prayer book for year-round use in synagogue and home. Its contents include the *Amidah* prayers for the weekday, Sabbath, Festival, and High Holy Day services but not the *piyyutim* (see p. 21), which are the distinctive feature of the Festival and High Holy Day liturgies. The holiday *piyyutim,* together with the standard prayers, are contained in a *Mahzor*—a prayer book containing the liturgies for the yearly cycle of Holy Days and Festivals. Though a High Holy Day prayer book contains only part of the "cycle" of liturgies, it is nonetheless referred to as a *Mahzor.*

What is intriguing and even astonishing about Judaism's liturgy is that though it has over fifty different rites, they all contain a common core of standard prayers which gives them all an identifiable, though not identical, schematic structure. The basic unity among all the liturgical rites is the result of the authority enjoyed by the liturgical material in the Babylonian and Palestinian Talmuds. By the end of the Amoraic period (*ca.* 500 C.E.), the basic prayers had received their definite form and formulation. Though no formal prayer books were in use until the eighth century, Jews were avid in their desire to abide by the prayer rules and texts developed in the academies of Babylonia and Palestine.

The first major work aiming to avert unwarranted liturgical deviations was the *Seder R. Amram,* in which Amram Gaon (Babylonia, *ca.* 850 C.E.) offered the texts of the required prayers for all occasions and laid down the rules of synagogue and home worship. His *Seder* became the foundation of an entire group of liturgical rites known as the "Sephardic" rites. Almost a century later, Saadyah Gaon (*ca.* 925 C.E.) issued his *Siddur,* with the prayers translated into Arabic, containing characteristic elements of the liturgical practices current in Egypt. At the end of the second book of his *Mishneh Torah,* Moses Maimonides (1135-1204) gives the text and the sequence of the prayers for the entire year. His text also won acceptance among Sephardic communities. The Sephardic group of rites include those of Spain, North Africa, Majorca, Sicily, and Egypt. A second group of liturgical rites, the "Ashkenazic," prevails in Germany, Poland, Hungary, and in an overwhelming majority of congregations in England, France, North and South America. By and large, the Sephardic rituals were under the liturgical hegemony of the Babylonian scholars, while the Ashkenazic ritual is based on the decisions of Palestinian scholars. The Ashkenazic rite is anchored in *Mahzor Vitry,* a comprehensive compendium of liturgical sources composed by R. Simhah b. Samuel of Vitry, France (*ca.* 1100 C.E.).

We shall have occasion in the discussion of the origin of the *piyyutim* to see more clearly how the Jews, mankind's most widely scattered religious group, held together by no tangible organizational discipline, maintained their spiritual unity through the liturgy. This was due to their loyalty and reverence for the Talmud and to their intuitive conviction that those elements of the liturgy which obtained among all rites represented the authentic collective aspirations of all Jews through the ages and throughout the world.

POETRY AND *PIYYUT:* VARIETY AMID UNITY

The High Holy Day liturgy is studded with *piyyutim* (from the Greek *poem*), which were composed in many lands during a period of about one thousand years. These devotional offerings are similar in their schematic structure, but they vary in meter, style, and literary quality. Some convey their religious fervor with a luminous clarity of expression. Others obscure their meaning through cryptic homiletic allusions, which afforded generations of learned worshipers the additional pleasure of successfully identifying their sources.

The popularity of the *piyyutim* was so well established that Amram Gaon (*ca.* 850 C.E.) and other guardians of the liturgy took pains to point out the distinction between the purely voluntary, permissive nature of the *piyyutim* and the mandatory claims of such basic elements of the liturgy as the *Shema* and the *Amidah.* The *piyyutim* are built into the classic structure of the liturgy, a structure prescribed by talmudic law and sanctified by wide usage. They are inserted into the midst of the fundamental sections of the liturgy, at vulnerable points where their intrusion was deemed by many scholars to be contrary to rules laid down in the Mishnah and the other talmudic sources. As *yotzrot,* the *piyyutim* interrupt the carefully delineated regulations for the "reading" of the *Shema* and its accompanying benedictions (Mishnah Ber. 2:1). As *kerovot,* they invade the highly sensitive territory of the *Tefillah,* the solemn prayers first recited while the congregation is standing, and then repeated by the reader. The *Tefillah* calls for a devoutness which the Mishnah underscores in these words: "Even if the king greets him [during the *Tefillah*] he may not return the greeting; and even if a snake were twisted around his heel he may not interrupt his prayer" (Mishnah Ber. 5:1).

How, then, did the *piyyutim* wedge their way into the prescribed service? Scholars, in ancient and in modern times, offered an intriguing explanation of the circumstances that supposedly accounted for the interpolation of the *piyyutim* into what had become virtually a closed canon of worship. In the Middle Ages and in earlier Geonic times, authorities posited a theory which was considered sound even by some modern scholars. The theory may be designated as "the persecution hypothesis." It is mentioned in *Sefer Haittim,* a work of the twelfth century by Judah ben Barzillai of Barcelona. He refers to a tradition, already of long standing, that the *piyyutim* arose in a time of persecution when Jews had been forbidden by "an oppressive government" to study Torah. Accordingly, the Jewish authorities then introduced "the practice of mentioning in the course of prayers the laws of the Sabbath and Festivals and of exhorting the people regarding these laws by means of hymns, thanksgivings, rhymes, and *piyyutim.*" It is generally assumed that reference is here being made to the Persian persecutions that lasted from 450 to 589 C.E. An even earlier reference to the persecution theory is found in a Genizah fragment of a work written by Pirkoi ben Baboi and published by Louis Ginzberg. Pirkoi ben Baboi undertook to resume a campaign which had been vigorously waged by his teacher Yehudai Gaon (head of the Sura Academy from 760 to 764 C.E.) against the retention of *piyyutim* in the liturgy. He cites his teacher's opinion to the effect that the *piyyutim* had originated under circumstances when

Palestinian Jews were forbidden by hostile governmental authorities to recite the required prayers, such as the *Tefillah*. They were, however, according to Yehudai Gaon, permitted to gather in the synagogues on Sabbath mornings "to recite and sing *maamadot*. The *maamadot* were none other than the *piyyutim* which, he claimed, had temporarily replaced the authentic liturgy. Yehudai contended that the *piyyutim* were meant to replace the original liturgy only during the particular emergency. Pirkoi proceeds to argue that "since the Kingdom of Edom [Rome] has, by the grace of God, been destroyed and has been replaced by the more friendly Arabs who have lifted the oppressive restrictions, everything in the service now has to be said exactly as ordained by the sages of the Talmud."

The persecution to which R. Yehudai Gaon alluded is the injunction issued by Justinian in 553 C.E. against the teaching of *deuterosis,* the oral interpretation of the Torah. Scholars had therefore assumed that when Judaism "went underground," certain *piyyutim* replaced the prescribed liturgy and that other *piyyutim* of a more legalistic content served as a means of circumventing Justinian's prohibition against teaching the Oral Law.

In his penetrating analysis of the Pirkoi fragment, Louis Ginzberg calls into question the validity of the theory that the *piyyutim* actually originated as a consequence of persecutions. Though he does not rule out the possibility that they may have served a special purpose in times when Judaism had to go into hiding, he contends that the *piyyutim* were a natural outgrowth of the desire for liturgical creativity. In one sense, Pirkoi was right in his assertion that the *piyyutim* originated in Palestine, for the Palestinian Talmud is more receptive to the creation of such prayers and to their inclusion in the liturgy. Thus, the Palestinian Amora Rabbi Aha (4th century C.E.) asserts that in the recitation of the *Tefillah* one should introduce something new "every day" (TP Ber. 8a).

By the end of the talmudic period (6th century) the text of the basic liturgy had become more or less fixed. The canon of the liturgy had been closed in order to guard against the intrusion of the heretical notions of sects that thrived in Palestine during the two centuries immediately preceding and those immediately following the rise of Christianity. Since textual variations could no longer be introduced into the standard prayers, the *piyyutim* became the sole means of self-expression on the part of gifted liturgical poets. In interpolating their hymns into the standard liturgy, they felt that they were introducing the ingredient of novelty recommended by Rabbi Aha and other sages who had cautioned against an inflexible regimen of prayers.

A unique feature of the *piyyutim* is the manner in which they interpret the portion of the Torah prescribed for a particular occasion. With remarkable ingenuity they combine prayer and instruction by weaving diverse midrashic sources into a tapestry of poetic allusions, yielding lessons of endurance, comfort, and hope.

The earliest *piyyutim* antedated Justinian's decree. The first of the *payyetanim* (composers of *piyyutim*), Yose ben Yose, whose *Avodah* for Yom Kippur is included in Saadyah's *Siddur,* may have flourished as early as the fifth century. Yannai, a prolific composer of *piyyutim,* lived in Palestine about the year 550 C.E. For each Sabbath of the year he composed *kerovot* that were based on the pentateuchal portions of the triennial cycle. In 1919 Israel Davidson uncovered and delineated the elaborate schematic structure of Yannai's *kerovot.* Not all of Yannai's compositions have come down to us. Those that have thus far been reclaimed from the Genizah, some eight hundred, were published in 1938 by M. Zulay. Yannai's literary architecture served as the model for other poets through the centuries.

Yannai's pupil, Eleazar Kalir (or Killir), occupies a pre-eminent place in the *Mahzor.* His *kerovot* enjoyed widespread popularity, though they were frequently criticized for their novel grammatical forms and neologisms. Yose ben Yose, Yannai, and Kalir were among the earliest of the *payyetanim,* and as Palestinians they must have found encouragement in the leniency of the Palestinian rabbinical authorities toward new liturgical creations.

Not such was the case among Babylonian Jewry. The authorities of the Babylonian academies were obdurate in their objection to liturgical innovations. Professor Ginzberg made the significant observation that the Academy of Sura was always under the influence of the Palestinian Talmud, while the Academy of Pumbedita leaned heavily toward the decisions of the Babylonian Talmud. This fact is relevant to Pirkoi Ben Baboi's quotation of the statement made by his teacher, R. Yehudai Gaon. Pirkoi was interested in affirming the spiritual hegemony of the Babylonian authorities over the Palestinian Jews. He therefore argued that the *piyyutim*, which, according to his theory, had been tolerated as an emergency device, should not enjoy permanent immunity, since their retention would run counter to the opinions of the Babylonian authorities. But his efforts were of no avail. There arose even among Babylonian Jewry many *payyetanim* whose fervent hymns and skillfully worded embellishments of the regular liturgy were warmly received in all the communities. Israel Davidson, who devoted a lifetime to the classification and identification of extant *piyyutim*, lists in his monumental *Thesaurus of Mediaval Hebrew Poetry* over 34,000 hymns by some 3,000 authors!

Despite the sharp difference of opinion regarding the *piyyutim*, Judaism was spared the agonies of divisive liturgical sectarianism. The *piyyutim* did not constitute a threat to the essential liturgical consensus which governs the basic service in all synagogues. In their choice of *piyyutim* the various *Mahzorim* vary considerably from one another. But as for the standard prayers, they all conform to the fundamental specifications of the Talmud. In the words of Shalom Spiegel:

The standard prayers, the oldest nucleus of the liturgy, always and everywhere became the center of Jewish worship, a bond of union despite geographic dispersal and a bridge across the ages linking the present with the past. At the same time, each period and place was left free, if not encouraged, to speak its own mind in new compositions added to or inserted within the ancient prayers. . . . Within the larger brotherhood of Israel and the stock of prayers common to all generations, the medieval synagogue attempts and maintains both a contemporary note and regional differentiation.[*]

The *piyyutim* are an embellishment and extension of the classic prayers and are drawn from many sources in Talmud and Midrash. Like the basic liturgy, they reflect

[*] *The Jews, Their History, Culture and Religion*, ed. Louis Finkelstein (3d ed.; New York: Harper & Row, Publishers, 1960), p. 866.

a passionate yearning for messianic redemption from exile, an unshaken faith in God's justice and mercy in the face of a precarious existence, a love for the Torah, and a firm belief in Israel as the vehicle of God's revelation to mankind. Despite their differences in time, place, and authorship, the *piyyutim* exhibit a remarkable unanimity of aspiration and conviction.

THE NEW YEAR (ROSH HASHANAH)

ROSH HASHANAH: AN INTRODUCTION

The Mishnah, the oldest code of Jewish law, on which the vast and monumental structure of the Talmud has been erected, begins with the question, "From what time in the evening may the *Shema* be recited?" (Mishnah Ber. 1:1) In the discussion of this passage, there was formulated Judaism's practice of reckoning each day from sunset to sunset. Hence the opening service of Rosh Hashanah is the evening service. Like every other day, Rosh Hashanah has three basic services: *Maariv* (Evening Service), *Shaharit* (Morning Service), and *Minhah* (Afternoon Service). As on all major holidays, an additional (*Musaf*) service is added on Rosh Hashanah to celebrate and commemorate the practice prescribed in the Torah, of offering in the Temple special sacrifices in addition to the regular daily offering. These additional sacrifices are prescribed in Numbers 29:1-6 (see discussion, pp. 133-34).

Why Rosh Hashanah is observed for two days

All congregations the world over, except most (though not all) of those affiliated with Reform Judaism, observe Rosh Hashanah for two days. This was not always the case. In his book on the differences between the Jews of Babylonia and the Jews of Palestine, Mordecai Margalioth marshals massive and convincing evidence that until the 11th century the Jews of Palestine observed Rosh Hashanah for only one day (not to speak of the Festivals, each of which they still observe one day less than do the Jews in the Diaspora).* The midrashic compilation, *Pesikta de Rav Kahana*, which was composed in Palestine about the sixth century and which contains homilies for all holiday and special Sabbaths, includes a homily only for the Torah reading prescribed by the Mishnah for a one-day observance of Rosh Hashanah (Mishnah Meg. 3:5). Kalir, the Palestinian *payyetan* who flourished in the sixth century, composed only one *kerovah* (a set of poetic interpolations into the *Amidah*) for Rosh Hashanah. This is silent testimony that only one day of Rosh

* Mordecai Margalioth, *Hillukim Sheben Anshe Mizrah Ubene Erez Yisrael* (Jerusalem, 1938), p. 162.

Hashanah was observed. In fact, with the exception of some outlying parts of Palestine, the older communities in Palestine adhered to the one-day observance until the eleventh century, when Provençal Jews settled in Palestine and instituted the two-day observance of Rosh Hashanah.•

There is a historical reason behind the now universally recognized two-day observance of Rosh Hashanah and the observance of Passover, Shavuot, and Sukkot for an additional day in the Diaspora, though not in Palestine. Originally, the beginning of each Jewish month was fixed by observation of the new moon. On the 29th day of every month, witnesses would observe when the first crescent of the new moon appeared and would bring their testimony to the Priestly Court and then to the Sanhedrin, at Jerusalem (Mishnah R.H. 1:7). Later the Sanhedrin established its authority for determining the intercalation of the month should the crescent of the new moon appear too late. The Mishnah describes how, originally, as soon as the new moon was officially announced by the Nasi (president) of the Sanhedrin, communities in outlying sections of Palestine and Babylonia were so informed by means of fire signals progressively kindled from mountain to mountain (Mishnah R.H. 2:2-4). When the Samaritans flared such signals at the wrong times in order to confuse the people regarding the exact day of the holiday, the authorities adopted the practice of sending messengers to the distant communities to inform them of the precise day of the new moon. The messengers could not reach the distant Babylonian communities and some regions of Palestine on time. Hence those distant communities, being in doubt whether the new moon was to be observed on the one day or on the next, observed two days, to avoid possible violation of a biblically prescribed holiday. Even after the Jewish calendar was fixed by precise calculations (during the fifth century C.E.), the Jews outside of Palestine continued to observe an extra day for each festival "to continue the practice of their forebears" (Beza 4b), while the Jews of Palestine observed only the number of days prescribed in the Bible.

• *Ibid.*

We have seen how Provençal Jews, who settled in Palestine during the eleventh century, prevailed on Palestinian Jews to observe Rosh Hashanah for two days. The Babylonian Talmud considers both days to be equally binding, on the claim that the two days are "like one long day" (Beza 30b). So anxious were the later authorities to fuse the two days of Rosh Hashanah into "one long day" that they seriously raised the question of the propriety of reciting Sheheheyanu ("who kept us in life") in the Kiddush of the second eve of Rosh Hashanah. Inasmuch as the two days were considered "one long day," a Sheheheyanu recited also on the second eve of Rosh Hashanah would be a "blessing recited in vain" (berakhah levatalah). To obviate this difficulty, they advised the wearing of a new garment during the Kiddush on the second evening, or the eating of a new seasonal fruit so that the Sheheheyanu would be a prayer of gratitude for new apparel or for the eating of the season's new fruit for the first time.

Before entering on a more detailed discussion of the Shaharit and Musaf prayers of Rosh Hashanah, we will offer a schematic outline of the Maariv and Shaharit liturgies, with a brief explication of their various sections.

ORDER OF THE MAARIV (EVENING) SERVICE OF ROSH HASHANAH

The Maariv Service consists of five divisions:

I. Barekhu: The call to congregational worship
II. The Shema and its blessings
III. The Amidah: The prayer recited silently in standing posture
IV. The Kiddush: The "Sanctification" of the day over the wine
V. Alenu: The prayer for the universal acceptance of God's sovereignty

Here is a brief description of each division:

I. Barekhu ("Bless ye the Lord who is to be praised")

This is the call to public worship to which the congregation responds: "Praised be the Lord who is blessed for all eternity." The presence of at least ten male adults is thus celebrated as an opportunity for worshiping God in and with the congregation (see p. 47).

II. The *Shema* and its blessings

The Mishnah (Ber. 1:4) stipulates that in the evening the reading of the *Shema* is to be preceded by two blessings and followed by two blessings.*

The two blessings before the *Shema* are:

1. *Hamaariv Aravim* ("Who brings on the evening twilight")

In the recurring cycle of day and night we see evidence of the Creator's design and wisdom. But man himself is more than just another phenomenon of nature. Though a part of nature, there is embedded in him a divine element, the image of God. This belief served to free man from the practice of magic whereby he endeavored to cajole the blind and capricious forces that were believed to determine his fate. When man seeks to relate himself to nature's Creator, he asserts the essential element of his humanity. In this prayer, we first render praise to God, the Author of nature, and then express the hope that our life may be lived under His sovereignty: "O Eternal, do Thou reign over us forever and ever."

2. *Ahavat Olam* ("With everlasting love")

We express our gratitude for the gift of the Torah and its commandments. In having been taught the ways of life ordained in the Torah, we deem ourselves to be the recipients of God's abundant love, for the Torah and the commandments are "our life and the length of our days."

For the discussion of the text of the Shema, *see pp. 67-79.*

The two blessings after the *Shema* are:

* For the morning, the Mishnah prescribes two blessings before the *Shema* and one blessing after it. The total of seven blessings for the *Shema* of the morning and the evening inspires R. Joshua b. Levi to invoke the verse, "Seven times a day do I praise Thee because of Thy righteous ordinances" (Ps. 119:164; TP Ber. 3c).

1. *Emet Veemunah* ("True and certain it is")

This prayer, in recollection of the exodus from Egypt, parallels *Emet Veyatziv* ("True and abiding"), a prayer of similar content, which follows the *Shema* in the morning service. Because it ends with *goal Yisrael* ("who redeemed Israel"), it is liturgically designated as *Geulah* (prayer of redemption) (See pp. 81-82).

2. *Hashkivenu* ("Grant that we lie down in peace")

Worry has been defined as the act of borrowing trouble from the future for present-day consumption; and courage has been defined as the act of borrowing hope from the future for present-day consumption. *Hashkivenu* is a prayer for Divine protection against the perils and fears of the unknown tomorrow. One of the by-products of religious faith is the hopeful outlook described by Isaiah: "The mind stayed on Thee, Thou keepest in perfect peace because it trusteth in Thee" (Isa. 26:3).

This blessing closes with: "Blessed art Thou O Lord . . . who spreads a canopy of peace over us, over all His people Israel, and over Jerusalem."

Tikeu Bahodesh Shofar

Intermediate between the *Shema* and the *Amidah* and after the *Hashkivenu,* we recite two verses from the Psalms: "Blow the *shofar* [horn] on the new moon, at the full moon [*bakeseh*] for our feast-day. For it is a statute for Israel, an ordinance of the God of Jacob" (Ps. 81:4-5).

The first verse refers to the sounding of the *shofar* on the new moon (Rosh Hashanah) and to its sounding again on the full moon, the fifteenth of the month, when Sukkot is celebrated. On both occasions it was sounded during the sacrificial rites, in conformance with the Torah's provision: "Also in the days of your gladness, and in your appointed seasons, and in your new moons, ye shall blow with the trumpets over your burnt-offerings, and over the sacrifices of your peace-offerings" (Num. 10:10).

The Rabbis, however, apply the two verses solely to Rosh Hashanah. Into the word *keseh,* which suggests the meaning "hidden," the Rabbis read a reference to Rosh Hashanah, which occurs on the first day of the month when the moon "hides itself" (R. H. 8b).

The second verse, "For it is a statute for Israel, an ordinance of the God of Jacob," is likewise given an interpretation relevant to Rosh Hashanah: "When it is a law (*hok*) for Israel, it is a judgment (*mishpat*) for the God of Jacob. Israel first sets the date of Rosh Hashanah and only then God ascends the Throne of Judgment" (R.H. 8b).

This midrashic interpretation suggests this insight: Our spiritual life is enhanced on Rosh Hashanah only to the degree to which we observe the day not as a calendar occasion, but as a momentous day dedicated to the contemplation of the most sublime purposes of human life and to an honest self-appraisal, as we submit our lives to God's judgment.

Hatzi Kaddish

To mark the conclusion of the *Shema* portion of the evening service, the partial *Kaddish* (*Hatzi Kaddish*) is here recited. The reader begins the *Kaddish* by a summons to the congregation to declare the greatness and grandeur of God in the world which He created. He voices the hope that soon, in our lifetime, the Kingship of God may be further extended and more widely accepted.

The congregation responds, "May God's name be praised forever and to all eternity," which is followed by the ecstatic declaration of the reader that God's name is to be praised and extolled above and beyond (*leela, leela*) any praises that are within man's capacity to utter.

The human incapacity for giving adequate expression to the praise of God inspired this homiletical rendering of a verse in the Psalms: "To Thee silence is praise" (65:2). Commenting on this and other passages, which praise the eloquence of such silence, Abraham Joshua Heschel says: "In a sense, our liturgy is a higher form of silence. It is pervaded by an awed sense of the grandeur of God which resists description and surpasses all expression. The individual is silent. He does not bring forth his own words. His saying the consecrated words is in essence an act of listening to what they convey. *The spirit of Israel speaks, the self is silent.*" •

• Heschel, *Man's Quest for God*, p. 44.

III. The *Amidah*

The use of the word *Amidah* (standing) is post-talmudic. In the Mishnah, the *Amidah* is designated as *Tefillah* (prayer), since it is the prayer par excellence, the recitation of which was deemed to be a religious obligation, though there was a difference of opinion about the obligatory nature of the evening *Tefillah* (see p. 34).

The Rabbis traced the origin of the thrice-daily recitation of the *Amidah* to the patriarchs. They said that Abraham originated the *Tefillah* of the *Shaharit;* Isaac the *Tefillah* of the *Minhah;* and Jacob the *Tefillah* of the *Maariv.* The hours of the day when these prayers are offered were said by the Rabbis to conform with the hours when the regular daily sacrifices were offered in the Temple (Ber. 26b).

The Seven Blessings of the Rosh Hashanah *Amidah*

The *Amidah* of the weekdays originally consisted of eighteen blessings and is therefore designated in the Mishnah (Ber. 4:3) as *Shemoneh Esreh* ("Eighteen"). On Sabbaths and holidays the *Amidah* consists of only seven blessings: the first three and the last three blessings are the same as the first three and last blessings of the "Eighteen." The middle blessings of the weekday *Amidah* are omitted on Sabbaths and holidays because they refer to the needs and concerns of the individual and the community, mention of which is deemed to be disturbing to the serene spirit of the Sabbath, the Festivals, and the High Holy Days.

The fourth, or middle, blessing of the Rosh Hashanah *Amidah* is called *Kedushat Hayom* ("Sanctification of the Day"), and its various elements are climaxed by a magnificent prayer, "Reign over all the universe in Thy glory," which gives exalted expression to the hope that all mankind would join Israel in acclaiming the Kingship of God.

Interpolations in the *Amidah*

The first three blessings receive their special High Holy Day adornment through the interpolation of *Zakhrenu*

Lehayyim ("Remember us unto life O King who delightest in life and inscribe us in the Book of Life . . .") into the first blessing; *Mi Kamokha Av Harahamin,* etc. ("Who may be compared to Thee, Father of mercy, Who in love rememberest Thy creatures unto life?) into the second blessing; and of three short paragraphs, each beginning with *Uvekhen,* into the third blessing: "Blessed art Thou, O Lord the holy King." The reference to God as "the holy King," a fitting change from the usual text "the holy God," emphasizes the thought that on the Holy Days God's Kingship manifests itself, in that all His creatures pass in judgment before Him. On Saturday night, there is inserted in the fourth blessing a *Havdalah* (separation) prayer, which speaks of the difference in the degree of sanctity between the Sabbath, which now departs, and the Holy Day, the Sabbath being of a higher degree of sanctity. Another insertion in the fourth blessing is the familiar *Yaaleh Veyavo* ("May our remembrance . . . come before Thee"), which makes specific reference to the hope that the people of Israel would be remembered "for deliverance and well-being on this Day of Remembrance."

Into the last two blessings there are interpolated two brief supplications: "O inscribe all the children of Thy covenant for a happy life," and "In the book of life, blessing, and peace, may we be remembered and inscribed before Thee . . ."

Since the *Amidah* of the *Maariv* is the same as that of the *Shaharit,* the detailed discussion of these prayers will be found in the *Shaharit* section (pp. 82-116). Here we shall outline only briefly the order and content of the seven blessings:

1. *Avot* ("Fathers")

We address God as "The God of our fathers, the God of Abraham, the God of Isaac, and the God of Jacob."

2. *Gevurot* ("Powers")

God's omnipotence is extolled. He is the Healer of the sick, Sustainer of the living, Redeemer of the oppressed, and the Decreer of life and death.

3. *Kedushat Hashem* ("Sanctification of the Name")

We refer to the celestial holy beings whom we on earth join in the praise of the Creator.

4. *Kedushat Hayom* ("Sanctification of the Day")

We speak of the privilege which is Israel's, to have been the first to proclaim the Kingship of God, and of the hope that all mankind may join us in recognizing God's sovereignty.

5. *Avodah* ("Worship")

We pray that the worship of our lips be favorably received, and that the Temple service be re-established at Jerusalem, its restoration being the prophetically promised event climaxing the redemption of Israel in a world at peace.

6. *Hodaah* ("Thanksgiving")

We offer thanks for the extraordinary blessings of life and love which are the "daily miracles" bestowed on us by God's beneficence.

7. *Berakhah* ("Benediction")

We pray that there descend on us the blessings of God's protection, favor, and peace, as expressed in the threefold benediction anciently offered by the priests in the Temple.

Elohai Netzor ("O God, Guard . . .")

When recited silently by the congregation, the *Amidah* closes with *Elohai Netzor* ("O my God, guard my tongue from evil"). This prayer of personal petition, by the fifth-century Babylonian sage Mar bar Rabina, is one of several such supplications suggested as fitting conclusions to the individual's recitation of the *Amidah* (Ber. 16b-17a).

"May the words of my mouth"

In the enumeration of the Psalms, some Rabbis considered Psalms 1 and 2 to be one psalm; others considered Psalms 9 and 10 to be one psalm. In either case the

present Psalm 19 was actually Psalm 18. The last verse
of that psalm is: "May the words of my mouth and the
meditation of my heart be acceptable before Thee, O
Lord, my Rock, and my Redeemer" (Ps. 19:15). The suggestion is therefore made that for this reason the same
verse which concludes the 18th Psalm also concludes the
Eighteen Blessings (Ber. 9b).

Why the *Maariv Amidah* is not repeated

The repetition of the *Amidah* by the reader aims to
enable those in the congregation who are not familiar
with the prayers to fulfill their liturgical obligations by
listening to the reader as he recites the prayers and by responding "Amen" after each blessing (see pp. 82). Why,
then, does the reader not repeat the *Amidah* of the
Maariv? The reason is that the recitation of the evening
Tefillah was deemed by some sages to be a permissive
rather than a mandatory duty (Ber. 27b).

Vayekhullu ("*And the heaven and the earth were fin-
ished*") and *Magen Avot* ("Shield of our Fathers")

When Rosh Hashanah occurs on a Sabbath eve, a short
form of the *Amidah* is recited by the reader immediately
after the silent *Amidah*. This abridged prayer consists of
Vayekhullu (Gen. 2:1-3) and a short form of the *Avot*
blessings, of which *Magen Avot* is a part. This, in turn, is
followed by *Retzeh Bimenuhatenu* ("Our God and God
of our fathers, accept our rest"), which is the *Kedushat
Hayom* ("Sanctification of the Day") of the regular Sabbath *Amidah*.

We have already said that the reader does not repeat
the evening *Amidah*. The abridged repetition of the Sabbath eve *Amidah* was instituted, not to imply that the saying of the *Amidah* was mandatory, but for an entirely
different reason. In talmudic days it was not customary
for people to say their evening prayers in the synagogue
at all on weekdays, since the synagogues were located on
the outskirts of the towns. They did, however, attend
synagogue on Sabbath eve. Inasmuch as those who lived
at a distance would come late, the service was prolonged
for their sake, through the addition of the abbreviated,
Sabbath *Amidah*. The congregation would thus be kept
waiting in the synagogue for late arrivals, that they might

leave together, so that no harm could befall them. (Shab. 24b; *see also* Rashi on *sakkanah* ad locum).• It is interesting to note that *Magen Avot* is not recited on the first evening of Passover when it occurs on a Sabbath, because on the first night of Passover, Israel is considered to have special divine protection, by virtue of the Passover night being a *lel shimmurim* ("night of vigil") when God Himself shields His people from danger (Exod. 12:42).

Magen Avot ends with: *mekaddesh hashabbat* ("who sanctifies the Sabbath") and makes no reference to the holiday. The reason given in the Talmud is that as the abridged *Amidah* is occasioned by the Sabbath, it properly makes reference only to the Sabbath (Shab. 24b).

Kaddish Titkabbal ("May Israel's prayers be accepted")

To mark the formal end of the *Amidah*, a *Kaddish* is here recited which includes a paragraph that opens with the phrase, "May the prayers and supplications of the house of Israel be accepted." The word for "accepted" is *titkabbal*. Hence this particular *Kaddish* is called *Kaddish Titkabbal*.

It is assumed by authorities of the history of the liturgy that the recitation of the *Kaddish* was originally instituted at the end of a period of Torah study, and that it later came to be recited at the end of a formal service. The main theme of the *Kaddish* is the hope for the speedy coming of the Messiah, when the Kingship of God would be universally recognized. It is regarded as Israel's special merit that through its prayers and through its study of the Torah (which in the *Kaddish* evoke the response, "May the name of God be praised forever and to all eternity") the Kingship of God is advanced. In the light of this we can appreciate the pathos expressed in this talmudic passage:

Every time Israel enters its houses of prayer and study and utters the response, "May the name of God be praised forever and to all eternity," the Holy One, blessed is He, nods His head and says, "Happy was the King when such praise was rendered Him in His own abode [the Temple]. Why did I exile My children? Sad indeed is the plight of My children who were exiled from their Father's table" (Ber. 3a).

• For a more detailed discussion of the origin of *Magen Avot*, see Saul Lieberman, *Tosefta Ki-Fshutah, Zeraim*, p. 34.

IV. The *Kiddush* (The "Sanctification" over the wine)

The recitation of the *Kiddush* over the wine really belongs to the home. The rule established by the Babylonian scholar Samuel (3rd century C.E.) is, "*Kiddush* should be recited at the time and place where the meal is eaten" (Pes. 101a). However, the recitation of the *Kiddush*, which according to some authorities originated in the synagogue, was continued there despite the rule formulated by Samuel. The reason was to enable travelers who were housed by the synagogue to hear the *Kiddush* (*ibid.*). When Rosh Hashanah occurs on a Saturday night, the *Kiddush* also includes a *Havdalah* prayer in recognition of the termination of the Sabbath. As at the beginning of all holidays, the *Kiddush* ends with the blessing *Sheheheyanu* ("Who has kept us in life"), in gratitude to God who sustained us in life and enabled us to observe this significant occasion.

In the Rosh Hashanah *Kiddush* the concluding blessing is: "Blessed art Thou . . . King of the Universe, who sanctifies [the Sabbath], Israel, and the Day of Remembrance (*Yom Hazikkaron*)." For the reason for the order in which the Sabbath, Israel, and the Day of Remembrance are here mentioned, see p. 111.

A distinctive phrase in the *Kiddush*, which occurs also in the *Kedushat Hayom* ("Sanctification of the Day"), is *udevarekha emet vekayyam laad* ("Thy word is true and stands forever"). For the significant thought to which this alludes, see p. 111.

V. *Alenu* ("Let us adore the Lord of all")

As will be seen later (pp. 180-81), this prayer originated as an introduction to the Kingship prayers of Rosh Hashanah, but because of its sublime tone and content, it was incorporated into the daily service.

Adonai Ori ("The Lord is my light")

Psalm 27 is read during the entire month of Elul and through the High Holy Day period until the holiday of Shemini Atzeret. The *Midrash Tehillim* associates the first verse with Rosh Hashanah and Yom Kippur through this interpretation: "The Lord is my light and my salvation" (Ps. 27:1). "The Lord is my light" alludes to Rosh

Hashanah, which is the Day of Judgment as Scripture says: "And He will make thy righteousness [vindication] to go forth as the light and thy right [judgment] as the noonday" (Ps. 37:6); "and my salvation" alludes to Yom Kippur, when we pray that God may come to our help and forgive our sins" (*Midrash Tehillim,* ed. S. Buber, p. 224).

The Mourner's *Kaddish*

This doxology of the *Kaddish* which, as we have seen, is chanted at the end of a service, is also recited by mourners after *Alenu* and after the recitation of a psalm. It has no reference to death, but it is nonetheless relevant as a mourner's prayer. It affirms the enduring significance of human life when it is dedicated to the sanctification of the Name of God. Originally, mourners recited the *Kaddish* during their *Shivah* (seven) days of mourning after a period of study.

Yigdal ("Praised and adored be the living God") and *Adon Olam* ("Eternal Lord")

A medieval poem, which is assumed by scholars to have been composed by Daniel ben Judah Dayyan (Rome, 14th century), *Yigdal* summarizes the Thirteen Articles of Judaism's Creed formulated by Moses Maimonides in his commentary on the tenth chapter of the Mishnah Sanhedrin. Originally, *Yigdal* was recited only at the beginning of the service, and it is still included at that point in the daily prayer book. It gradually became a favorite closing hymn, alternating with *Adon Olam* ("Eternal Lord"), which gives exquisite poetic expression to man's quest for the living God. Originally, *Adon Olam* was read only on Yom Kippur, but it appears in many manuscripts at the very beginning of the daily service. In printed editions of the Prayer Book, it now appears with *Yigdal* at the very beginning of the service. It is customary in most synagogues to recite *Yigdal* as the closing hymn of the evening service and *Adon Olam* as the closing hymn of the morning service. The authorship of *Adon Olam* is unknown.

ORDER OF THE *SHAHARIT* (MORNING) SERVICE OF ROSH HASHANAH

The *Shaharit* Service consists of four main divisions:

I. *Birkhot Hashahar* ("Morning Blessings")
II. *Pesuke de-Zimra* ("Verses of Praise")
III. The *Shema* and its blessings
IV. The *Amidah*

Here is a brief description of each division:

I. *Birkhot Hashahar*

Preliminary prayers and blessings, in which the individual, upon rising, expresses gratitude for the renewal of his mental and physical capacities. This section also contains a token fulfillment of the obligation to study Torah, by means of brief selections from the Bible and the Talmud. There is also an abbreviated reading of the *Shema* at this earlier part of the service—fulfilling the requirement that the morning *Shema* be recited not later than the third hour after sunrise (Mishnah Ber. 1:2).

II. *Pesuke de-Zimra* ("Verses of Praise")

Psalms and other passages from the Bible, in praise of God. The selections include *Ashre* (Ps. 145) and the psalms which follow it, to the very end of the Book of Psalms. The antiquity of this part of the *Pesuke de-Zimra* can be seen from the prayer of Rabbi Jose ben Halafta (Palestine, 2nd century C.E.): "May my portion in life be among those who recite the concluding psalms of the Book of Psalms every day" (Shab. 118b). As part of the "Verses of Praise," *Az Yashir,* the fifteenth chapter of Exodus, which is the song sung by Moses and the Israelites at the Red Sea, is read. Originally this was chanted only on Sabbaths (R.H. 31a).

The *Pesuke de-Zimra* open with the blessing *Barukh Sheamar* ("Praised is He who by His command created the world"), and are concluded with *Yishtabbah* ("Praised be Thy name . . . forever"). On Sabbaths and holidays,

Yishtabbah is preceded by *Nishmat* ("The breath of every creature shall bless Thy Name"), which is identified by Rabbi Johanan (3rd century C.E.) as *Birkat Hashir* ("The Blessing of the Song, i.e., the *Hallel*), since *Nishmat* was originally and still is recited during the Passover Seder at the conclusion of the *Hallel* Psalms (Pes. 117b).

III. The *Shema* and its blessings

The Mishnah stipulates that in the morning, one recites two blessings before the *Shema* and one blessing after it (Mishnah Ber. 1:4).

The two blessings before the *Shema* are:

1. *Yotzer Or* ("Creator of light and darkness")

This begins with *Barukh attah . . . yotzer or uvoreh hoshekh oseh shalom uvoreh et hakol* ("Blessed art Thou . . . Creator of light and darkness, Maker of peace and Creator of everything"), and concludes with *Barukh attah . . . yotzer hameorot* ("Blessed art Thou . . . Creator of [the] light"). God's goodness is extolled as manifesting itself in the recurring cycle of light and darkness whereby Creation "is renewed daily."

In liturgical terminology this blessing is referred to as the *Yotzer* blessing. Hence all *piyyutim* (poetic compositions) interpolated into this section of the *Shaharit* are designated as *Yotzrot* (*Yotzer* poems). In the *Yotzer* division is included a doxology called *Kedushah de-Yotzer*, which will be discussed later (pp. 60-61).

2. *Ahavah Rabbah* ("With great love")

The content of this blessing is similar to that of *Ahavat Olam* in the evening service (p. 28). As a blessing before the "reading" of a portion of the Torah (that is, the *Shema*), *Ahavah Rabbah* celebrates the giving of the Torah which evidences God's love for His people. *Ahavah Rabbah* ends with: *Barukh attah . . . haboher beammo Yisrael beahavah* ("Blessed art Thou . . . who in love hast chosen Thy people Israel"). The last word in the Hebrew text, *beahavah* ("with love"), is a fitting link with the *Shema* (see p. 69), which in the *Veahavta* section speaks of Israel's love for God.

The blessing after the *Shema* is:

Emet Veyatziv ("True and certain")

This begins with *Emet Veyatziv* ("True and certain") and ends with *Barukh attah . . . goal Yisrael* ("Blessed art Thou . . . who redeemed Israel"). Like the corresponding blessing in the evening *Shema* (see p. 29), this too is called *Geulah* (redemption), since it speaks of God as Israel's Redeemer from Egyptian bondage.

IV. The *Amidah*

The structure and the wording of the *Shaharit Amidah* are the same as that of the *Maariv* service (pp. 32-33) except for the text of the last blessing, which in the *Shaharit* begins with *Sim Shalom* ("Bestow Thy peace"). *Sim Shalom* is fittingly connected with the Priestly Benediction which immediately precedes it in the reader's repetition of the *Amidah*. *Sim Shalom* is not said at *Minhah,* as the Priestly Benediction is not recited at *Minhah* time; however, *Shalom Rav* is substituted. The reason given in the Talmud is that since that service is held in the afternoon, after the main meal of the day, the *Kohanim* may be in a condition under which they are forbidden to function (Taan. 26b). On public fast days, when this could not be the case, the Priestly Benediction and the *Sim Shalom* are recited during the *Minhah* service.

Avinu Malkenu ("Our Father, Our King")

The reader's repetition of the *Amidah* is followed by *Avinu Malkenu* which is, in turn, followed by *Kaddish Titkabbal* (p. 35), marking the end of this section of the service.

On the origin of the *kerovot,* which are interpolated into the reader's repetition of the *Amidah,* see pp. 83-85.

Piyyutim

For a period of over one thousand years, poets of all lands expanded the standard liturgy by the interpolation of their own poetic compositions, or *piyyutim* (see our discussion of their origin, pp. 16-21), which, as *yotzrot,* were inserted into the *Yotzer* division of the *Shaharit,* and, as *kerovot,* were inserted into the *Amidah*.

Opening of the ark

During the recitation of certain *piyyutim,* the ark is opened and the congregation stands. It appears that the ark was originally opened to draw attention to a significant interpolation into the standard liturgy. The frequency of such occasions and the designation of the places in the service when the ark is opened are not governed by any mandatory rules. As prayer books were published, the printer indicated a *petihah* (opening of the ark) before those *piyyutim* which, in his opinion or in the practice of his synagogue, called for a heightened sense of exaltation which would be induced by the opening of the ark and the consequent rising of the entire congregation.

THE *YOTZER* PRAYERS: ROSH HASHANAH

הַמֶּלֶךְ

O King! Thou who art seated on a high and lofty throne

The word *Hamelekh* ("the King") is intoned and accentuated as a sort of musical overture charged with alternating feelings of trembling awe, deep humility, and heightened expectancy. Thus we are introduced into the main motif of the High Holy Day liturgy, in which the Kingship of God is again and again proclaimed.

What is the abiding meaning of the frequent reiteration that God is enthroned on high, that His name is exalted and holy? It is a declaration that our life is committed to the supreme authority of our moral and spiritual imperatives. These "spell out" for us the will of God. The will of God is made known to us through the conscientious study, clarification, and application to our own life, of the cumulative insights of the Torah. To acknowledge God as King means to make all our inner "drives" and impulses, as well as all external claims on our loyalty, subservient to His sovereignty and His will. It means to repudiate and resist attitudes and actions which contradict or compromise our manifest duty. Because God is holy, only those whose lives testify to His reality can offer Him the praise acceptable to Him:

> By the mouth of the upright Thou art praised;
> By the words of the righteous Thou art lauded;
> By the speech of the faithful Thou art extolled
> Among the holy Thou art sanctified.

Although it may be purely coincidental, the point at which the reader begins to read the concluding words of *Nishmat* strikes an appropriate note for each occasion. On Sabbath, as *Nishmat* is concluded, the reader begins with *Shokhen Ad,* celebrating God's eternity as the Creator. On Festivals he begins with *Hael,* acclaiming Him as the omnipotent Protector of His people; and on Rosh Hashanah and Yom Kippur he begins with *Hamelekh,* proclaiming Him as Sovereign and Judge.

וּבְמַקְהֲלוֹת רִבְבוֹת עַמְּךָ

In the assemblies of the tens of thousands of Thy people in the house of Israel, Thy name shall be glorified . . .

Jewish worship requires at least a *minyan* (ten males above the age of thirteen) for the recitation of certain portions of the liturgy, such as *Barekhu, Kedushah,* and *Kaddish.* A *minyan* is also required for the reading of the Torah. No *minyan* is required for the early part of the daily service prior to *Barekhu.* The individual is required to recite the prescribed liturgy of the *Shema* and the *Amidah* by himself, when he cannot attend public worship. But so highly was public prayer regarded that those who could not attend the synagogue service were urged to recite their prayers at the same time as the service was going on in the synagogue: "May my prayer be offered unto Thee in an acceptable time" (Ps. 69:14). And the Talmud says: "When is the time when prayer is most acceptable? The time when the congregation is at worship. He who occupies himself with the study of Torah and with deeds of kindness and also recites his prayers with the congregation, is considered as if he had redeemed God and redeemed His children from the exile and from the oppression of the nations" (Ber. 8a).

The origin of the Synagogue

The merit that Judaism attaches to public worship is an example of the stress it places on religion as a shared experience of the community, rather than as that "which a man does with his solitariness." Not isolation and insulation from society, but active participation in its destiny and its concerns is the norm that is lauded. For this reason, if a person was engaged in performing a communal service, he was exempt from the time strictures relating to the *Shema* and the *Tefillah* (*Tosefta Ber.*, 2:6).

It is generally agreed among scholars that the synagogue arose during the Babylonian exile and that it coexisted with the Temple in Jerusalem during the period of the Second Temple. The ancient institution of *Maamadot* throws some light on the early beginnings of the local synagogue. We are told in the Mishnah that in order to have the people represented at the daily sacrifices in the Temple, the prophets enacted the *Maamadot,* by means of which the priests, the Levites, and the people at large were arranged into twenty-four geographical divisions. Each division was assigned a period when it was to participate in the service of the daily sacrifice. Contingents of lay Israelites were present at the Temple service in Jerusalem, to represent the geographical division to which their communities belonged. While the Temple service was going on, a special *Maamad* service was also conducted in the local communities represented by the particular *Maamad* at the Temple (Mishnah Taan. 4:2). Long before the destruction of the Temple, synagogues had already been established throughout Palestine and also in the Diaspora. Thus the Synagogue was well prepared to assume its post-exilic role as the center of Jewish education, worship, and communal welfare. That the people recovered so quickly from the traumatic effects of the destruction of the Temple was due to the fact that for some centuries before 70 C.E., the Synagogue had been a functioning institution with a reasonably well-established liturgy. The Rabbis tell us that God prepares the healing before the hurt (*Song of Songs Rabbah,* 4:5).

The Synagogue's availability as the successor to the Temple can be said to be an illustration of the truth of this observation.

שֶׁכֵּן חוֹבַת כָּל הַיְצוּרִים

For it is the duty of Thy creatures . . . to give thanks unto Thee and exalt, adore, and bless Thee

Prayers of praise and appreciation

> Praise the Lord from the earth,
> You sea-monsters, and all deeps;
> Fire and hail, snow and vapour,
> Stormy wind, fulfilling His word;
> Mountains and all hills,
> Fruitful trees and all cedars;
> Beasts and all cattle,
> Creeping things and winged fowl.
>
> Psalm 148:7-10

There are numerous midrashic texts which enlarge on the theme of this and many other psalms—that all nature is filled with adoration of God. The heavens, the earth, the rivers, the brooks, the mountains, and the hills—these comprise the cosmic chorus. Each living creature and each phenomenon of creation utters its distinctive sound. The sounds of nature and its creatures form a litany of song which the psalmist articulates and the Midrash elaborates. Thus the heavens "declare the glory of God, and the firmament showeth His handiwork" (Ps. 19:2); the trees in the forest "sing for joy before the Lord" (Ps. 96:12-13); and the wild animals, according to the Midrash, say: "Thou art good, and doest good; teach me Thy statutes" (Ps. 119:68). One of these texts, *Perek Shirah* ("Chapter of Song") is included in some editions of the Prayer Book as an individual meditation to precede the morning prayers. In citing the verses suggested by the songs of nature, *Perek Shirah* implies that as man alone can give verbal expression to the praise of God, his is the duty and the privilege to dedicate his gift of speech to the service of his Maker.

Commenting on the manner in which man so often

abuses this unique endowment of speech, Rabbi Abba bar Kahana offers this parable:

A certain king built a palace and had it entirely occupied by deaf mutes. Though they could not express their gratitude in words, they did express it by the use of sign language. Not a day would pass without their solicitous inquiry after the welfare of their royal benefactor. So touched was the king by their devotion that he reasoned that if mutes are so appreciative, those who speak would be all the more eager to express their appreciation. He therefore arranged for the palace to be inhabited by people who were able to speak. Little time elapsed before they rebelled against the king and seized the palace. Therefore the king decreed that the palace be again inhabited by mutes. When the world was created, the waters of the earth glorified the Lord, for Scripture tells us: "The floods have lifted up, O Lord, the floods have lifted up their voice, the floods lift up their roaring" (Ps. 93:3). When God heard this, He thought that if the waters, which are speechless, glorify Him, how much more would be nature's adoration of Him if He would create man and endow him with speech. But after man was created, he sorely disappointed his Creator by using his gift of speech for slander, lying, and acrimony (Gen. Rabbah, 5:1).

Mordecai M. Kaplan drew attention to the coincidental, but striking similarity between this parable and a vignette of Anatole France's. France's skit tells of a judge who married a woman of great beauty and of distinguished ancestry. His happiness would have been complete were it not for her inability to speak. Every day he was tempted by this thought: "If she is so sweet and so considerate without being able to utter a word, what blessing would be mine if she could speak her thoughts!" A friend of his who knew of his sorrow told him of a doctor who possessed the skill of restoring speech to the speechless. The doctor was at once summoned, and the long-wished-for cure was effected. But the judge's dreams were frustrated, for she drove him nearly insane by her ceaseless nagging.

Nine synonyms for "praise" are mentioned in the paragraph beginning with *Uvemakhalot: lehodot, lehallel, leshabbeah, lefaer, leromem, lehadder, levarekh, lealleh lekalles.* The last, *lekalles,* is from the Greek *kallos* (beau-

tiful), rather than from the Hebrew word *kalles,* which
has a derogatory meaning.[*]

יִשְׁתַּבַּח שְׁמְךָ

Praised be Thy Name, O our King, forever

Until Abraham our father came into the world, God was King
only over the heavens, for Scripture quotes Abraham as saying:
"The Lord, the God of heaven who took me from my father's
house" (Gen. 24:7). But when Abraham came into the world,
he proclaimed Him King over heaven and earth as is said in
Scripture: "I shall make you take an oath by the Lord God of
heaven and the God of the earth" (*ibid.,* 23:3) (*Sifre Haazinu,*
313).

When He created man, God said, "I open the tongue and
mouth of all men that they may praise Me daily and acknowledge Me as King over the entire world. Were it not for the
daily hymns offered by man, I would not have created the
world" (*Alphabet of R. Akiba,* 12:13).

The notion, found frequently in rabbinic literature,
that God seeks the prayers of man, suggests that man
serve as the terrestrial ambassador of God's justice, forbearance, and beneficence. By serving Him as witness,
man praises God in deed as well as in word, and thereby
testifies to His reality. In dedicating himself to such
praise of God, man achieves the ecstatic delight described
by the psalmist:

> For Thy love is better than life.
> My lips shall praise Thee,
> As long as I live I shall bless Thee.
> I will call on Thy Name as I lift up my hands.
> My soul is satisfied as with marrow and fat
> When my mouth praises Thee with joyful lips.
>
> Psalm 63:4-6

Yishtabbah concludes the section of the "Verses of
Praise" (*Pesuke de-Zimra*), even as *Barukh Sheamar*
("Blessed is He who spoke") introduces this section. Be-
cause a distinct segment of the service ends here, the
Hatzi Kaddish is recited at this point.

---

[*] Saul Lieberman, "Kalles, Killusin," *Allei Ayin, Schocken Jubilee
Volume* (Jerusalem, 1950), pp. 75-81.

בָּרְכוּ

Bless ye the Lord, who alone is to be praised

This might be designated as the "call to worship," to which the congregation responds: "Praised be the Lord who is blessed for all eternity."

Both the *Barekhu* and the congregational response are omitted when a *minyan* is not present at the service.

The reader's call to worship is the same as the opening words of the blessing one recites when called to the Torah. The propriety of the wording of this blessing is questioned in the Talmud, as the reader seems to call on others to worship, rather than to associate himself with the congregation. This would run counter to the teaching that a person must not separate himself from the community. The call to join in the blessing after meals is cited as a fulfillment of this principle, for there the leader says: *Nevarekh* ("Let us bless God of whose bounty we have partaken"). In defense of the propriety of *Barekhu* as the call to worship, the Palestinian Talmud takes the word *hamvorakh,* with which the call ends, to mean: "Whom all of us praise" (TP Ber. 10b-c). The repetition of the congregational response by the reader is also intended to confirm his association with the community when he calls them to worship.

בָּרוּךְ אַתָּה . . . עֹשֶׂה שָׁלוֹם וּבוֹרֵא אֶת הַכֹּל

Praised art Thou . . . Who makest peace and createst all things

From Chaos to Creation

> Surely the Lord's mercies are not consumed,
> Surely His compassions fail not.
> They are new every morning,
> Great is Thy faithfulness.
>
> Lamentations 3:22-23

In the morning, as we perceive the light of a new day, we are moved to extol the Creator whose wisdom and power are apparent in all creation. Light and darkness alike testify to His supremacy. Amidst the triumphs and tragedies of our earthly existence, we praise the living God who daily renews the miracle of creation. The tension between good and evil, between light and darkness, is in itself a manifestation of the boundless creativity of Him who transformed primeval chaos into a pattern of order and harmony.

The juxtaposition of "peace" and "all things" inspired this midrashic comment:

Precious is peace, for it is equated with all Creation, as we say in our prayers: He who makes peace and creates all things (*Num. Rabbah*, 11:7).

Wishing to answer the disturbing question of why a beneficent and omniscient God created evil, Persian and Hellenistic thinkers interposed an intermediary force between God and the world; to this force they ascribed the evil in the universe. Some called it the demiurge, while others personified it as Satan, the creator of evil. All these concepts were condemned by the Rabbis as forms of the heresy which consisted in the positing of two primal powers (*shetei reshuyot*). Judaism unequivocally held fast to the undiluted monotheism which is implied in the biblical passage from which the prayer *Yotzer Or* ("Creator of Light") is derived: "I form the light and create darkness, I make peace and create evil" (Isa. 45:7). Even so seemingly innocent a prayer as "Thy mercy extends even to the sparrow's nest, and because of the good that emanates from Thee, be Thy name remembered" was condemned because it seemed to imply that there must be another cosmic power who is the creator of evil. One who in leading the congregation in prayer says: "*Modim, modim*" ("We acknowledge, we acknowledge") must be silenced, for he is then suspected of having acknowledged "two powers" (Mishnah Ber. 5:3).

A fully satisfactory explanation for the persistence of evil in a world ruled solely by God has not been offered. We know, however, that man would not appreciate light were he never to know the experience of darkness, nor could he conceive of good health were he not subject to illness. If the tongue that lies were immediately to lose its power of speech, if the hand that steals were quickly to become paralyzed, and if the eye that covets were instantly to lose its sight, man would cease to be a free moral being. He is free precisely because he can make choices—to resist evil and to transmute evil into good. Because the world has potentialities for evil as well as for good, we can serve God as persons who are morally free and responsible.

"Who makest peace and createst all things"

The verse from which this blessing is taken, reads as follows: "I form the light and create darkness, I make peace and create evil" (Isa. 45:7); however, in our prayer, the concluding phrase has been changed to "and createst all things." The Talmud explains the reason for this to be the need for a more felicitous expression, suiting the mood of prayer (Ber. 11b).

As indicated above, despite its encounter with the ancient Persian belief in two gods—one of light and goodness, the other of darkness and evil—Judaism never succumbed to a dualistic theory of the government of the universe. It is the One God who controls the universe. Satan, the personification of evil, is always portrayed in biblical literature as an instrument of the Divine (I Kings 11:14; Ps. 109:6; Job 1:6). All power and sovereignty reside with God.

In the morning we say: *Yotzer or uvoreh hoshekh* ("Who formest light and createst darkness"), and in the evening we say: *Golel or mipne hoshekh vehoshekh mipne or* ("rolling away the light from before the darkness"). This is in accordance with the rule that when we pray in the morning we should refer to God *also* as the Creator of light and when we pray in the evening we should refer to Him *also* as the Creator of darkness (Ber. 11b).

אוֹר עוֹלָם בְּאוֹצַר חַיִּים

Yea, everlasting light is in God's treasury of life;
let light replace the darkness, and there was light.

Scholars see in this brief strophe the opening part of a *piyyut* by Yose ben Yose, one of the earliest Palestinian liturgical poets (*ca.* 400 C.E.). The text of this fragment should read:

אור עולם אוצר חיים
אורות מאפל אמר ויהי

The everlasting light, the source of life, commanded the lights [sun and moon] to emerge
out of darkness and so it came to pass

That the opening words, *Or Olam*, can refer to God is
evident from the verse in Isaiah in which the prophet
assures his people that in the future "The Lord will be
your *or olam*—your everlasting light" (Isa. 60:19). One
could, however, also interpret this passage to mean: The
primordial light is the treasury of everlasting life. God
commanded the luminaries to appear out of the darkness
and so it came to pass. According to this, reference is
being made here to the rabbinic concept that the light
which was created when God said, "Let there be light,"
was treasured up for the use of the righteous in the world
to come. This light was so supernal that by means of it a
person could survey all creation at one glance (*Gen.
Rabbah*, 3:1). When this primordial light was hidden,
darkness did not take its place, for on the fourth day of
creation, by God's command, there appeared the sun, the
moon, and the stars.

Mordecai M. Kaplan made the observation that there
is something appealing in the conception that in the future there will be a more perfect light, "when the light
of the moon shall be as the light of the sun, and the
light of the sun shall be sevenfold, as the light of the
seven days [of the week]" (Isa. 30:26). This interpretation
is in contrast to the doleful notion that nature is in a
continuous process of decay, and that all life is destined
to become extinct.

מֶלֶךְ אָזוּר גְּבוּרָה

O King, girt with power
(A *yotzer* for the first day)

Many manifestations of the One God

In various passages, the Midrash tells us that God's unity
is not compromised by the diversity of His manifestations:

"The voice of the Lord is powerful [with power]" (Ps. 29:4). The voice of the Lord comes not with "His power" but "with power," that is, in accordance with the perceptive power of each person. At Sinai each person heard the Divine voice in accordance with his own capacities. Said God to Israel: "Think not that because there are many voices there must be as many gods. I am the Lord! I am the same God of each of you (*Yalkut Shemot*, 286).

Rabbi Hiyya b. Abba said: "God appeared to the people of Israel in keeping with the circumstance and need of each occasion. He appeared at the Red Sea as a mighty warrior, at Sinai as a teacher of children, in the prosperous times of Solomon as tall and sprightly as the cedars of Lebanon and in Daniel's time as a sage of the Torah" (*Mekilta,* ed. Lauterbach, II, 231).

> In countless visions did they imagine Thee,
> But through all the visions Thou art One.
> *Hymn of Glory*

A similar motif animates this poem, the *Melekh Azur,* by Eleazar Kalir. When God manifests His regal power, diverse aspects of His being are exposed, yet He remains One. At times He is girded with might, and He dons the vestments of retribution. At other times He is robed in majesty, wrapped in light, or adorned with splendor. Now garbed in righteousness and then enveloped in glory, He appears also in crimsoned garments, when He treads down the arrogant. Pure white are His vestments when He is clad in the mantle of indignation as He goes forth to vindicate the oppressed. Awesome indeed is He, as He proceeds to judge man, for searching and penetrating is His knowledge of the motives of men and peoples. But love is the measure of His dealing with those who pursue mercy. Such is the Eternal God and King whom Israel, the eternal people, acclaimed at the Red Sea when it declared "The Lord shall reign forever."

Comments on the text

The Ten Garments

Kalir derived the idea of the ten garments from a passage in the *Pesikta de Rav Kahana* (ed. Buber, p. 264). In that passage God is depicted in various roles. He brought destruction on the corrupt generation of the Flood, gave the Torah to Israel, decreed the doom of the Babylonians, the Persians, the Medes, and the Greeks—each of whom in turn planned to establish their hegemony over all mankind and to crush Israel. The final act of retribution which will precede Israel's redemption will be the war of Gog and Magog described by the prophet Ezekiel (Ezek. 38:14-22). Then universal peace will be established and God's power will be recognized by all the nations (*ibid.*, 23). In this midrashic description of the unfolding of history, God is depicted as wearing a garb of different color on each occasion.

Acrostics

Alphabetical acrostics occur as early as the biblical books of Psalms, Proverbs, and Lamentations. In ancient times when texts were not readily available, they served as aids to the memory. The daily recitation of the *Ashre* (Pss. 144:15; 145) is highly commended by the Rabbis because of the special efficacy attached to the alphabetical order of its verses (Ber. 4b). Solomon is praised because he composed full alphabetical acrostics and added to the acrostics five additional letters, these being the five final letters of the Hebrew alphabet (*Song of Songs Rabbah,* I:1,7).

In his *Hellenism in Jewish Palestine* (pp. 79-81), Saul Lieberman informs us that in the second millennium B.C.E. the device of the name acrostic (where the first letter of each line when read consecutively forms the name of the author) was already in use. He submits convincing evidence in support of his conjecture that even the early Alexandrian grammarians sought acrostics for the purpose of establishing the authorship of certain poems in the Iliad and Odyssey. In early rabbinic literature, however, Lieberman tells us, this kind of acrostic is not mentioned. While he does cite two instances in midrashic literature where name acrostics are alluded to, he considers them to be later interpolations.

In rabbinic fancy and symbolism, the letters of the alphabet were personified, and they were pictured as vying with each other for the distinction of being the first letter of the Torah. The following description of the parade of the alphabet was probably a pedagogic means of making elementary instruction interesting to the young:

Said Rabbi Akiba: The twenty-two letters of the alphabet with which the Torah was given to Israel, are engraved with a pen of flaming fire on the awesome and august crown of God. When God was about to create the world, all the letters descended and stood before God. One after another, in reverse order, each presented its claim, that the world be created through it. The first to step forward was the letter *tav* claiming that it be given priority since the word Torah begins with a *tav*. Said God, "I cannot create the world with you, since it is with a *tav* that I shall mark the sign of death upon the foreheads of sinners" (Ezek. 9:4). Then the letter *shin* stepped forward and based its claim on the fact that the word *Shaddai* (Almighty God) begins with a *shin*. Unfortunately it also forms the first letter of *sheker* (falsehood), and therefore it was rejected. *Resh* had no better luck because it forms the first letter of *ra* (wicked), which cancelled out the fact that it is the first letter of *rahum* (merciful God). The *kaf* was rejected because its association with *kelalah* (curse) outweighed the fact that it is the first letter of *kadosh* (holy). *Zade* lost its case because it heads the letters of the word *zarah* (trouble). *Pe* was declared unfit because it evokes the word *pesha* (transgression). *Ayyin* reminds one of *ervah* (unchastity). *Samakh* was rejected because it heads the verse "They made (*samu*) Jerusalem into heaps" (Ps. 79:1). *Nun* was not accepted because it opens the punitive verse: "The lamp (*ner*) of the wicked shall be put out" (Job 21:17). Though *mem* starts *Melekh* (King), one of the titles of God, it was deemed unfit because it is also the first letter of *mehumah* (confusion). *Lamed* had a strong claim in that with it came *luhot,* the tablets of the commandments, but as those tablets were to be smashed to pieces, *lamed* was denied the honor it sought. *Kav* had formidable claims because of the words: *kisseh* (God's throne), *kavod* (God's glory), and *keter* (God's crown). But these claims did not avail since, because of the sins of Israel, God would smite hand on hand (*kaf*) to give vent to His anger at Israel (Ezek. 21:22). *Yod* was ruled out because it evokes the phrase *yetzer hara* (the evil inclination). *Tet,* though it forms the word *tov* was rejected because of the word *tamme* (unclean). *Het's* claim that it is the first letter of *han-nun* (the gracious One), was offset by its place in the word *het* (sin). *Zayyin* means a weapon and was therefore rejected. *Vav's* claim was rejected because of its central place in the word *taavah* (lust), for which the Israelites were severely punished (Num. 11:34). *He* occurs twice in the ineffable Name and is therefore too exalted a word to be pressed into the service of a mundane world. *Dalet* stands for *din* (strict justice) under which, without mercy, the world could not exist. Because *gimmel* is a reminder of the severity of *gemul* (retribution), its plea was rejected. Next came the *bet* and claimed that it is the key letter of the word *barukh,* the word with which every *berakhah* (blessing) opens. Whereupon God said to the *bet:* "*Barukh haba* (Blessed be he that comes). With you I shall create the world." This is why the Torah begins with the *bet* of *bereshit* ("in the beginning"). In its modesty the *aleph* did not even put forth its claim, and for this it was rewarded with the distinction of first place in the Ten Commandments: "I (*anokhi*) am the Lord Thy God" (*Midrash Alphabet of Rabbi Akiba,* II).

Even the shapes of the letters were used as a homily. Thus the Talmud asks: "Why is the *gimmel* so shaped that it looks as if it runs after the *dalet*? Because *gimmel* reminds us of a *gomel* (giver of charity) who must run after the *dal*" (the poor man) to help him and not wait till he is asked (Shab. 104a).

Abraham Joshua Heschel (*Man's Quest for God,* p. 29), observes that in prayer "we often arrive at thoughts that lie beyond our power of expression. . . . Its beginning lies on this side of the word but the end lies beyond all words. . . . At times all we do is to utter a word with all our heart yet it is as if we lifted up a whole world." A Hasidic folk tale illustrates this insight with singular poignancy: An untutored boy could not read the prayers, but his heart welled forth with love for God and with an irresistible urge to pray to Him. Hence, declaiming the entire alphabet: *aleph, bet, gimmel, dalet,* etc., he said, "O God! I do not know how to read the words of the *Siddur.* All I know is the alphabet. Here are all the letters of the alphabet and I beg of Thee O God, to string them together into words expressing my love for Thee."

מֶלֶךְ אָמוֹן מַאֲמָרְךָ מֵרָחוֹק מָצָּב

Thy word standeth steadfast from of yore
(A *yotzer* for the second day)

Original repentance and forgiveness

Because man is subject to human frailties, God, the merciful King, provided him with a means of release from the bondage of circumstance and the shackles of habit. Before man was created, repentance was ordained as the corrective law of human life, for repentance enables man to channel the impulses that threaten to degrade his humanity. By repentance we can avert and even annul the evil of our deeds. When we conscientiously seek to obey the imperatives that are of God, when the quality of our life testifies to His reality, when we yearn for His presence, then we find Him. The observances and prayers of the New Year can lead us to a heightened awareness of our collective duty and destiny as a people. The *shofar* blasts evoke for us the merit of Isaac's sacrifice, even as they make vivid the recollection of our collective consecration at Sinai. Expectantly, we await the sounding of the *Shofar* of Liberation, when Zion will be free to receive its exiled children from all parts of the earth. Elevated by that hope we resolve to live nobly and triumphantly in "the land of the living."

"Thy word stands forever"

For the Torah reading of Rosh Hashanah, the Mishnah prescribes the portion beginning with the verse: "In the seventh month, in the first day of the month, shall be a solemn rest unto you a memorial proclaimed with the blast of horns" (Lev. 23:24). The present readings, Genesis 21 for the first day of the New Year, and Genesis 22 for the second day, were instituted (*ca.* 250-500 C.E.) in Amoraic times (Meg. 31a). The *piyyut* under discussion was composed for the second day of Rosh Hashanah by Rabbi Simon ben Isaac ben Abun of Mayence (11th century). But its content was drawn from a midrashic homily on the Torah portion prescribed in the Mishnah. The homily opens with the verse: "Forever O Lord Thy word stands fast in heaven, Thy faithfulness is unto all generations" (Ps. 119:89). On this verse Rabbi Eliezer comments that the world was created on the twenty-fifth day of Elul, and that on the first day of Tishri, man was created. Rosh Hashanah is, therefore, the birthday of mankind. Rabbi Eliezer then proceeds to give an "hour by hour" account of what transpired on the day when Adam was created:

In the first hour the idea of creating man arose in God's mind. In the second He consulted the angels. In the third He assembled the dust out of which man was to be formed. In the fourth hour he kneaded it into clay, the fifth He shaped it, the sixth He made it into a solid form and set him on his feet. In the seventh hour He blew a breath of life into him. In the eighth hour He placed him in the Garden of Eden. In the ninth hour He commanded him. In the tenth hour Adam disobeyed God's command. In the eleventh hour he was judged and in the twelfth hour, he was pardoned. Said the Holy One, blessed is He, "You are a symbol and a hope for future generations. Just as you stood in judgment before Me on this day, so will your descendants be judged by Me on this same day. Just as you were pardoned, so will your descendants emerge with a full pardon" (*Pesikta de Rav Kahana,* ed. Buber, p. 269).

The concept of "original forgiveness," which is implied here, is based on the teaching that repentance was among the things created even before the world came into being (Pes. 54a).

Among the many references to the idea that on the Day of Judgment man is given the opportunity to mend his ways and win divine pardon is this phrase found in the *Kiddush* for Rosh Hashanah, as well as in the *Kedushat Hayom* of the *Amidah: Udevarekha emet vekayyam laad* ("Thy word is true and stands forever"). This is a reference to the midrashic account, just cited, of the pardon extended to Adam on the first, the primeval, Rosh Hashanah. The "word" is the promise that, through repentance, man will always be given the opportunity to win divine pardon. The concept of "original forgiveness" which the Rabbis associated with the story of Adam, is in sharp contrast to the concept of "original sin" so fundamental in Christianity and also associated with the story of Adam. The Rabbis never forfeited an opportunity to express the belief that God is merciful in judgment and that, for the repentant sinner, the Day of Judgment can become a day of spiritual regeneration when he becomes, as the Rabbis phrase it, a "new creature."

Comments on the text

Rabbi Simon ben Isaac ben Abun

Kalir did not compose a *yotzer* and a *kerovah* for the second day of Rosh Hashanah, because in his time, only one day of Rosh Hashanah was observed in Palestine. The *yotzrot* and *kerovot* for the second day are by Rabbi Simon ben Isaac ben Abun of Mayence (11th century C.E.). Rabbi Simon's *piyyut* consists of two sections, with

three stanzas. Each stanza consists of three strophes. Each
of the two sets of stanzas is arranged around the words
melekh (king), *zekhor* (remember), and *shofar* comprising
the themes of the Rosh Hashanah liturgy: *Malkhuyot,
Zikhronot, Shofarot,* with the seventh stanza repeating
the key word, *melekh.*

Each stanza has a concluding couplet. The first two
couplets contain an acrostic of the author's name:

שמעון בר יצחק

שומרי מצות עדיך ועובדיך

נטלם ונשאם להרבות כבודך

ברחמים יקר צעירי הצאן חקם הטריפם

The concluding couplets of the third and fourth
stanzas carry this acrostic of the name of the author's
son:

אלחנן בני יחי לארך ימים

לחיי עולם יכתב אמן סלה

May my son Elhanan be inscribed for eternal life. Here
are the lines that form the name acrostic:

אל חנן נחלתו בנעם להשפר

ידעם קרא קרבנותיו במספר

יראה פעלך והדרך לתמימים

חיות בצלך לארך ימים

לחיי עולם יכתבו אמוני

יזכו לחזות בנעם ה'

אמרי נחומיך שעשעוני בכפלים

סלה לעבדך בכל גבולים

Several legends, whose historic element is not defi-
nitely known, have been woven around the life of this son.
The basic legend is that when he was a child, Elhanan
was stolen by a Christian maid and baptized. He rose to
great prominence in the Church and was elevated to the
papacy. At this point there appear two different traditions regarding the occasion for the reunion between

father and son. One tells of his father's coming to Rome to plead for the lifting of severe restrictions imposed on the Jews by his son, now pope. This legend proceeds to tell that the son then made himself known to his father and secretly went back to Mayence to return to Judaism. The other version tells that Elhanan, having been told of his origin, sent for his father, avowed his loyalty to Judaism before him, and then jumped to his death from the top of a tower. That Elhanan must have died a martyr's death can be seen from these words of the acrostic referring to him: "Elhanan my son, may he be granted everlasting life, Amen."

תִּתְבָּרֵךְ צוּרֵנוּ . . . בּוֹרֵא קְדוֹשִׁים

**Be Thou blessed, O our Rock . . .
Creator of ministering angels**

Why God prefers the praises of man

This section is known as *Kedushah de-Yotzer* because it contains the *Kedushah* preceding the blessing: *Yotzer Hameorot* (Creator of Light). Its theme is inspired by the mystic visions described in the sixth chapter of Isaiah and in the first chapter of Ezekiel.

The heavenly hosts, ministering angels of the Most High, daily offer a service of song to their Creator. As they proclaim and acknowledge God's universal sovereignty, they sanctify His name, singing in unison with sweet melody: "Holy, Holy, Holy is the Lord of Hosts, the whole earth is full of His glory." The response of the celestial retinue is: "Blessed is the glory of God from His abode." Thus the inhabitants of the heavens praise God as He daily renews creation.

Our sages were intrigued by the idea expressed in the *Kedushah*, that man is moved to "sanctify God's name on earth even as it is sanctified by angelic beings in heaven." These beings are all pure and eager to obey the will of the Creator. Yet, the Rabbis averred, in the eyes of God, man's worship takes precedence over that of the celestial beings. Here are some of the midrashic passages in which this rather astonishing sentiment is expressed:

God's greatest delight is to hear Israel recite the *Kedushah,* for the very breath of their mouth is like sweet savor to Him (*Hekhalot Rabbati,* 9).

Wherever you find the mark of man's footsteps there I am before thee (*Mekilta,* ed. Lauterbach, II, 133).

The angels objected to the creation of man and said, "What is man that Thou shouldst remember him?" (Ps. 8:5). God replied to the angels, "Man, whom I am about to create, will excel you in wisdom" (*Midrash Tehillim,* 8:2).

"Then a spirit lifted me up, and I heard *behind me* the voice of a great rushing: 'Blessed be the glory of the Lord from His place'" (Ezek. 3:12). *Behind me* (*aharai*) really means *after me.* Only after man has praised God in the midst of his fellow worshipers did the heavenly hosts respond (*Gen. Rabbah,* 65:21).

When the angels desire to sing praise to their Creator . . . God bids them wait, as He prefers to hear first the worship of Israel assembled in its synagogues (Hullin 91a).

When Israel prays, you do not find all the people praying at the same time. Each assembly of worshipers prays separately, first one, then the other. When they have all finished, the angel who was appointed over prayers collects all the prayers that have been offered in all the synagogues, weaves them into garlands and places them on the head of God (*Exod. Rabbah,* 21:4).

Man is all the more precious to God precisely because his morality is fashioned out of the struggle between his impulses, on the one hand, and a heroic exercise of will and decision, on the other. Man's worship is sweeter to Him, even more than is the song of the angels, for where they are pure by nature, man must struggle to achieve his measure of purity. It is thus in the very tension out of which man's morality emerges that the Rabbis also see his true prestige and nobility. They tell us that when Moses ascended to heaven to receive the Torah, the angels asked God: "What is he who is born of woman doing here?" When informed that Moses was about to be given the Torah, they remonstrated: "Will you give to flesh and blood this most precious possession that you have treasured for 974 generations before Creation?" At God's request Moses answered their objection. He pointed out that angels do not need the Torah since they are not liable to the temptations of idolatry, false swearing, murder, stealing, and adultery (Shab. 88b).

כֻּלָּם אֲהוּבִים

The heavenly hosts are beloved

The description given here of the harmony and peace that prevails among the heavenly court, may have been inspired by the following passage:

The Holy One blessed is He, made peace on high. What is the peace which He made on high? He did not name ten angels Gabriel, ten Michael, ten Uriel, ten Raphael, the way men often name ten individuals with the same name—ten being named Reuben, ten Simon, ten Levi and ten Judah. Had He done what men do, then when He called one of them, they would all have come before Him envious of each other. Instead, He named one angel Gabriel, one Michael. When He calls for one of them, that one comes and stands before Him, and He sends him wherever He pleases.

How do we know that they revere and respect one another? For when they open their mouths and recite the Song one says to the other: "You begin, for you are greater than I," and the other says: "You begin, for you are greater than I." This is not the way human beings behave. Among human beings, one says to the other, "I am greater than you," and the other says to the first, "I am greater than you." Some sages say that the angels recite the Song, group by group, one group saying to the other: "You begin for you are greater than I," for it is said, "And one called to the other and said, 'Holy, Holy, Holy is the Lord of Hosts' " (Isa. 6:3) (*Abot of R. Nathan,* 12).

קָדוֹשׁ קָדוֹשׁ קָדוֹשׁ ה' צְבָאוֹת

Holy, Holy, Holy, is the Lord of Hosts

Jewish liturgy contains three forms of the *Kedushah* doxology. They are inspired by the visions of the heavenly retinue described in the Book of Isaiah (Chapter 6), and of the chariot and the wheeled and winged creatures described in the Book of Ezekiel (Chapters 1 and 3).

Louis Ginzberg (*Legends of the Jews*, V, 25) informs us that the underlying motivation behind the *Kedushah* doxology is that the same liturgy recited by the celestial hosts in praise of their Creator is also recited on earth by the congregations of Israel who, like the angels in Isaiah's vision, declare to one another: "Holy, Holy, Holy is the Lord of hosts, the whole earth is full of His glory" (Isa 6:3); and like the winged creatures in Ezekiel's vision, they respond: "Blessed is the glory of the Lord from His abode" (Ezek. 3:12).

Kedushah de-Yotzer

The first of the three forms of *Kedushah* doxology is designated as *Kedushah de-Yotzer,* because it is inserted into the *Yotzer* blessing of the *Shaharit.* The second *Kedushah* is inserted into the reader's repetition of the *Amidah.*

Kedushah in the *Amidah*

It is quite understandable why, before the reader's repetition of the third blessing, "The Sanctification of the Name," the *Kedushah* theme was introduced.

The *Kedushah* of the *Amidah* was originally recited in Palestine only on Sabbaths, but when, in the eighth century, the hegemony of Babylonian scholars predominated in Palestine, the Babylonian practice of reciting the *Kedushah* in the daily *Amidah* prevailed.

For a fuller discussion of the Kedushah, *see pp. 171-73.*

Kedushah de-Sidra

The third form of *Kedushah* doxology is known as *Kedushah de-Sidra.* The merit ascribed to the recitation of this *Kedushah* can be seen from the comment which a fourth century Babylonian Amora made on a statement attributed to Rabbi Joshua, a Tanna who lived in Palestine in the second century. Rabbi Joshua's statement was to the effect that from the day that the Temple was destroyed, there is no day without its malediction: the dew no longer offers its full blessing, and fruits have lost their luscious taste (Mishnah Sotah 9:12). To this reflection on the calamitous effect of the destruction of the Temple, Raba (Babylonia, 4th century C.E.) adds the observation that the despair increases day by day. The question is raised: How then does the world survive in the face of such doleful circumstances? The answer given is that the world survives because Israel recites the *Kedushah de-Sidra* (the *Kedushah* following Torah study) and the *Kaddish* doxology which follows it (Sotah 49a). This tribute to the merit of study is explained by Rashi as follows: "The *Kedushah de-Sidra* which consists of biblical verses was introduced into the liturgy to enable all Jews to engage in a minimum study of Torah."

We do not know what form the *Kedushah de-Sidra* took in talmudic days. As the liturgy took shape, it came to be inserted into the *Uva Letziyyon Goel* ("May a redeemer come to Zion"). This prayer opens with two consecutive verses from the Book of Isaiah (59:20-21). The first verse refers to the hope and assurance of Israel's redemption from exile, and the second refers to the covenant which God made with Israel, that the study of the Torah must never cease among them and their descendants through the generations. These two verses are followed by the *Kedushah* which, as a doxology, concludes the *sidra* (study) of verses from the prophetic books. According to Abudraham (Spain, 14th century) this additional opportunity for reciting the *Kedushah* was offered to latecomers who had missed its two earlier recitations. A much earlier scholar, Rabbi Natronai Gaon (Babylonia, 10th century), had already offered an explanation for inclusion of the Targum, which here is essentially an Aramaic paraphrase of the *Kedushah* verses in the *Uva Letziyyon*. According to him, ten verses from the Prophets were originally read, and these were followed by the reading of their Aramaic Targum. The conclusion of the "study" of the ten verses was followed by the verses of the *Kedushah* and their Targum paraphrase. In time, only two of the ten verses were retained.

The *Kedushah* of the *Amidah* is recited only in the presence of a *minyan*, the required quorum of at least ten males above the age of thirteen. Rabbi Saadyah Gaon and other authorities require a *minyan* even for the *Kedushah de-Sidra*, but the practice is to limit the *minyan* requirement to the *Kedushah* of the *Amidah*.

כְּבוֹדוֹ אִהֵל

Tentlike this day the King stretched out the sky

Enlarging on the word *kevodo,* Eleazar Kalir elaborates in this alphabetical acrostic the rabbinic teaching that when God created the world, He tempered the attribute of strict justice with the attribute of mercy in order that the world might exist. The Creator knows the frailty of human nature; therefore He offers His merciful forgiveness to all who sincerely seek Him on that day—the Day of Judgment—which commemorates the creation of the world. Conscious of our own unworthiness, painfully aware of the distance between what we are and what we ought to be, we invoke the merit of Abraham, Isaac, and Jacob, the founders of our people and of our faith. Our awareness of being their spiritual descendants accentuates our sense of unfulfilled potentialities. Bearing the credentials of our *Zekhut Avot* ("the merit of our patriarchs"), we pray that we may ever merit the nearness of Him whom we acknowledge as our God and King.

לָאֵל בָּרוּךְ נְעִימוֹת יִתֵּנוּ

בָּרוּךְ אַתָּה . . . יוֹצֵר הַמְּאוֹרוֹת

To the blessed God, they offer sweet song . . .
Blessed art Thou . . . Creator of the lights

The sense of wonderment

In this prayer we express gratitude for the daily renewal of creation attested to by the rising of the sun. To our forebears, the rich colors characteristic of the skies of Palestine gave daily emphasis to a deep and ecstatic awareness of the miracle of Creation. In mishnaic times the pious were scrupulous about rising early in order to recite the *Shema* at sunrise (Ber. 9b). Each day, as they praised the Creator of the lights, they experienced a fresh appreciation for God's work of renewal. The sheer delight of beholding the dawn of each new day elevated the secular to the sublime, and the recurrence of the orderly processes of nature testified to the extraordinary munificence of God.

Modern man suffers from a grievous disadvantage. He has a diminished sense of wonder before the universe. In the daily recurrence of light and darkness, in the perennial sequence of the seasons, he apprehends the operation of the impersonal laws of nature. True, these laws are in themselves wondrous—knowing them, man can extend his physical security, devise ingenious means for enhancing his mobility and comfort, sophisticate his capacity to control the elements and forces of nature. But people have become so "thing-minded" that their sensitivity to the source and vitality of natural life has been dulled. We seem to have lost our sense of wonderment and amazement at the infinitely greater marvels of nature which scientific knowledge has uncovered. We need to recapture that sense of wonder which will enable us to behold in every sunrise a daily renewal of God's beneficence —to see the marvelous in the mundane, the fabulous in the familiar, the ultimate in the immediate. "How great are Thy works O God!" would then be our spontaneous response to the daily miracle of Creation. We are, however, impeded by the fact that the enormity of the works of man tends to obscure the works of God. The verdure of the fields has been replaced by highways; tall buildings eclipse the light of the sun, and man's massive machines and mighty inventions seem to scream, "How marvelous are the works of man!" For modern man—thing-obsessed creature that he is—the heavens do not declare the glory of God, and the firmament no longer displays His handiwork. The spiritual focus of modern man is blurred and unsure. In the nineteenth century he lost faith in God as he rebelled against the social abuses and doctrinal obscurities practiced by organized religion or condoned by it; nevertheless he preserved his faith in man. He even directed his worship to human reason. In the twentieth century, as man has accelerated his domination over nature, he seems also to have lost faith in himself. He may boast of his ability to handle other people, to "manipulate" them and to persuade them, but his capacity to control himself and to behave as a morally responsible being has perceptibly weakened. We need to reclaim our faith in God the Creator. But that faith should not lead to resignation, quietism, and passivity. The Rabbis taught that God left the world in an unfinished state so that man might serve as His "partner" in its perfection. They were even so bold as to say that man can improve that which God has created. This idea is expressed in the following rabbinic passages:

Tineus Rufus asked Rabbi Akiba: "Who makes more beautiful things, God or man?" Rabbi Akiba answered: "Man makes more beautiful things" . . . He showed him ears of grain and cakes and said, "The ears of grain are God's work, the cakes are man's. You see that man's works are more beautiful." Then he brought him raw flax and some finished linen garments of Bet Shean. He said to him "You see again that what man creates is more beautiful" (*Tanhuma Tazria*).

Whatever was created by God during the six days of Creation needs further improvement; for example, mustard needs sweetening, vetches need sweetening, wheat needs grinding. Even man is subject to improvement (*Gen. Rabbah*, 11:6).

אַהֲבָה רַבָּה

With abounding love hast Thou loved us, O Lord our God, and with exceeding compassion hast Thou shown us Thy mercy

Having praised God for the daily renewal of Creation, we now extol Him for the light that comes to us from the Torah. The light of the sun comes without effort on our part, for it is God's free gift. The light of the Torah, however, comes to us only in response to our desire "to understand, learn, teach, and practice" the insights derived from its study. Such an eagerness for the divine light emanating from the Torah is evinced by the psalmist when he says: "Open Thou mine eyes, that I may behold wondrous things out of Thy Torah" (Ps. 119:18).

In intent as well as in content, *Ahavah Rabbah* is a blessing preceding the study of a portion from the Torah. The Torah portion which here occasions the blessing is the *Shema*. Samuel, the Babylonian Amora of the third century, actually refers to *Ahavah Rabbah* as *birkat hatorah*—the blessing over the Torah (TP Ber. 3c). We do not "pray" the *Shema*. We *read* it as a biblical lesson. Hence we speak of *keriat shema*—the reading of the *Shema*.

וּבָנוּ בָחַרְתָּ מִכָּל עַם וְלָשׁוֹן

Us hast Thou chosen from all peoples and tongues

The Chosen People

The concept of the "Chosen People" is a central teaching in Judaism, and the liturgy is replete with references to it. It is always accompanied by the qualifying statement that Israel was chosen to receive the Torah and is sanctified by the way of life ordained by the *Mitzvot*. The doctrine of the chosenness of Israel thus expresses our collective responsibility as a covenanted people to exemplify a life of holiness and integrity.

It would be impossible to explain fully the riddle of Jewish history and the endurance of the Jew, without taking into account the power, the strength, and the stamina that belief in his chosenness afforded him. Nor can there be an intellectually satisfying rationale for continued Jewish survival unless, at the core of our religious convictions, there is retained the awareness of an indissoluble covenant between God and Israel—not merely a vague feeling of communal solidarity, but a sense of collective commitment and historic purpose.

The belief in Israel's unique role as a "God-elected" people whose purpose is to testify to God's reality and to exemplify the moral demands He makes of man, has its roots in Scripture and its fruits in the Talmud. Abraham is singled out by God, "that he may command his children and his household after him that they may keep the way of the Lord to do righteousness and justice" (Gen. 18:19). Israel is to be God's treasured possession among all the peoples: "Indeed all the earth is Mine; but you shall be to Me a kingdom of priests and a holy nation" (Exod. 19:5-6).• The prophets spared no effort in refining and clarifying this concept. They emphasized the heightened responsibility and culpability it demanded. "You only have I singled out of all the families of the earth; therefore, I will call you to account for all your sins" (Amos 3:2). The wider global concern of Israel as God's collective servant is expressed by the Prophet of the

---

• This is the new translation given in *The Torah* (Philadelphia: The Jewish Publication Society of America, 1962).

Exile in these verses: "It is too light a thing that you
should be My servant, to establish the tribes of Jacob and
to restore the remnants of Israel. I appoint you as a light
to the nations, that My deliverance may reach to the end
of the world" (Isa. 49:6).

The Talmud sees in Israel's possession of the Torah
evidence of its being a people most favored by God, as
well as the very means whereby Israel fulfills its universal destiny. "When God created the world," said Resh
Lakish, "He made a condition with all Creation that if
Israel accepts the Torah, well and good, but if not, He
would cause the whole world to revert to primeval chaos"
(Ab. Zarah 3a). The Rabbis taught that the entire world
exists because of the breath of children studying the
Torah (Shab. 119b), for it was their belief that the universe is sustained through the study of the Torah and
through the practice of its "laws of life."

THE *SHEMA*

The *Shema* and the Ten Commandments

Long before the liturgy became comparatively fixed, the
order of worship in the Temple at Jerusalem included
the recitation of the *Shema,* and this was preceded by the
recital of the Ten Commandments (Mishnah Tamid
5:1).

After the rise of Christianity, the reading of the Ten
Commandments was abolished. The reason given in the
Jerusalem Talmud is that the Christians contended that
only these commandments and no others were given at
Sinai (TP Ber. 3c). The "proof" of their contention lay
in the fact that the *Shema* contains the verse, "And
these words which I command thee this day shall be
upon thy heart" (Deut. 6:6). As the text of the *Shema*
does not specify what is meant by "these words," the
juxtaposition of the *Shema* and the Ten Commandments
offered seemingly irrefutable evidence that "these words"
are none other than the Ten Commandments which are
designated in the Torah (Deut. 10:4) as the "Ten Words"
(*Aseret Hadevarim*).

The Talmud tells us that when attempts were made in
the Babylonian academies of Sura and Nehardea to institute the daily reading of the Ten Commandments, the

historic precedent was invoked in each case, that "the reading of the Ten Commandments had long been abolished because of the contentions of the Christians" (Ber. 12a). The fact that there were no Christians in Babylonia (Pes. 56a) may have accounted for the attempt to reinstate the reading of the Ten Commandments in the daily service. The historic association of the *Shema* with the Ten Commandments was, however, retained, and it led the Palestinian scholar Rabbi Levi to seek and to find in various phrases of the *Shema* these allusions to all the Ten Commandments:

"Hear O Israel" is an allusion to "I am the Lord your God." "The Lord is One" reflects the commandment, "You shall have no other gods before Me;" "You shall love the Lord your God" alludes to: "You shall not take the name of the Lord your God in vain," for one who really loves God will not lie or swear falsely in His name. "Remember the Sabbath Day to keep it holy" is mirrored in the phrase: "that you may remember all My commandments," for the importance of the Sabbath has been equated with that of all the *mitzvot* of the Torah combined. "Honor your father and your mother" is implied in the expression "that your days and the days of your children may be prolonged," for this is the reward assured to those honoring their parents (Deut. 5:16). "You shall not kill" can be deduced from "And you shall quickly perish," for he who kills is eventually executed. "You shall not commit adultery" is in "that you go not astray after your heart and your eyes," for indeed the heart and the eyes are the agents of sin. "You shall not steal" is deduced from "You will gather in your corn," for this means that you may gather your corn and not that of your neighbor. "You shall not bear false witness against your neighbor" is indicated in "I am the Lord your God," for to bear false witness against another person is tantamount to denying that God created heaven and earth. "You shall not covet your neighbor's house" is evident from "And you shall write them on the doorposts of your house," as the Torah here specifies *your* house, not your neighbor's house (TP Ber. 3c).

שְׁמַע יִשְׂרָאֵל

וְאָהַבְתָּ

Hear O Israel! The Lord is our God, the Lord is One. And you shall love the Lord your God with all your heart, with all your soul and with all your might

The first section (Deut. 6:4-9) affirms that God alone is to be our God. When we say that God is One, we declare that all our loyalties are conditioned by the primary loyalty owed to Him alone. We are to love God with all that we have and with all that we are. If love, any love, is to be more than a casual experience, it must be founded on the consciousness of the proximity of the beloved. The love of God is articulated in the nearness of God, in the fact that it will inspire diligent efforts to teach "these words" to our children, to make these teachings the guideposts of our daily life, evening and morning, when at home and when abroad. As reminders of this supreme loyalty, "these words" are to be placed on the forehead (*tefillin*) and inscribed on the doorposts (*mezuzah*).

וְהָיָה אִם שָׁמֹעַ

If ye shall hearken diligently to My commandments

The second section of the *Shema* is also taken from the Book of Deuteronomy (11:13-21). In the context in which it is found, Moses tells the people that unlike the soil of Egypt which was cultivated largely by irrigation, the land of Canaan which they were about to occupy depended on rain—which is a gift of God. There follows the warning that these rains would come down regularly and plentifully if the Israelites would obey God's commandments, but they would be withheld if Israel allowed itself to be lured into the worship of strange gods. As further punishment for the violation of their covenant with God, they would be driven into exile from the very land which God had given them. As frequent reminders of the promise and the warning, "these words" are to be inserted in the capsules of the *tefillin* and inscribed on the parchment of the *mezuzah*. However unsophisticated the second paragraph of the *Shema* may be, it offers a concrete warning that the moral law cannot be violated with impunity.

Modern history has confirmed all too accurately that in the wake of idolatries based on racial and class imperialisms, severe economic hardship and tragic dislocations of peoples result. The interdependence of moral integrity and physical security can be seen to have a global significance, for the effects of the maltreatment of the weak by the strong offer horrifying validation of the warning here expressed with such simple profundity.

וַיֹּאמֶר

The Lord said to Moses: "Speak to the Israelites and tell them to make fringes on the corners of their garments."

In this, the third section of the *Shema*, mention is made of the fringes (*tzitzit*) "with a blue thread on the fringe of each corner" which the Israelites are to put on their garments. When looking at them, the Israelites will remember "all the commandments of the Lord and do them" (Num. 15:39).

Perhaps because he was apprehensive that the literal meaning of this verse might lead to the telescoping of all the commandments into the one *mitzvah* of the *tzitzit*, Rabbi Meir allegorized it in this comment:

The verse does not say: "And you shall look at them" (namely, the *tzitzit*), but rather "and you shall look at Him (*oto*)." We are here told that one who observes this *mitzvah* is as if he were greeting the Divine Presence, for the blue thread in the *tzitzit* is comparable to the sea, the sea to the verdure, the verdure to the firmament, and the firmament is comparable to the Throne of Glory (TP Ber. 3a).

Comments on the text

El Melekh Neeman

When the *Shema* is read in private devotion, the words: *El melekh neeman* ("God the faithful Sovereign"), forming the acrostic *Amen*, are read before the *Shema*. When one recites the *Shema* at a congregational service, these three words are omitted. Instead, the reader concludes the *Shema* with the words: *Adonai elohekhem emet* ("the Lord your God is faithful"). The reason offered is that there are 245 words in the text of the *Shema,* and by adding three words the total becomes 248, symbolizing the 248 parts of the human body and thus indicating that one should love God with every portion of his being (*Tur Orah Hayyim,* 61).

Ehad

The custom of covering the eyes with one's hand as the word *ehad* is pronounced, is first mentioned as the practice of Rabbi Judah Hanasi (Palestine, 3rd century C. E.), the compiler of the Mishnah (Ber. 13b). The pronunciation of *ehad* is prolonged, as one affirms the uncompromising unity of God and His sovereignty over heaven and earth (*ibid.*). The unity of God is so absolute a principle in Judaism that one is not permitted to recite the *Shema* twice in succession, as such repetition might be taken as compromising monotheistic belief (Ber. 33b).

In the Sefer Torah and in many editions of the Prayer Book, the *ayyin* and the *dalet,* the last letters of the words *shema* and *ehad* respectively, are enlarged to form the word *ed* (witness). Abudraham says that the purpose is to remind every Jew that it is his duty to serve as a witness to God's unity and to His sovereignty in human life.

Barukh Shem Kevod Malkhuto

The recitation of the verse: "Hear O Israel the Lord is our God the Lord is One" was regarded by the Rabbis as "the acceptance of the kingship of God" (Mishnah Ber. 2:2). For this reason the declaration *Barukh shem kevod* . . . ("Blessed is the glorious majesty of His kingship for ever and ever") follows immediately after *Shema Yisrael.*

According to Rabbi Abbahu, the Palestinian Jews recited the *Barukh Shem* aloud all during the year to offset the accusation made by early Jewish Christians that the Jews were silently interpolating some heretical doctrine into the *Shema.* In Babylonia, however, where there were no Christians, *Barukh Shem* was recited in an undertone because it is a non-biblical passage interpolated into a section of biblical verses which, as such, are of a higher degree of sanctity (Pes. 56a). This is the practice today.

For the reason that *Barukh Shem* is recited aloud on Yom Kippur, see pp. 223-24.

On pronouncing the *Shema*

The Mishnah rules that the *Shema* be spoken with the meticulous pronounciation of every syllable in each word (Mishnah Ber. 2:3). Both in the Palestinian and in the Babylonian Talmud, one is cautioned against the conflation of certain words and syllables, and against the mispronunciation of certain words (TP Ber. 4d; Ber. 15b). One of these cautions relates to the correct pronunciation of the *zayyin* in *lemaan tizkeru* ("that you may remember"). With the articulate pronunciation of the *zayyin*, the verse means: "That you may remember to observe all My commandments . . ." But with the *zayyin* mispronounced as an "s," the verse would seem to say: "In order that you may be rewarded (*tiskeru*) for observing all My commandments" (TP Ber. 4d).

The order of the three sections

The three sections of the *Shema* are not recited in the order in which they occur in the Torah, the third section, from the Book of Numbers, being recited after the two sections from the Book of Deuteronomy. Rabbi Joshua ben Korhah offers this explanation:

Why do we read *Shema* before *Vehayah im shamoa*? Because one must first accept the yoke of the Kingship of God and then accept the yoke of the *Mitzvot*. Why does *Vehayah im shamoa* precede *Vayyomer*? Because the latter makes reference to the *tzitzit*, a *mitzvah* which is to be observed only during the day, while in *Vehayah*, we are told "And you shall teach them to your children," and the *mitzvah* of studying and teaching the Torah devolves on us both day and night (Mishnah Ber. 2:3).

Rabbi Simon ben Yohai suggests this additional reason:

The sections are arranged in the descending order of their comprehensiveness. The first section is most important because it stresses the threefold duty to learn, to teach, and to practice. The second accentuates the twofold duty to learn and to practice, while the third underscores only the duty to practice (Ber. 14b).

"Thou shalt love the Lord thy God" (Deut. 6:5)

Our relationship to God must be anchored in a love for Him and in a passion to serve Him with heart, soul, and mind. Some anthropologists say that religion originated in the fear of the unknown. If so, Judaism, at an early stage, graduated from that primitive fear to an enthusiastic pursuit of God's presence.

"When thou sittest in thy house" (Deut. 6:7)

Judaism is a "portable religion." Its practice is not dependent upon a sanctuary or enjoined only for special times and seasons. Wherever we are, at all times, and in all places and relationships, our actions must be consistent with what God demands of us.

"bind them . . . write them . . ." (Deut. 6:8)

Man is in a constant state of tension. Though sentient and rational, he is still an animal; though an animal, he nevertheless possesses the faculties and capacity to transcend his animality. The tension of the divine image and instinctual nature is sustained in the life of man. Man needs therefore to cultivate those qualities which express the divine aspect of his nature. Religious symbols, such as *tzitzit* and the *mezuzah*, are not magical in purpose. They are intended to serve as permanent reminders of the link between man and God.

"If ye shall hearken diligently" (Deut. 11:13)

The Hebrew word for "obey" also means to "hear" and to "understand." Judaism is not content with ignorant and uninformed obedience. It insists on the entire people being "learned of the Lord." The central symbol of Jewish reverence is the scroll of the Torah. The only aristocracy that Judaism recognizes is the aristocracy of learning, open to all—rich and poor alike. Indeed a person of illegitimate birth who is learned in the Torah is deemed by the tradition to take precedence over an ignorant high priest (Mishnah Hor. 3:8).

"I will give the rain of your land in its season"
(Deut. 11:14)

Judaism's love of life and its appreciation of material blessings are illustrated in this passage. Although the Bible often expresses the belief that a people's rectitude leads to physical abundance and security, the Rabbis took occasion to state that material blessings may be a result, but must not be the motive of obedience to God. "Be like servants who serve their master without expectation of a reward" (Abot 1:3).

"after which ye use to go astray" (Num. 15:39)

To live a life of principle, means to relate one's actions to an all-embracing purpose. That purpose is always in danger of being obscured because of the appeal of distracting and unworthy preoccupations. Too often we fail to view the task of the hour in the perspective of the centuries, and we yield to the momentary temptations of the heart and the eye. The *tzitzit* are here depicted as symbols of our dedication to the service of God, and as reminders not to default in the duties that accompany it.

Rabbinic comments on the text

"Thou shalt love the Lord thy God" (Deut. 6:5)

When we approach a mortal ruler, we submit our request with great trepidation and feel greatly relieved upon leaving his presence. Because we fear him, we avoid too frequent contact with him. Very different is our relationship to God. Our fear of Him is suffused with love—the love a person feels for an intimate friend (*Sifre Vaethannan, 32*).

"Thou shalt love the Lord thy God. . . ." really means, "You shall make the Lord your God beloved." Because of you the name of God should become beloved. How can the name of God become beloved because of you? When a person studies the written and the oral Law, attends on the disciples of the Torah, is honest in his dealings with people and courteous toward all, what do people say? "Happy is the father who taught him Torah, alas for those who do not study Torah. This man studied Torah, see how fine are his ways, how ethical his deeds! Of him Scripture speaks when it says: 'Thou art my servant, Israel in whom I will be glorified' " (Isa. 49:3). But when one who studies Torah and attends on the disciples of the wise is dishonest in his dealings with others and is rude in his behavior toward people, what do people say? "Woe unto him who studied Torah, woe unto his father, woe unto his teacher . . . This man studied Torah. Look how corrupt are his deeds, how reprehensible his ways" (Yoma 86b).

"with all thy heart" (Deut. 6:5)

The word for heart here is *levav*, not *lev*. This suggests that we must love God with two "hearts," with evil inclination as well as with our good inclination, by dedicating all our impulses and capacities to His service (Mishnah Ber. 9:5).

"And thou shalt love the Lord thy God . . . with all thy soul" (Deut. 6:5)

When the Romans brought out Rabbi Akiba to execution, they began to comb his body with iron combs. As it was time for reading the *Shema*, he began its recitation, and despite the tortures to which he was being subjected, he continued to take upon himself the yoke of the Kingship of God [i.e., to recite the text of the *Shema*]. His disciples said to him, "Master! thus far?" [Meaning, "Why, amid such agonies, do you concentrate upon saying the *Shema*?"] Rabbi Akiba answered them: "Throughout my life I was troubled with this verse: 'And thou shalt love the Lord thy God . . . with all thy soul.' This means: even if He takes your life. I have been thinking: 'When will I have the opportunity to fulfill this?' Now that the opportunity is mine, shall I not fulfill it?" He prolonged the word *Ehad* (One) and the word was on his lips as he expired. A heavenly voice then proclaimed, "Happy are you, Rabbi Akiba, that you died with *Ehad* on your lips" (Ber. 61b).

"with all thy heart . . . soul . . . might" (Deut. 6:5)

Rabbi Eliezer said: "After we are told to love God with our whole life, why are we then told to love Him with all our might, i.e., our wealth? There are persons to whom life is more precious than wealth. They are admonished to love Him with all their life. But there are others whose actions indicate that wealth is dearer to them than life. Such people are bidden to love God with all their wealth" (Ber. 61b).

"with all thy might" (Deut. 6:5)

Meod, which means "might," suggests the word *middah* (measure). From this we can deduce that whatever measure God metes out to us, be it one of joy or sorrow, we should be grateful to Him (Mishnah Ber. 9:5).

"which I command you this day" (Deut. 6:6)

You must not regard my commandments as obsolete decrees to which nobody pays attention. They must be to you something ever new and precious, relevant decrees for "this day" which a person is most anxious to read and obey (*Sifre Vaethannan,* 33).

"if ye will hearken diligently" (Deut. 11:13)

This means "hearken to understand." By being cognizant of what we have already learned, we become receptive to new learning and thus acquire a deeper insight into the Torah (*Sifre Ekev,* 48).

"this day, to love the Lord your God" (Deut. 11:13)

Beware lest you be tempted to think: "I shall study in order to acquire wealth, or to have the honor of being addressed as Rabbi, or that I may earn a reward in the world to come." The Torah says, "to love." All that you do, must have the pure aim of expressing your love for God (*Sifre Ekev,* 48).

"this day" (Deut. 11:13)

Say not: "I cannot master the entire Torah and observe all its *mitzvot.*" For are we not told that "the measure thereof is longer than the earth and broader than the sea"? (Job 11:9). Such fallacious thinking is reflected in the following parable: A king asked his son to hire two men to fill a deep pit. The first, a stupid worker, upon looking into the pit, exclaimed in despair, "How can I fill so deep a cavern?" The other, a wise worker, said, "What concern is it of mine that the pit is so deep? I am hired by the day and I shall therefore perform my day's work." So God says to us: "What concern is it of yours that the Torah is so extensive and that there is so much to learn? You are hired to do My work from day to day. All that I expect of you is to perform a full day's work in the study of Torah" (*Yalkut Ekev,* 863).

"grass in thy fields for thy cattle, and thou shalt eat" (Deut. 11:15)

It is forbidden to partake of any food before one has fed his animal. First provide grain for your cattle and then you may eat (Ber. 40a).

"eat and be satisfied. Take heed . . ." (Deut. 11:15)

When a person is fully satiated, he tends to rebel against God . . . An example of the perils of material prosperity were the people of Sodom who said, "We have surplus food, let us therefore deny all wayfarers the right to enter our city" (*Sifre Ekev*, 43).

"turn aside and serve other gods and worship them" (Deut. 11:16)

When a person forsakes God and His Torah, he is prone to worship idols (*Sifre Ekev*, 43).

"lay up [samtem] these My words in your heart" (Deut. 11:18)

Vesamtem calls to mind *sam tam*, which means: "a perfect tonic." The Torah is a tonic which gives vitality to all who partake of it. It imbues man with strength to master his evil inclination (Kid. 30b).

"teach them to your children" (Deut. 11:19)

Rabbi Joshua ben Levi said: "He who teaches Torah to his grandchild is considered as if he were personally receiving the Torah at Sinai. This we learn from the passage in the Torah, "Make them known to your children and your children's children," which is followed by the verse, "The day that *thou* stoodest before the Lord *thy* God in Horeb" (Deut. 4:10) (Kid. 30b).

Rabbi Hiyya ben Abba saw that Rabbi Joshua ben Levi was wearing festive clothes as he was bringing his grandchild to the school. He asked, "Why this festive attire?" Rabbi Joshua answered "Is this not an occasion of supreme importance? Is not the act of bringing a grandchild to the study of the Torah likened to the revelation at Sinai?" From that time on, Rabbi Hiyya would not partake of his morning meal till he had taught his son a Torah lesson (Kid. 30b).

Why are we told in another verse, "Make them known unto thy children and thy children's children"? (Deut. 4:9) This serves to teach us that he who educates his child in the knowledge of the Torah is considered as if he were giving Torah instruction to his children, his grandchildren, and indeed, to future generations for all time to come (Kid. 30b).

"bid them make . . . fringes" (Num. 15:36)

Why is this section a part of the prescribed *Shema*? Because it speaks of five important subjects: The *mitzvah* of *tzitzit*, our liberation from Egyptian bondage, the duty of observing the Commandments, the warning to abstain from lust, and the warning to abstain from idolatry. The first three are directly mentioned, while the last two are implied in the words: "That ye go not about after your own heart and your own eyes, after which ye use to go astray" (Num. 15:39) (Ber. 12b).

"in the corners of their garments" (Num. 15:37)

In ancient days, a slave carried on his person the seal of his master. The fringes are the sign and seal of our complete submission to the will of the Holy One, blessed is He (*Tosefot, Men.* 43b).

"look upon it and remember all the commandments of the Lord, and do them" (Num. 15:39)

Seeing alerts the memory and memory leads to action (*Men.* 43b).

"after which ye use to go astray" (Num. 15:39)

This can be explained by the following parable: A man fell from a boat into turbulent waters and was struggling for life. The pilot threw him a rope and said, "Take hold of this rope and don't let it slip from your grasp, for if you let go, you will not live." So said God to Israel: "As long as you hold fast to the *Mitzvot,* you will survive" (*Tanhuma Shelah,* 15).

There is always the danger that a passing object of lust or cupidity may tempt us to go astray. This is especially true when a person finds himself distant from the friends and counselors whose respect he seeks to retain. The *Mitzvot* have the efficacy of restraint, of deterring us—as the parable suggests—from sinking into the sea of moral indifference. Religious people who are ashamed "before God" will shrink from doing that which is reprehensible. The Prayer Book expresses this thought in these words: "A man should always be God-fearing, in private and in public."

"I am the Lord your God" (Num. 15:41)

Why is this phrase repeated? Because God remains our Sovereign regardless of time and circumstance. He will never relinquish His claim upon us. There is no way in which Israel can repudiate its covenanted relationship to Him who redeemed it from Egypt. . . . "I am the Lord your God" under all circumstances (*Sifre Shelah,* 115).

We are bound to God, Israel, and the Torah, through a covenant which can be disobeyed but cannot be denied. Many who repudiated the covenant and denied that

Israel still has a providential role to play in history came to learn the "brotherhood of suffering" which binds them to Israel. But such a feeling of common peril is surely not enough. "Our existence is either superfluous or indispensable to the world; it is either tragic or holy to be a Jew. . . . We were not born by mere chance as a by-product of a migration of nations or in the obscurity of a primitive past. . . . To be a Jew is to be committed to the experience of great ideas." •

אֱמֶת וְיַצִּיב

True and firm

God in history

After the *Shema,* we find this vigorous affirmation of Judaism's belief in God's enduring power to redeem. This prayer is the subject of the following mishnaic statement by Rabbi Elazar ben Azariah, quoted in the Passover Haggadah:

Said Rabbi Elazar ben Azariah: "I was already seventy years old and had still not understood the reason for our reference to the liberation from Egypt in the evening service, until Ben Zoma derived it from the interpretation of the verse, "That you may remember the time you departed from Egypt, all the days of your life." The words "All the days of your life" mean to teach us that the liberation from Egypt must be mentioned also in the evening (Mishnah Ber. 1:5).

According to Saul Lieberman, the Mishnah here refers to *Emet Veyatziv,* which introduces the theme of the Exodus. *Emet Veyatziv* is specifically mentioned as a very old element of the liturgy recited in the Temple (Mishnah Tamid 5:1), and the Talmud refers to it as a familiar and standard part of the liturgy (Ber. 12a). *Emet Veyatziv* was originally recited in the evening service as well (TP Ber. 2d).

Judaism added a new dimension to religion when it identified the Creator of the universe with the Sponsor of history. The historical consciousness of the ancient Israelites effected a radical transformation in the original nature festivals of the Near East. It linked these

• Abraham Joshua Heschel, *op. cit.,* p. 421.

festivals to crucial events in the history of the people. Passover, though retaining its original agricultural association in the "counting of the omer," became more emphatically "the time of our liberation." Shavuot, the harvest festival of the first fruits, became primarily "the time of the giving of our Torah," and Sukkot, the festival of ingathering, became more prominently a historic commemoration of the wanderings of Israel in the wilderness. Thus nature worship, with its concomitant rites of magic and licentiousness, was suppressed in the very early stages of the religion of Israel.

Judaism's notion that the intention and will of God manifests itself in history does not compromise man's moral freedom and responsibility. It falls neither into fatalism nor into an otherworldly postponement of redemption. Judaism is firm in its teaching that man is a free agent, and that by his action he can either advance or impede the work of redemption. So unwilling were the Rabbis to accept a fatalistic view of life, that they had the daring to affirm that when man performs God's will, he strengthens God's power, and when he repudiates God's will, he weakens His power (*Sifre Haazinu*, 319). They were not upset by the evident paradox of God's omnipotence and man's freedom, for as Rabbi Akiba defined it: "Everything is foreseen yet freedom of choice is granted" (Ab. 3:15).

עַל אֲבוֹתֵינוּ וְעָלֵינוּ

As for our fathers, so also for us, for our children, for our generations, and for all the descendants of the seed of Israel

In all ages God's sovereignty is made manifest when the arrogant are humbled, when the captives go free, and when the oppressed are redeemed. God's reign is acclaimed wherever human freedom is advanced.

גָּאַל יִשְׂרָאֵל

Who redeemed Israel

This blessing, known as that of *Geulah* (redemption), is recited by the reader in an undertone, to obviate the necessity of the congregation's responding "Amen." The congregation thus proceeds directly to the recitation of the *Tefillah*, without any interruption. This is done to conform with the rule that the *Geulah* blessing must be followed immediately by the *Tefillah* (TP Ber. 2d).

Comments on the text

Louis Ginzberg, in his commentary on the Jerusalem Talmud, proposes a fascinating theory about the origin of the Islamic practice of praying five times daily. From the Talmud's insistence that the *Amidah* should follow immediately after the *Geulah* blessing, we can deduce that the aim was to counteract an earlier custom of the people—to recite the *Amidah* apart from the *Shema* and its accompanying blessings. This was indeed the earlier practice. The pious would recite the *Shema* at dawn and follow immediately with the *Tefillah*. But most others would recite the *Shema* at home, upon rising at dawn. After attending to some of their daily tasks, they would go to the synagogue for the *Tefillah*, which, according to Rabbi Judah, could be read till four hours after sunrise (Mishnah Ber. 4:1). The evening service also has a *Geulah* blessing which precedes the *Tefillah*. Thus there were originally five daily "services": (1) the morning *Shema;* (2) the morning *Tefillah;* (3) the *Minhah* service; (4) the evening *Shema;* (5) the evening *Tefillah*. In time, the five were telescoped into three: (1) *Shaharit;* (2) *Minhah;* (3) *Maariv*. To fortify this practice, the rule was adopted: *tekhef ligeulah tefillah*, "the *Tefillah* must be recited immediately after the *Geulah* blessing."

The Arabian Jewish tribes, from whom Mohammed derived many of the beliefs and practices which he incorporated into the faith he founded, were still following the earlier tradition. This may have been because they were not in close contact with other Jewish communities and were unaware of later Jewish practice. Ginzberg surmised that it was from them that Islam derived the practice of praying five times a day.*

The Talmud takes pains to explain that the verse, "O Lord, open Thou my lips; and my mouth may declare

* Louis Ginzberg, *A Commentary on the Palestinian Talmud* (New York: The Jewish Theological Seminary of America, 1941), English introduction, p. lxxii.

Thy praise" (Ps. 51:17), recited before the silent *Amidah,* is to be regarded as an extension of the *Geulah* blessing (*Geulah arikhta*), and not as an interruption of it. It explains in like manner the inclusion of *Hashkivenu* ("Grant that we lie down in peace") after the evening *Geulah* blessing, as being an extension of the *Geulah* blessing (Ber. 4b).

READER'S REPETITION OF THE *SHAHARIT AMIDAH:* ROSH HASHANAH •

Sheliah Tzibbur: The emissary of the congregation

The Talmud deems recital of the *Amidah* to be obligatory for every person in the congregation. Hence the *Amidah* is first recited by each person as he stands in silent devotion. Since prayer books were not used till the eighth century C.E., and since many people did not know the text and the order of the blessings of the *Amidah,* the practice of repeating the *Amidah* was instituted. The repetition of the *Amidah* is designated as *hazarat hashatz* ("the repetition by the reader"), *shatz* being an abbreviation of *sheliah tzibbur* ("the emissary of the congregation"). By listening to the repetition of the *Amidah* as it is rendered by the "emissary of the congregation," persons unfamiliar with the prayers can fulfill their obligation as they say "Amen" after each blessing. We are told that in Hellenistic Alexandria the synagogue was so large and its congregation so huge that a beadle would stand on the pulpit with banners in each hand. He would raise the banners to signal the congregation at points in the service where an *Amen* response was due (Suk. 51b).

Being the emissary of the congregation, the *sheliah tzibbur* was expected to be supremely conscious of his awesome responsibility. In fact, upon being asked to lead the prayers, one was expected to declare in all humility that he was unworthy of the honor and to proceed to the lectern only if asked for the third time (Ber. 34a). The

• The "silent" *Amidah* is the same as that of the *Maariv,* with *Sim Shalom* replacing the shorter *Shalom Rav* (See p. 40).

requirements for a *sheliah tzibbur* were highly idealized. He was expected to be a man whose conduct during his youth was unblemished, a hard-working man, with a large family and a modest income. Such a person would be more likely to pray sincerely for himself and for the congregation. He was also required to have a pleasant voice, to be able to offer a melodious rendition of the prayers, and to have a flawless command of all the *berakhot* and of the required biblical readings for all occasions (Ta'an. 16a).

The need for humility in prayer was symbolized in the location of the reader's stand. When called upon to lead the congregation in prayer, a person was addressed in the words: *red lifne hatevah* ("go down before the lectern"). Originally *tevah* referred to the ark, as is evident from the mishnaic rule that on communal fast days the *tevah* (the ark) should be taken to the public square where a service of prayer and penitence was to be held. Later, the word *tevah* came to be applied to the lectern before which the *sheliah tzibbur* "went down." Its place was not on a raised "pulpit" but on the floor level of the synagogue. According to one opinion, the place of the lectern had to be recessed below the synagogue floor (Ber. 10b) in compliance with the verse: "Out of the depths have I called Thee" (Ps. 130:1).

THE *KEROVAH*

The word *kerovah* stems from an Aramaic root that is already mentioned in the Talmud: "When one is invited to lead the service at the lectern, they do not say to him 'Go and pray' but 'Go and sing' (*karev*)" (TP Ber. 8b). *Kerovah* connotes a set of *piyyutim* woven into the text of the *Tefillah*.

The *Shaharit Amidah* for the first day of Rosh Hashanah is adorned with a *kerovah* composed in the main by Eleazar Kalir. This *kerovah* is known as *At Hil* ("The day of awe has arrived"), after the opening words of the first part. It is preceded by *Yareti Bifetzoti* ("I tremble as I plead"), which, as a *reshut*, is a plea for permission to interpolate poems into the *Amidah*, and which

was composed by Rabbi Yekutiel ben Moses of Speyer
(11th century). Each stanza of this *reshut* ends with the
syllable *hil,* suggesting the Hebrew word for trembling.
Its closing words are *beet at hil* ("my heart palpitates as
the dread day arrives") lead directly to the opening
words of Kalir's *kerovah: At Hil Yom Pekudah* ("The
dread day of judgment has come").

The *reshut* for the second day, equally stirring in
power and pathos, begins with the words *atiti lehanenakh*
("I have come to supplicate Thee"), and is by Rabbi
Simon ben Isaac ben Abun of Mayence (11th century)
who is also the author of *Imratekha Tzerufah* ("Thy
word is pure"), the *kerovah* for the second day.

Besides being an extension and embellishment of the
blessings of the *Amidah,* a *kerovah* includes a midrashic
interpretation of the Torah reading and of the *Haftarah*
(prophetic portion) prescribed for the particular day.
Thus, the *kerovah* for the first day of Rosh Hashanah
has *piyyutim* referring to the birth of Isaac, which is the
theme of the Torah reading for the day. The *piyyutim* of
the *kerovah* for the second day refer to the *Akedah* (The
binding of Isaac), which is the content of the reading of
the Torah on that day. The pattern of the *kerovah* is almost effaced in modern versions of the *Mahzor* which
omit many of its structural *piyyutim.*

The first three blessings of the *Amidah* are called *Avot*
(Patriarchs), and the *piyyutim* associated with them refer
to the merit of the patriarchs. The first *piyyut* before the
blessing *Magen Avraham* ("Shield of Abraham") refers
to Abraham; the second, before *Mehayyeh Hametim*
("He who revives the dead"), refers to Isaac; and the
third, before *Hamelekh Hakadosh* ("The Holy King"),
to Jacob. Thus, in the *Shaharit Amidah* for the first day,
the first *piyyut, At Hil,* refers to the midrashic idea that
Abraham was the prototype of an ideal humanity; the
second, *Taalat Zu,* has midrashic allusions to Isaac's life;
and the third, *Even Hug,* extols the virtues of Jacob.
(All three *piyyutim* are omitted in modern abridgements
of the *Shaharit*).

The patriarchal *piyyutim* expatiate on the unconditional love of God evidenced by the three patriarchs. The
"merit of the patriarchs" (*zekhut avot*) is invoked as our
claim to God's merciful consideration. Such a claim re-

flects a deep sense of humility—an awareness of the insufficiency of one's own worth.

The closing section of a *kerovah* is known as the *Silluk* (finale). It brings the ecstatic mood of the service to a crescendo, as it leads directly into the *Kedushah*.

בָּרוּךְ אַתָּה ה'

Blessed art Thou O Lord

The word *barukh* is almost a refrain in the Prayer Book. The translation: "Blessed art Thou" employs the word "blessed" in the sense of "praised" or "praiseworthy." Jacob Emden (German Talmudist, 1697-1776), in the introduction to his commentary on the Prayer Book, equates the grammatical form of *barukh* with that of *rahum* and says that as *rahum* means "the source of all love" (or mercy), so *barukh* means "the source of all blessings." Another nuance of the word *barukh* is conveyed in the blessings of gratitude which are classified as *Birkhot Hanehenin,* in which we express gratitude for material, aesthetic, or spiritual delights. In such a context *barukh* means "We thank Thee" or "Thanks are due to Thee."

אֱלֹהֵינוּ וֵאלֹהֵי אֲבוֹתֵינוּ

Our God and God of our fathers

Man is much like other animals in his physiological structure. But he is much more unlike them in that his consciousness is reflexive, turned inwards, and full with self-awareness. The worth of human personality and man's intimate relationship to the Creator are expressed in the Prayer Book when we address God intimately as *Barukh Attah,* "praised art Thou." However, the avowal of our closeness to God and of His accessibility to each individual is fraught with the dangers of excessive mysticism and of withdrawal from society. We therefore invoke God also as "the God of our fathers," the God who is revealed in the living tradition of our people. In thus addressing God, the individual affirms his personal identification with a long historic experience which traces its origin to Abraham, Isaac, and Jacob. The verse "This is my God and I will glorify Him, my father's God and I will exalt Him" (Exod. 15:2) suggests a similar polarity of the individual Jew's quest for God, and of the need to serve Him in the context of the collective and cumulative historic experience of the covenanted people of Israel.*

אֱלֹהֵי אַבְרָהָם אֱלֹהֵי יִצְחָק וֵאלֹהֵי יַעֲקֹב

God of Abraham, God of Isaac and God of Jacob

The God whom we address in prayer is not a philosophical abstraction. We experience Him in a more intimate relationship than as the "Self-moved Mover" or the "Great Mathematician." There are many modes of conceptualizing Him. But in prayer, we approach Him as the intimate and accessible "God of Abraham, Isaac, and Jacob." He is the God who manifests Himself in history and whom the individual confronts when he comes to view his selfhood in a wider framework of significance.

"The term 'God of Abraham, Isaac, and Jacob,'" says Abraham Joshua Heschel, "is semantically different from such a term as 'the God of truth, goodness and beauty.' Abraham, Isaac and Jacob do not signify ideas, principles or abstract values. Nor do they stand for teachers or thinkers, and the term is not to be understood like that of 'the God of Kant, Hegel, and Schelling.' Abraham, Isaac and Jacob are not principles to be comprehended but lives to be continued. The life of him who joins the covenant of Abraham continues the life of Abraham. For the present is not apart from the past. 'Abraham is still standing before God' (Gen. 18:22). Abraham endures forever. We are Abraham, Isaac and Jacob." • •

הָאֵל הַגָּדוֹל הַגִּבּוֹר וְהַנּוֹרָא

The great, mighty and awesome God

The following anecdote reflects an earlier period when the text of the *Amidah* was still in a fluid state, and when

---

* Cf. Saul Lieberman, *Tosefta Ki-Fshutah, Zeraim* (New York: The Jewish Theological Seminary of America, 1955), p. 60, n. 11.
• • Abraham Joshua Heschel, *God in Search of Man* (New York: The Jewish Publication Society of America, 1955), p. 201.

the reader of the service was permitted to vary the text of each prayer providing that he concluded each element of the *Amidah* with the prescribed *Barukh Attah* blessing:

A certain person led the congregation in prayer in the presence of Rabbi Haninah. He prayed as follows: "O God! the great, the mighty, the awesome, the glorious, the powerful, the majestic and exalted God." Said Rabbi Haninah, "Have you exhausted all the praise due to your Master? Were it not for Moses having used the first three of the attributes which you mentioned, the great, mighty and aweful God and for the Men of the Great Synagogue having fixed them in the liturgy, we should not venture to utter them. It is as if an earthly monarch had a million dinars of gold and one praised him for possessing much silver. Would this not be an insult?" (Ber. 33b).

Rabbi Haninah was objecting to the proliferation and multiplication of adjectives in praise of God, because he regarded excessive laudation not as an act of piety but almost as one of blasphemy, in that such proliferation of words implied that it is possible for man to apprehend and express in words the infinite and incomprehensible nature of God. Hence he insisted that in the recitation of the *Amidah,* reference to God's majesty should be limited to the adjectives: *hagadol, hagibbor,* and *hanora* (great, mighty, and awesome).

There are times when God seems to hide Himself and when a feeling of frustration and helplessness besets even the devout, as they fail to discern a meaningful pattern in the cataclysmic course of history. Such a feeling is described by Rabbi Joshua ben Levi with disarming honesty in this utterly frank passage:

The Men of the Great Synagogue were so named, because they restored the Crown to its pristine glory. Moses said: "The great, the mighty and the awesome God" (Deut. 10:17). Then came Jeremiah and said, "Alien peoples are occupying His Temple, where then are His awesome deeds?" Therefore, in praising God he omitted the word *nora* (awesome), saying only, "The great, the mighty God" (Jer. 32:18). Then came David and said, "Strangers are oppressing His children, where then are His mighty deeds?" Therefore when he prayed, he said, "The great and the awesome God" (Daniel 9:15), omitting the word *hagibbor* (the mighty One). Then came the Men of the Great Synagogue and said: "God is indeed mighty in that He restrains His wrath so as to give the wicked time to repent. He is indeed awesome in that, in the face of fierce persecution by all the nations, His people has through His power, survived." By what authority did Jeremiah and Daniel modify what Moses has enacted? Said Rabbi Elazar: "Knowing that God demands utter sincerity in prayer, they could not utter superlatives which did not echo their true feeling" (Yoma 69b; cf., TP Ber. 10c).

When, in our prayers, we express faith in the power of God and in His goodness, we do not presume to see clearly the pattern and plan of His providential government of the world. Often, in moments of frustration and despair we are in the mood of exclaiming with the psalmist: "Nay, but for Thy sake are we killed all the day; We are accounted as sheep for the slaughter. Awake, why sleepest Thou, O Lord? Arouse Thyself, cast [us] not off forever" (Ps. 44:23-24). But then, we regain our composure and banish despair. Even though we do not yet understand the meaning of the agonizing events in which we are involved, we muster our endurance and call up our courage as, with the same psalmist, we say: "Arise for our help, and redeem us for Thy mercy's sake" (Ps. 44:27). Judaism enables such hope by its teaching that the individual Jew can play a meaningful, even if humble, part in the drama of history, by committing his life to the realization of the ideals which the prophets and sages of Judaism delineated as the grand obsession and divinely ordained purpose of the Jewish people.

גּוֹמֵל חֲסָדִים טוֹבִים

Who bestows loving-kindness . . . and is mindful of the virtues of our patriarchs

"The day is short, but the task is great," says Rabbi Tarfon (Ab. 2:15). Human life is transitory, but God is eternal. His everlastingness validates the sacrifices of those who dedicate their lives to His service, and to the service of the welfare of humanity. Because the covenant with Abraham, Isaac, and Jacob is sealed with the seal of God's eternity, our own limited span of life can assume enduring significance.

מְסוֹד חֲכָמִים

By the permission of the learned and under-standing sages

This is a *reshut* in which permission is asked by the reader to introduce *piyyutim* into the *Amidah*. It is assumed that it antedates Kalir and is included in each *Amidah* before the first poetic interpolation.

On Rosh Hashanah and Yom Kippur the concluding stanzas of this *reshut* differ, reflecting in their difference the respective themes of these days. On Rosh Hashanah the concluding words read: "I open my mouth in prayer and supplication to entreat and implore the Presence of the King of Kings and the Lord of Lords." On Yom Kippur they read: "I open my mouth in prayer and supplication, to entreat and implore mercy from the Presence of the King who is full of compassion, who pardoneth and forgiveth iniquity."

יָרֵאתִי בִּפְצוֹתִי

With trembling I rise to implore
Thine awesome presence

Reshut for the first day

This is intended as a supplication by the reader for the acceptance of the prayers he renders. Supremely conscious of his own inadequacy and unworthiness, he voices the hope that his rendition of the liturgy be authentic and not artificial. Apprehensive lest, as the emissary of the congregation, he fails to win forgiveness for them, he seeks solace in the promise made to Moses "in a cleft of the rock" (Exod. 33:22), that whenever Israel would appeal to God's mercy, its petition would not be rejected (R. H. 17b). Though awed by the Day of Judgment and depressed by his own lack of merit, the reader, nevertheless, draws courage from the thought that because of the merit of the patriarchs, his prayers would be favorably received.

This acrostic is by Rabbi Yekutiel ben Moses of Speyer (11th century). The first letters of its strophes spell out

the name of the author יקותיאל בר משה and a brief
personal supplication חזק ואמץ יחי ("May he be strong
and of good courage and live"). Skillfully the author ends
each strophe with the syllable *hil,* thus setting the mood
for Kalir's *kerovah, At Hil* ("The dread day of judgment
has come") which follows this *reshut* in unabridged editions of the *Mahzor.*

אָתִיתִי לְחַנְנָךְ

**I come to supplicate Thee with a heart rent
and agitated.**

Reshut for the second day

The author, Rabbi Simon ben Isaac ben Abun, gives expression in this prayer to the trepidation with which the
sheliah tzibbur (reader)* approaches the ark to entreat
God that His justice be tempered with His mercy. He is
filled with consternation by the knowledge that he lacks
the piety and character expected of a worthy emissary of
the congregation. But pray he must, for he must fulfill
the sacred mission which has been entrusted to him. It is
his hope that despite his deficiency in the requisite
eloquence and erudition, his prayers would win help and
healing for the people which has deputed him to be their
emissary.

This alphabetical acrostic conceals the name of he
author שמעון in the words of the last stanza:

שלח מאתך עזר ותרופה
נאמיך ישיגו לחזק ולתקפה

Each stanza closes with a biblical quotation.

זָכְרֵנוּ לְחַיִּים

Remember us for life

The God of life

It was reported that an Italian, on his 104th birthday,
toasted the sky with a glass of grappa and said: "Up there

* See discussion of *sheliah tzibbur,* p. 82.

they have forgotten about me." The old man's toast re-
flects the mind of many people who think that when God
"remembers" us, He calls us to the "beyond," and when
He "forgets" us, we remain alive. Judaism pays its tribute
to God as the Author of life by reversing the vocabulary.
When we are alive we are actively in the thought of God.
When life is in peril, the psalmist exclaims, "How long,
O Lord, wilt Thou forget me for ever? How long wilt
Thou hide Thy face from me?" (Ps. 13:1).

לְמַעַנְךָ אֱלֹהִים חַיִּים

For Thy sake, O living God

When we pray that God may remember us for life, we
express much more than the "will to live." We desire a
life "for Thy sake, O living God." Judaism stresses the
incalculable worth of a life dedicated to the Most High.
The tragedies which our forebears experienced in so large
a measure, never moved them to renounce life, for they
felt as the psalmist felt when he said: "I will praise the
Lord while I live; I will sing praises unto my God while
I have my being" (Ps. 146:2).

אַתָּה גִּבּוֹר . . . סוֹמֵךְ נוֹפְלִים

Thou art mighty . . . sustainest the living . . .
supportest the falling . . . healest the sick . . .

We usually associate might with the ability to harm, but
here it connotes the power to heal. When Moses pleads
for God's forbearance with Israel, he says: "And now, I
pray Thee, let the power (koah) of the Lord be great,
according as Thou hast spoken, saying: 'The Lord is slow
to anger and plenteous in lovingkindness, forgiving iniquity and transgression' " (Num. 14:17-18). Human beings imitate the Divine when they use their power for
"sustaining the living, supporting the falling, and healing the sick." They then serve as messengers (malakhim)
of God, whom the psalmist extols as "Ye Mighty in
strength, that fulfill His word" (Ps. 103:20).

מְחַיֵּה הַמֵּתִים

Who revives the dead

The Mishnah (Ber. 5:2) ordains that during the rainy season there be inserted into the blessing of *Tehiyyat Hametim* ("The resurrection of the dead") the reference to God as: *Mashiv haruah umorid hagashem* ("He who causes the wind to blow and the rain to fall"). This insertion is called *Gevurot Geshamim* ("The wondrous power of God as manifested in the rainfall"). In the talmudic discussion of the exact time when the rainy season begins, reference is made to this statement by Rabbi Yohanan (Palestine, 3rd century):

> Three keys are kept in the hands of the Holy One, blessed is He, and they were never given over to an agent. They are: the key to rain, the key to childbirth, and the key to resurrection (Taan. 2a).

Rabbi Yohanan's statement helps us discern the underlying motif of the second blessing of the *Amidah*. God is acclaimed as the Source and Sustainer of life, who validates our hope for a future life. The origin of life is a great miracle and a great mystery. The persistence and renewal of life in nature is deemed a manifestation of God's *Gevurot*—His extraordinary powers. Man's quest for immortality is caused by the surmise that his all too brief stay on earth is only part of a fuller cycle of life, the key to which is in the hands of God, among whose *gevurot* is that of *tehiyyat hametim,* resurrecting the dead.

The resurrection of the dead is so strongly affirmed that the Mishnah lists among those to be excluded from the world to come, the person who states that "there will be no resurrection of the dead" (Mishnah Sanh. 10:1). But in the liturgy, *Tehiyyat Hametim* is mentioned as one of several manifestations of God's love and power. He sustains the falling, heals the sick, releases those in bondage, and revives the dead. Immortality is thus cited more as a testimony to God's power and goodness than as a source of human solace. By affirming belief in an afterlife, we avow our faith that God will, in His own good time, provide a rectification of the martyrdom and suffering endured by the righteous during their life on earth. Belief in resurrection is also a corollary of Judaism's doctrine that every person is individually responsible and accountable to God for the quality of his life on earth. *Tehiyyat Hametim* asserts that at life's end we shall stand in judgment before God, even as it affirms that before God the individual has an enduring worth which transcends the contradictions and compromises of time and history.

Talmudic personalities were as conscious as we are that for the human mind, immortality is a vast and unexplorable continent. Hence, they were vague in "spelling out" the nature of immortality. *Tehiyyat Hametim* always remained, as Max Kadushin puts it, "an indeterminate belief," necessitated by our faith in God but concretized in diverse ways. Rab, for example, was fond of this word picture of the future life:

In the world to come, there is neither eating nor drinking, neither procreation nor preoccupation with business, neither jealousy nor hatred nor rivalry, but the righteous sit with their crowns on their heads and derive joy out of the splendor of the Divine Presence (Ber. 17a).

In all rabbinic verbalizations of the intimations of immortality, some reference is made to the resurrection of the body. It is much more credulous to conceive of a bodily resurrection than to conceive of a disembodied soul coming to life. But the consistent association of the resurrection of the body with the afterlife may have implied a protest against the denigration of the human body which leads to excessive asceticism and self-denial. The Rabbis were averse to a strict dichotomy of body and soul. Their insistence that the body and the mind of man together account for and are accountable for his moral conduct is strikingly expressed in this parable:

Antoninus said to Rabbi (Judah the Prince): "Body and soul can escape from divine judgment. How? The body can say: 'It was the soul that sinned, for ever since I separated from it, I lie in the tomb silent as a stone.' The soul can say: 'It was the body that sinned, for ever since I separated from it I am soaring in the air like a bird.'" The sage replied: "Let me give you a parable. A human monarch had a splendid park in which there were fine new fruits, and he stationed in it two keepers: one lame and the other blind. Said the lame man to the blind one,

'I see fine early fruits in the park; let me climb up upon you
and we will get them and eat them.' So the lame man rode
on the back of the blind man and they got the fruits and ate
them. Sometime later, the king came and said to them:
'Where are the fine early fruits?' The lame man said, 'Have I
then legs to walk with?' The blind man said, 'Have I then eyes
to see?' What did he do? He made the lame man mount on
the shoulders of the blind man and punished them together.
So God will bring the soul, infuse it into the body and judge
them together" (San. 91a-b).

אַתָּה הוּא אֱלֹהֵינוּ

Thou art our God

This alphabetical acrostic, originally the fourth part
of Kalir's *kerovah* for Rosh Hashanah, celebrates the
majesty of God, His incomparable purity, His eternity,
and His power. He is Creator of all that is and the Be-
stower of life upon all that lives. Garbed in righteousness,
He brings retribution on those who defy His will. Near
to those who call upon Him in truth, He is God, ever-
living, everlasting, awesome, Most High, and Most Holy.

אַדֶּרֶת מַמְלָכָה

A tyrannical conqueror hurled the kingdom of
Israel to the ground. The downtrodden children of the Most High will yet see the end of
the arrogant oppressor and be restored to glory
as of old.

Israel was driven into exile because it rebelled against
God, its true King, and went astray after strange gods.
The heathen conquerer, proud that he destroyed the
sanctuary and devastated the Holy Land, arrogantly
boasted: "Who besides me rules the world? I alone am
master of all creation." Because Israel broke its covenant
with God, it was given over to a heartless tyrant for
chastisement, but not for long will the pretender boast
with pride. As Israel sounds the *shofar,* and heeds the call
to repentance and self-renewal, the Eternal King will
make manifest His saving power and His sovereignty.

The *piyyut, Aderet Mamlakhah* is inspired by the opening words of the Torah reading: "And the Lord took note of Sarah." It is recited only on the first day of Rosh Hashanah, when that day falls on a week-day, and on the second day when the first day of Rosh Hashanah falls on Sabbath. The reason is that its concluding refrain *Tair Vetaria* makes specific reference to the sounding of the *shofar* which is omitted on Sabbaths.

This encloses an acrostic of the full name of the author אֶלְעָזָר בִּירִיבִּי קִילִיר spelled out by the first letters in each stanza.

שְׁמוֹ מְפָאֲרִים

His name is extolled by His people. His praise is pronounced by His heavenly assembly. In His Temple all say: "Glory!"*

This is a *piyyut* which celebrates the power and efficacy of prayer. God's congregation on earth joins the heavenly hosts in praise of His name. The piety of the scholars and the integrity of the faithful adherents of the Torah are observed on high. In response to their prayers, the heavenly mandate is clearly heard: "Better in the sight of the Lord is the noble life and the worthy deed than the choicest offerings on the sacrificial altar." The people, which has remained loyal to God's commandments, will yet wend its way to the holy mountain, there to worship in His sanctuary. On that momentous day of redemption, a loud *shofar* will be sounded. Once again, Jerusalem will resound with the joyful worship of God. Heaven and earth will then also acclaim His name, the forests will clap their hands and offer sweet melody; the heavenly hosts and the stars of the dawn will join the human chorus in the triumphant exclamation, "The Lord has done wondrous things throughout the earth. The Lord shall be King over all the earth!"

Many of the *piyyutim* were composed by poets who had witnessed the humiliation of their faith by Judaism's daughter-religions, Christianity and Islam. But the repeated assertions by adherents of these faiths that God had rejected Israel and had annulled His covenant with

---

* *Shemo Mefaarim* is recited on the Sabbath and the second day, with the exception of Sunday.

them, that the Synagogue had been deserted by God for
the Church or the Mosque, did not avail to shake their
faith in Judaism. They preserved their self-respect and
their sanity, by invoking the vision of their restoration as
God's covenanted people, and they clung firmly to the
belief that it was Israel's destiny to inspire all humanity
to proclaim with it: "The Lord has done wondrously on
the earth, the Lord shall be King over all the earth."

Each stanza of this *piyyut* by Simon ben Isaac ben
Abun contains an acrostic of the name שמעון In the
first acrostic these letters can be discerned as follows:

שמו מפארים עדת חבלו ונערץ

A similar structure governs the other stanzas. The third
strophe of each stanza is a biblical quotation.

In some abridged editions of the *Mahzor* there are ap-
pended to this *piyyut* the last three stanzas of an alphabetical acrostic אדר והוד by the same author.

אֶתֵּן לְפוֹעֲלִי צֶדֶק

**I will proclaim the justice of my Maker on this
day set aside for the scrutiny of the deeds of
men**

This *piyyut* is likewise an integral part of a *kerovah*
composed by Rabbi Simon ben Isaac ben Abun for the
second day of Rosh Hashanah. We have already seen
(pp. 56-58) that the poet, whose personal life was one of
unrelieved hardship, was very active in the community,
traveling to Rome to secure for his people some ease-
ment from oppressive measures decreed against them. In
his *piyyutim,* Rabbi Simon expresses the agonies as well
as the dreams of his tormented people, but he draws hope
from a confident vision of their future redemption. The
piyyut before us is an alphabetical acrostic concluding
with an acrostic of the author's name שמעון בר יצחק חזק

An old tradition relates that on the wall of Rabbi
Simon's house there were three mirrors so that he could
symbolically view the present in the light of the past and
in that of the hopes of the future. Believing that though

the arc of the universe is vast, it nevertheless bends towards justice, he had a firm faith that the covenant made
with the patriarchs would, under God's providence, be
fulfilled in the lives of their descendants.

אַדִּירֵי אֲיֻמָּה

**In the celestial heights the angels acclaim God
as Eternal Sovereign. On earth, in resounding
tones, Israel echoes this acclaim.**

This *piyyut* by Eleazar Kalir prepares the setting for
the *Kedushah*. The poet envisions a vast congregation of
fiery celestial beings exclaiming aloud: "The Lord is
King, the Lord was King, the Lord shall be King, forever and ever." On earth the proclamation of the eternal
sovereignty of God is, in resounding manner, echoed by
God's earthly hosts—the congregations of His people
Israel. Israel is here characterized by such endearing terms
as: "the noble nation, the learned sages, the heirs of the
precious Torah, the students of God's teaching, the faithful people of the covenant."

A rhythmic type of alliteration is formed by a three-fold
alphabetical acrostic, each line concluding with the sono-
rous refrain *bekol,* "with a loud voice," inspired by the
phrase in the *Kedushah: Az bekol raash gadol* ("Then
with a loud and mighty sound").

The opening phrase *Addire Ayummah* was suggested
by a midrashic interpretation of the Song of Songs (6:10),
which sees in the phrase *ayummah kanigdalot* ("The
bannered hosts of heaven") an allusion to Israel.

The *piyyut* reflects the enduring patience of the Jewish
people. Israel saw in every oppressor an incarnation and
continuation of the Roman Empire that destroyed the
Temple in Jerusalem and exiled the people. The abasement and humiliation heaped upon them did not crush
their spirit. Viewing their sad plight as a chastisement for
their own failures, they regarded the tyrant as a usurper
who dared enthrone himself in defiance of God's justice.
The people which he so cruelly crushed has nevertheless
retained its regal bearing. They still harbor an invincible
faith that God, the Most High King, will punish the
oppressor and rule the world with equity.

מֶלֶךְ עֶלְיוֹן

**God our Most High King is our stronghold and
refuge. He promises and performs as He extends
His mercy to all who implore Him***

The limitless power and wisdom of God, the *Melekh
Elyon* ("The Most High King"), is here contrasted with
the impotence and helplessness of man, the *melekh evyon*
("The inconsequential king"), to whom people are wont
to give obeisance. The "Most High King" has complete
sway over all Creation; His knowledge of the motives and
ways of man is searching and His compassion is abundant
and abiding. The "inconsequential king" is, however,
evanescent in his plans, ephemeral in his power, and is
destined for the oblivion of the grave.

Only two *melekh evyon* stanzas are found in printed
editions of the *Mahzor*. Originally, however, each *Melekh
Elyon* stanza alternated with a *melekh evyon* stanza, and
together they comprised a full alphabetical acrostic. A
full complement of *melekh evyon* stanzas is to be found
in the compilation of the *piyyutim* of Rabbi Simon ben
Isaac ben Abun published in 1938 by A. M. Haberman,
though the *bet* and *tav* stanzas which alone have survived
in our *Mahzor* are of a different wording. The confusion
caused by opening the ark before each *Melekh Elyon*
stanza and closing it before each *melekh evyon* stanza
may account for the deletions.

כָּל שִׁנְאַנֵּי שַׁחַק

**All the hosts of heaven proclaim that the Lord
is King****

The *Kedushah* theme is elaborated again: the heavenly
and earthly beings join in the proclamation of God's
eternal sovereignty and in the rendering of praise to
Him. Each stanza opens with a different characterization
of the celestial hosts. Among these designations are: "the
forces of heaven, the inhabitants of celestial space, the

---

* *Melekh Elyon* is recited on the second day.
** *Kol Shinnane Shahak* is recited only on the second day.

supremely intelligent beings, the divine council of efful-
gent beings." In the second line of each stanza the author
is equally resourceful in his allusions to the earthly congregations that join in the song and sanctification. They
are variously designated as beings whose "destiny is
silence, whose life is transitory, but whose loyalty is constant, who are honored students of the Torah, and who
are assembled in holy congregations." The third line of
each stanza carries the refrain *Elu Vaelu*—the celestial
together with the terrestrial hosts acknowledge and affirm
in ecstatic song that "the Lord is King, the Lord was
King, the Lord forever shall be King."

Rabbi Simon ben Isaac ben Abun of Mayence, exer-
cised his ingenuity in embedding in the first two lines of
each stanza the letters which form an acrostic of his name
שמעון בר יצחק חזק Each letter of the name occurs four
times. Thus, *shin,* the first letter of the name, occurs four
times in words of the first two lines:

כל שנאני שחק . . .

כל שוכני שקט . . .

In addition, the two concluding words of each line
form a double alphabetical acrostic, as, for example, in
these two lines:

כל שנאני שחק באמר מאדירים

כל שוכני שקט בברכה מברכים

לָאֵל עוֹרֵךְ דִּין

**All acclaim sovereignty to Thee; to Thee, God,
who orders judgment**

This alphabetical acrostic of Kalir's *kerovah* for the first
day is also recited on the second day because of its appealing content.

The hymn climaxes the liturgical interpolations in
preparation for the *Kedushah,* which immediately follows. The refrains *beyom din* ("on the day of judgment") and *badin* ("in judgment") induce a mood of

solemnity and even trepidation. But the intent of the
poem is to give comfort and reassurance. On the Judgment Day, God searches our hearts, probes our thoughts,
and fathoms our secrets. But even in judgment, He reveals His love, remembers His covenant, extends His
mercy, restrains His wrath, and assures forgiveness and
renewal to the truly repentant.

For our discussion of the Kedushah *which follows here,*
see pp. 60-62.

וּבְכֵן תֵּן פַּחְדְּךָ

And therefore, O Lord our God, let Thine awe
be manifest in all Thy works, and a reverence
for Thee fill all that Thou hast created

The three *Uvekhen* prayers

The three *Uvekhen* prayers, included in each *Amidah*
of the High Holy Days, are ascribed to Rabbi Johanan
ben Nuri who lived during the Hadrianic persecutions,
about six decades after the destruction of the Second
Temple. The terror and tyranny with which Rome ruled
its far-flung empire, and the brutality with which its
officials in Palestine pursued the extermination of Judaism, gave rise to these prayers.

In the oppression practiced by the Roman empire, our
sages saw an attempt to unite all mankind by force, exploitation, and ruthlessness. They envisioned and hoped
for the time when humanity would be united by man's
fear of God rather than by man's fear of man. By the fear
of God they meant a universal recognition of the inexorable consequences of the violation of the will of God,
which is the moral law. The fear of God not only would
serve as a deterrent to man's inhumanity, but would
lead to a banding together of all men "to perform God's
will with a perfect heart."

It is a fundamental biblical teaching that there is a
universal moral law obligatory on all peoples. Even before Israel came into being, all men were enjoined to
obey that law. The Flood was brought on the world because "the earth was filled with violence" (Gen. 6:11), and
the Sodomites were punished because they were "wicked
and sinners against the Lord" (Gen. 13:13). Interesting

indeed is the fact that the term *yere Elohim* (a God-fearing man) is by no means limited to Israelites; it connotes a person with basic moral scruples. When Abimelech asks Abraham why he refrained from admitting that Sarah was his wife, Abraham answered, "Because I thought: surely the fear of God is not in this place" (Gen. 20:11). Likewise, when the Amalekites attacked the Israelites in a cowardly manner, the Torah characterizes their act as follows: "Remember what Amalek did unto thee by the way as ye come forth out of Egypt; how he met thee by the way and smote the hindmost of thee, all that were enfeebled in thy rear, when thou wast faint and weary; and he feared not God" (Deut. 25:17-18). The prophet Amos severely castigates heathen nations for their brutal conduct to other peoples (Amos 1:3; 2:4). That a God-fearing man is essentially one who obeys the moral law can be seen from this description given by the psalmist: "Come, ye children, hearken to me; I will teach you the fear of the Lord. . . . Keep thy tongue from evil, and thy lips from speaking guile. Depart from evil, and do good; seek peace, and pursue it" (Ps. 34:12-15).

וּבְכֵן תֵּן כָּבוֹד . . . . לְעַמֶּךְ

And therefore, O Lord, grant glory to Thy people, joy to Thy land, gladness to thy city, and redemption to all whose hope is in Thee

With vivid imagery, and reflecting the rabbinic vision of the messianic hope, the second *Uvekhen* articulates for us, as well, the ideal of *Eretz Yisrael* as an autonomous homeland for Jews and Judaism, and as a part of a world community of peoples at peace with one another. There is no conflict between the ideal of a united humanity and that of the continuation of the Jews as a distinct entity among the peoples of the world. Indeed, we can consider the second *Uvekhen* as a prayer for the liberation of all peoples, for the Jews have rightly been characterized as the "barometer of civilization." "Whenever joy is about to come upon the world, the people of Israel is the first to feel it; even as when distress is about to come upon the world, Israel is the first to feel it" (*Midrash Ekhah*, ed. Buber, 2:3). The unity of mankind does not call for a

global uniformity of culture and creed and the oblitera-
tion of distinctive historic traditions. A striking example
of the kind of unity which must be the basis of a universal accord is given in a celebrated passage in Isaiah, in
which three peoples who in the prophet's time were implacable enemies of one another are thus spoken of:

In that day shall Israel be the third with Egypt and with Assyria, a blessing in the midst of the earth, for that the Lord of
hosts has blessed him saying "Blessed be Egypt My people and
Assyria the work of My hands, and Israel Mine inheritance"
(Isa. 19:24-25).

וּבְכֵן צַדִּיקִים יִרְאוּ וְיִשְׂמָחוּ

**And therefore, the righteous shall see and be
glad, the just exult, and the pious rejoice in
song, while iniquity shall close its mouth. . . .**

When wickedness will have vanished like smoke and
when the "kingdom of arrogance" (which referred originally to Rome) will have been vanquished, joy will come
to all men of moral constancy.

This prayer can serve to remind us that the ennobling
of the individual must be the ultimate goal of society.
Society must develop the conditions wherein its citizens
may become *tzaddikim,* socially responsible; *yesharim,*
men of integrity; and *hasidim,* spiritually dedicated men.

Comments on the text

It is assumed by scholars that originally the *Uvekhen*
prayers reflected a difference of opinion between Rabbi
Johanan ben Nuri and Rabbi Akiba about the place-
ment of the prayers and verses in celebration of God's
universal kingship in the *Musaf Amidah* of Rosh Hashanah. According to Rabbi Johanan ben Nuri, the *Malkhuyot* prayers are to be inserted into the *Kedushat Hashem*
("The Sanctification of the Name"), the third blessing of
the *Amidah.* According to Rabbi Akiba, they are to be
inserted into the *Kedushat Hayom* ("Sanctification
of the Day"), the fourth blessing of the *Amidah* (Mishnah
R. H. 4:5). The opinion of Rabbi Akiba prevailed, and
our liturgy is arranged accordingly. However, because of
their appealing and exalted content, the three *Uvekhen*

prayers have been retained and are recited during the third blessing of each *Amidah* not only on Rosh Hashanah, but on Yom Kippur as well.

In his *Orhot Hayyim* (22a), Rabbi Aaron ben Jacob ha-Kohen of Lunel (14th century) sees in the first *Uvekhen* a reflection of the theme of *Malkhuyot* in that it speaks of a world under the kingship of God; in the second, that of *Zikhronot,* in that it prays for the joy which would come to Jerusalem when God "remembers" His people and His land; and, in the third, that of *Shofarot,* since it speaks of the time when the end of "kingdom of arrogance" would be heralded by the *"shofar* of Liberation."

אַתָּה בְחַרְתָּנוּ

**Thou hast chosen us from all people. . . .
Thou hast sanctified us by Thy commandments**

Living in God's companionship

We avow that we deem it a privilege to be members of the household of Israel. This implies no national arrogance, no desire for supremacy or dominion over others. To have been chosen from among the nations, and to have been singled out among all tongues, means that upon us devolves the duty of a life of holiness, of serving as emissaries and witnesses of God, by whose Name we have been called. To live in the constant companionship of God is the meaning and purpose of our chosenness.

The closeness and constancy of the community of God and the Jew are reflected in this charming talmudic anecdote:

A ship filled with pagan passengers was sailing the Mediterranean. On board was one Jewish lad. A severe storm arose and the terrified passengers proceeded to pray, each to his own idol. As their prayers were of no avail, they turned to the Jewish lad and said to him, "We have heard that your God answers you when you pray to Him and that He is all-powerful. Pray then to your God for all of us." The boy proceeded to pray with all his heart. God accepted his prayers, and the storm subsided. As they came to a strange island they went ashore to purchase provisions. They said to the lad, "Do you wish to purchase something?" Said the lad "What can we get in this

lonely place?" They answered: "It is not you who are in a
lonely place but we. Some of us are here while their god is in
Babylonia, others are here while their god is in Rome. Still
others are here and while their idol is with them, he is im-
potent. But as for you, wherever you go, your God is with
you" (TP Ber. 13b).

וְקִדְּשָׁתָנוּ בְּמִצְוֹתֶיךָ

Thou hast sanctified us by Thy commandments

The idea of the holy in Judaism

The word *kadosh,* which is the key to this familiar and
recurring phrase, means "to be set apart" and, hence, to
be dedicated to God's service. We declare that our lives
take on the dimension of holiness through the observance
of the *Mitzvot.* God dedicated Israel to Himself by means
of the *Mitzvot* and these transform it into a holy people.

One understands more clearly the implications of this
concept if one attends to Max Kadushin's analysis of
"The Commonplace and the Holy" (*The Rabbinic Mind,*
pp. 167-188). He shows how the Talmud classifies certain objects as being intrinsically holy, these objects being
for the most part associated with parchments containing
the Name of God. They are actually called *kedushah.* In
the category of *kedushah* are a scroll of the Torah, *tefillin,* a *mezuzah,* and scrolls of the Prophets or the Writings. In addition, the receptacles or covers for such holy
objects, classified as *tashmishe kedushah* (accessories of
holiness) must, like the *kedushah* objects themselves, be
treated with special reverence and not thrown aside care-
lessly (Meg. 26b). Apart from these objects of *kedushah*
and *tashmishe kedushah,* there is a second group of ritual
objects which can freely be thrown away when they are
no longer being used (Meg. 26b). They are known as
tashmishe mitzvah (objects used in performing a *mitzvah*)
and are not intrinsically holy. A *sukkah* is not holy after
Sukkot, and the same is true of a *lulav.* A *shofar* or *tzitzit*
belong to the same category of *tashmishe mitzvah* in
that, though they are used in the performance of a *mitzvah,* they are in themselves not considered to be holy.

This leads us to an important aspect of Judaism's concept of holiness. It is not the "ritual object" that is holy

(unless it be related to that on which God's Name is written), but it is *man* who becomes holy when he performs a *mitzvah*. This is clearly the meaning of *veki-dashtanu bemitzvotekho* ("Thou hast made us holy through Thy *Mitzvot*").

When we perform a *mitzvah* we have experienced an event of holiness and each *mitzvah* is symbolic of the entire sacred system of *Mitzvot* whereby our lives partake of the dimension of the holy. For this reason the blessing before the performance of a rite begins with the mention of the sanctifying nature of all the *Mitzvot:* "Blessed art Thou, O Lord our God, King of the universe, who hast sanctified us by Thy *Mitzvot.*" Then the blessing continues with a reference to the particular commandment about to be performed.

What is the nature and content of the *Mitzvot* whereby our lives are sanctified? What is the full meaning of the rabbinic statement in which God says to Israel, "Be holy, for as long as you fulfill the *Mitzvot* you are sanctified, but if you neglect them you are profaned"? (*Num. Rabbah,* 17:7) It is commonly assumed that the *Mitzvot* are "ritual" observances, and this widespread impression seems to be confirmed by the fact that a *berakhah* is recited only before the prescribed performance of some religious ritual, such as that of putting on *tefillin,* entering a *sukkah,* or sounding the *shofar.* But these "ritual" *Mitzvot* do not at all exhaust the concept of *Mitzvah.* It is also a *mitzvah* to give charity, to visit the sick, to show respect for the aged, to dower the bride, and to accompany the deceased to his final resting place. These righteous acts, no less than the ritual acts, make us holy. Why then do we not recite a *berakhah* before such acts? A number of reasons have been suggested. One is that while ritual observances need a *berakhah* to invest them with sacred significance, ethical acts are intrinsically sacred. Another reason is that one does not, as in the case of giving charity or visiting the sick, say a blessing for a *mitzvah* occasioned by another person's misfortune. A third reason may be that the ethical *Mitzvot* devolve on non-Jews as well, and that a *berakhah* is recited only on the performance of *Mitzvot* which are obligatory only upon Jews.

It is essential for a true understanding of Judaism that we avoid diluting the word *mitzvah* by limiting it to the ritual observances, indispensable as these are. In the Bible it is made abundantly clear that righteousness must precede the observance of the rite.

This idea is one of the main teachings of the prophets. Thus Isaiah addressed to a multitude that thronged the Temple courts these pertinent words:

To what purpose is the multitude of your sacrifices unto Me? Saith the Lord; I am full of the burnt-offerings of rams, and the fat of fed beasts; and I delight not in the blood of bullocks, or of lambs, or of he-goats. When ye come to appear before Me, who hath required this at your hand, to trample My courts? Bring no more vain oblations; it is an offering of abomination unto me; New moon and sabbath, the holding of convocations —I cannot endure iniquity along with the solemn assembly. Your new moons and your appointed seasons, My soul hateth; They are a burden unto Me; I am weary to bear them. And when ye spread forth your hands, I will hide Mine eyes from you; Yea, when ye make many prayers, I will not hear; Your hands are full of blood. Wash you, make you clean, Put away the evil of your doings from before Mine eyes, cease to do evil; learn to do well; seek justice, relieve the oppressed, judge the fatherless, plead for the widow (Isa. 1:11-18).

Jeremiah delivers a similarly fearless charge to the people assembled at the Temple:

Amend your ways and your doings and I will cause you to dwell in this place. Trust ye not in lying words saying, "The Temple of the Lord, the Temple of the Lord, are these." Nay, but if ye thoroughly amend your ways and your doings; if ye thoroughly execute justice between man and his neighbor; if ye oppress not the stranger, the fatherless, and the widowed, and shed not innocent blood in this place, neither walk after other gods to your hurt; then will I cause you to dwell in this place. . . . (Jer. 7:3-7).

In the Psalms, moral purity is made a requirement for entrance into the sacred precincts of the Temple. One psalm suggests the following "entrance requirements":

Who shall ascend into the mountain of the Lord?
And who shall stand in His holy place?
He that hath clean hands and a pure heart;
Who hath not taken My name in vain,
And hath not sworn deceitfully.

Psalm 24:3-4

Another psalm expresses the same thought with even greater clarity and power:

> Lord, who shall sojourn in Thy tabernacle?
> Who shall dwell upon Thy holy mountain?
> He that walketh uprightly, and worketh righteousness,
> And speaketh truth in his heart;
> That hath no slander upon his tongue,
> Nor doeth evil to his fellow
> Nor taketh up a reproach against his neighbor. . . .
>
> Psalm 15:1-3

The Targum translates the first verse of this psalm as follows:

> Lord, who is *fit* to sojourn in Thy tabernacle?
> And who is *fit* to dwell upon Thy holy mountain?

The implication of the Targum's rendition is that a person earns the right to appear before the Lord only by striving to live up to the highest moral standards. Prayers and the observance of religious sancta are an abomination when one disregards righteousness and merely invests himself in the sacerdotal garb of ritualism. Of such a person the Book of Proverbs speaks when it says, "He that turneth away his ear from hearing the law, even his prayer is an abomination" (Prov. 28:9).

Solomon Schechter pointed out that the Talmud is just as unequivocal in stressing the preeminence of ethical conduct in the Jewish way of life:

Holiness is the highest achievement of the Law and the deepest experience as well as realization of righteousness . . . In its broad features holiness is but another word for *Imitatio Dei,* a duty intimately associated with Israel's close contact with God . . . The holiness of Israel is dependent on their acting in such a way as to become God-like . . . The profession of the Holy One, blessed is He, is charity and loving-kindness, and Abraham who will command his children and his household after him "that they shall keep the way of the Lord" (Gen. 18:19), is told by God: "Thou hast chosen my profession; wherefore thou shalt also become like unto me, an ancient of days" (*Gen. Rabbah* 58:9). The imitation receives practical shape in the following passage: "The members of the house of Israel are in duty bound to deal with one another mercifully, to do charity, and to practice kindness. For the Holy One, blessed be He, has only created this world with loving-kindness and mercy, and it rests with us to learn from the ways of God." •

A teaching by the *Hafetz Hayyim*

The importance of the ethical *Mitzvot* is illustrated in the following anecdote about Rabbi Israel Meir ha-Kohen of Radin (died 1933), popularly known as the *Hafetz Hayyim*•• for having written a treatise against gossip and slander. Once a poor man came to the rabbi's home and after giving him a sumptuous meal, the rabbi, in his zeal to observe the *mitzvah* of hospitality, proceeded to make the bed for him. When his son offered to assist him, the saintly rabbi said, "I would not think of accepting assistance in putting on my *tefillin*. The *mitzvah* of hospitality is no less important, and I wish to perform it entirely by myself."

יַעֲלֶה וְיָבֹא

May our remembrance and that of our ancestors and the remembrance of the Messiah the son of David Thy servant and Jerusalem Thy holy habitation . . . ascend before Thee . . . on this day

Past and present are here merged in a continuum of historic memory and future redemption. Implicit in this prayer is the belief that God remembers what man resolves to bring to remembrance before Him. Out of the persistent hopes which we express in prayer, God fashions the future. Our generation has been witness to this truth, for the "remembrances" which Jews invoked before God during the past nineteen centuries have come to fruition in the renewal of *Eretz Yisrael*. The *Yaaleh Veyavo* is included in every *Amidah* and in the grace after meals

---

• Solomon Schechter, *Aspects of Rabbinic Theology* (New York: Schocken Books, Inc., 1961), pp. 199, 202.
•• The name *Hafetz Hayyim* is derived from a verse in Psalm 34:

> Who is the man that desireth life,
> And loveth days, that he may see good therein?
> Keep thy tongue from evil,
> And thy lips from speaking guile.

Psalm 34:13-14

on the days (other than the weekly Sabbath) when *Musaf* is recited: Passover, Shavuot and Sukkot, Rosh Hashanah, Yom Kippur, and Rosh Hodesh (Shab. 24a).

מְלוֹךְ עַל כָּל הָעוֹלָם

Reign over all the universe in Thy glory . . . that every living creature may understand that Thou hast created it and declare The Lord God of Israel is King and His Kingship rules over all

The Kingship of God

The meaning of Judaism's concept of the "Kingdom of God" or, more correctly, the "Kingship of God" is illuminated by this prayer. We pray for the day when all men will acknowledge God as their Maker, accepting His sovereignty and declaring wholeheartedly: "The Lord God of Israel is King and His Kingship rules over all."

The idea of the "Kingdom of God" has been given an otherworldly accent which is not authentic in Jewish tradition. During the tragic decades of Roman rule over Palestine, certain sects, founded on despair, believed and taught that since the world was in the hands of the "dominion of arrogance" mankind was doomed to punitive annihilation. During that cataclysm, the righteous would be transported to a safe, otherworldly abode and enjoy in the hereafter what was denied them in this life. With the end of this world and of "the kingdom of arrogance" which ruled it, there would be established in heaven the Kingdom of God. Sectarians, whose outlook was colored by their pessimistic persuasion, renounced and denigrated man's earthly strivings and hopes and, therefore, located God's kingdom in heaven. They found seeming confirmation in the phrase: *Malkhut Shamayim* (literally: Kingship of Heaven). But in reality, *shamayim* is here an epithet for God. Why is this epithet used? The Mishnah (Sanh. 10:1) proscribes the explicit pronunciation of the *Shem Hameforash* (Tetragrammaton). The reason may have been to discourage the use of the Name in the performance of magical rites. During the *Avodah* service on Yom Kippur, the Name was spoken by the

High Priest ten times (*Tosefta Yoma,* 2:2). The Talmud makes reference to the Name of twelve letters and another of forty-two letters which were later substituted for the Tetragrammaton when the priests pronounced the benediction. We are informed by Rabbi Tarfon that the twelve-letter Name was deliberately drowned out by the singing of the priests (Kid. 71a). Even the articulation of *Adonai,* the word which was substituted for the explicit pronunciation of the Name, was restricted to prescribed prayers and to citations of verses from Scripture. For other purposes, the practice was to resort to such circumlocutions as *Hashem* (the Name), *Hakadosh Barukh Hu* (the Holy One, blessed is He), *Ribbono Shel Olam* (Master of the Universe), *Hamakom* (the Place), and other metonyms. Reverence for God was thus expressed by the restrictive use of *Adonai* and also *Elohim.* The same reverential motive is displayed in an interesting Yiddish circumlocution which alludes to God as "He whose Name I am not fit to mention." In the light of this practice, we can understand how the Kingship of God came to be referred to as *Malkhut Shamayim* rather than *malkhut Adonai.*

In the Jewish conception, the "Kingdom" of God is not that which is to be established "at the end of time" or "beyond history" or in an otherworldly existence. The "Kingdom" of God is already here now. God's sovereign will established and maintains the laws of heaven and earth (Jer. 33:25), and by His will the destiny of men and nations is decreed. It is therefore not the "Kingdom" of God which man must affirm but His *Kingship.* Man's moral freedom necessitates his being given the choice of obeying the moral law or of rebelling against it. He must of his own volition "accept the Kingship of God" by ordering his life in accordance with the imperatives and disciplines whereby God's will becomes the rule of man's conduct. In the prayer before us, the hope is expressed that the day would be speeded when God would rule over the whole universe with His glory, and when all mankind would declare that the Lord God of Israel is King and His dominion extends over all.

As Israel prays for the day when the Kingship of God would be recognized by all mankind, it is determined to pursue its lonely vocation as it regulates its life under

God's sovereignty. In Judaism, *Mitzvot* are the means whereby life can be lived "under God," and whereby it is responsive to that which is holy. For us, the *Mitzvot* are the means whereby we declare that God "not only reigns in the world, but that He also governs our personal lives."

At the conclusion of the present prayer, we supplicate God to purify our hearts to serve Him in truth, and climax that supplication with the ringing declaration that God is King over all the earth and that from Him stems the sanctity of Israel and the sacredness of the Day of Remembrance.

Comments on the text

This prayer, *Melokh Al Kol Haolam*, closes with: "Who sanctifieth [the Sabbath], Israel, and the Day of Remembrance." This concludes the blessing *Kedushat Hayom* ("the Sanctification of the Day").

This particular order, in which the Sabbath is mentioned first, then Israel, and then the holiday, is that which was practiced in the ancient Babylonian Academy of Pumbedita. In Palestine, and in the Sura Academy (Babylonia), which followed many Palestinian practices, the order was: "Who sanctified Israel [and the Sabbath] and the Day of Remembrance." The Babylonian Talmud gives the following reasoning behind the order that obtains in our liturgy: God sanctified the Sabbath before Israel came into being (Gen. 2:3); therefore, the Sabbath is mentioned first. Since the dates of the holidays were fixed by Israel through its central court (*bet din*), the blessing first refers to Israel's having been sanctified, and only after this does it make reference to the sanctity of the holiday (Pes. 117b).

"Sanctify us by Thy commandments"

For the discussion of this phrase, see p. 104.

"And Thy word is true and stands forever"

For the discussion of this phrase, see pp. 54-55.

רְצֵה

O Lord our God, look with favor on Thy people
Israel and on their prayer. Restore the worship
to Thy sanctuary and receive in love the offerings and supplications of Israel.

This blessing is denoted as *Avodah* (Service) because it
pleads for the restoration of the sacrificial order of worship in the Temple in Jerusalem. It is the oldest of the
blessings of the *Amidah*, having originally been the prayer
offered by the priests for the acceptance of their offering
of the daily morning sacrifice (Mishnah Tamid 5:1). With
the destruction of the Temple, the text was altered by the
addition of the phrase, "Restore the worship to Thy
Sanctuary," thus transforming the prayer into a supplication for the restoration of the Temple and its service.
The concluding blessing originally read: "Blessed art
Thou, O Lord, whom alone we worship in awe" (*Yalkut
Samuel,* 80). It is still recited instead of "Who restores
His presence to Zion" when the *Kohanim* (the priestly
descendants of Aaron) ascend the pulpit to recite the
Priestly Benediction.

We shall have occasion later (pp. 177-78) to comment
on the contemporary significance of the liturgical references to the sacrifices. We must always bear in mind the
saying of Simon the Just (*ca.* 200 B.C.E.), "By three things
in the world sustained: by the Torah, by the Temple
service, and by deeds of loving-kindness" (Ab. 1:2). The
communal sacrifices offered twice daily were regarded as a
concomitant of sincere repentance and as an expression of
obedience to God's will. With the suspension of the
Temple worship, the Rabbis looked upon the restoration of the sacrifices as the effect of Israel's repentance
and of its reconciliation with God. The association of
repentance with the restoration of sacrifices is clearly seen
in the fifth blessing of the *Shemoneh Esreh:* "Bring us
back, O our Father to Thy Torah and draw us near, O
our King, to Thy Service and restore us unto Thee in
wholehearted repentance." With the cessation of the
sacrificial cultus, the greatest stress was put on the indispensability of repentance as a means of nearing the
day when God, whose Presence (*Shekhinah*) had gone into

exile with His people, would return to Zion and again be worshiped by His people as in ancient times. The opinion was even ventured that one whose spirit is broken through remorse and contrition is deemed to be as meritorious as if he had gone up to Jerusalem, rebuilt the Temple, erected its altar, and offered the prescribed sacrifices. The symbolism of the sacrifices is illustrated in this passage from the *Pesikta de Rav Kahana:*

The sacrifices of God are a broken spirit; a broken and contrite heart, O God, Thou wilt not despise (Ps. 51:19). Zabdi ben Levi and Rabbi Jose ben Petros (both flourished in Palestine, 3rd century C.E.), and the Rabbis comment on this verse. One of them said: "David said before the Holy One, blessed is He: 'If Thou wilt accept my repentance I shall know that my son Solomon will arise, build the Sanctuary, erect the altar and offer upon it all the (prescribed) sacrifices.' This lesson we derive from (the sequence of) these verses: *The sacrifices of God are a broken spirit; a broken and contrite heart, O God, Thou wilt not despise. Do good in Thy favor unto Zion; build Thou the walls of Jerusalem. Then wilt Thou delight in the sacrifices of righteousness, in burnt-offering and whole offering; Then will they offer bullocks upon thine altar"* (Ps. 51:19-21).

The other said: "Whence do we know that if a person repents, God accounts it to him as if he had gone up to Jerusalem, built the Temple and the altar and offered all the sacrifices? From the (sequence of) these verses: *A broken spirit . . . Do good in Thy favor unto Zion . . . Then wilt Thou delight in the sacrifices . . .*" (*ibid.*)

The concluding section of this passage contains the oldest version of the *Retzeh* prayer in the *Amidah:*

The Rabbis said: "Whence do we know that he who goes down before the ark should make mention of the rebuilding of the Temple and of the sacrifices and then to bow down? From the following blessing: 'Take delight in us, O Lord our God and dwell in Zion Thy city and may Thy children worship Thee in Jerusalem'" (*Pesikta de Rav Kahana,* ed. B. Mandelbaum, pp. 352-53).

מוֹדִים

We thankfully acknowledge that Thou art the Lord our God. We are grateful unto Thee for Thy miracles which are daily with us.

Affirmation and gratitude

The root of the word *modim* is used in this prayer in two distinct meanings: affirmation and gratitude. We first affirm that God is "our God and the God of our fathers, the Rock of our lives and the Shield of our salvation." Then we declare that throughout the generations, thrice daily—evening, morning, and noon—we offer thanks (*nodeh lekha*) for His protecting care and for His miracles which are daily with us.

Modim thus reflects a mood of gratitude for our daily blessings. Judaism instructs us to be grateful for all the blessings of life and to see in them miraculous manifestations of God's beneficence. God owes us nothing. We owe Him everything. Every living moment is a free gift from Him. The material, intellectual, and aesthetic satisfactions which come to us, the presence of our loved ones, the companionship of our friends—all these are, to cite a phrase in the *Birkat Hagomel,* a prayer recited when one escapes a great peril—"God's goodness to the undeserving." When, in our prayers, we place before God our needs, our anxieties, and our hopes, we do not presume to make demands on Him, for what we already have is beyond our true desert. We simply give expression to that which surges forth from our hearts, and rely on Him to do what is in accordance with His will.

Our sages warned against the tendency to regard prayer as a *quid pro quo* and against arrogant calculation on God's acquiescence to our wishes. Such an automatic, business-like religion, they believed, was suitable to pagans, who renounce their gods when their wishes are not granted, but improper for Jews. This thought was expressed by Rabbi Akiba when he said:

"You shall not do so with Me" (Exod. 20:23).

This verse means that you shall not deal with Me as pagans deal with their gods. Only when good comes to pagans do they honor their gods . . . but as for you, when I bring good upon you, give thanks and also when I bring suffering upon you, give thanks. Thus David says, "I will lift up the cup of salvation and call upon the name of the Lord" (Ps. 116:13); and he says too: "I found trouble and sorrow, but I called upon the name of the Lord" (Ps. 116:3-4) (*Mekilta,* ed. Lauterbach, II, 277).

We are to believe in God even when He sees fit to delay or even deny the fulfillment of our prayers. Eliezer, when he was traveling, would recite this prayer:

May Thy will be done in heaven above, give peace of mind to those who fear Thee and do what is pleasing in Thy eyes. Blessed art Thou, who hearest prayer (*Tosefta Ber.,* 3:7).

The Rabbis even say that he who calculates that every prayer of his will be answered is among those who invoke the recollection of their sins (Ber. 55a).* The following prayer by Bahya Ibn Pakuda (Spain, 11th century) is an example of a pure prayer expressed in complete surrender to God's purpose:

Thou knowest what is for my good. When I recite my wants, it is not to remind Thee of them, but only that I may understand better how great is my dependence upon Thee. If then, I ask Thee for things that do not make for my well-being, it is because I am ignorant. Thy choice is better than mine and I submit myself to Thy decrees and Thy supreme direction.

A deep sense of obligation to God for even the most elementary satisfactions of life is underscored in this statement:

One must not taste anything without uttering a blessing to God, for Scripture says: "The earth is the Lord's and the fullness thereof" (Ps. 24:1). He who partakes of the bounties of this life without saying a prayer is considered as if he had made unlawful use of that which belongs to God (*Tosefta Ber.,* 4:1).

Modim de-Rabbanan

The shorter *Modim,* recited by the congregation in an undertone, is known as *Modim de-Rabbanan,* the "Mo-

---

* In this passage the term *iyyun tefillah* means the expectation that God would grant the wishes expressed in our prayers. In most other talmudic contexts, the phrase carries the laudable connotation of devotion and sincerity in prayer. (See *Tosefot,* on *iyyun tefillah,* R. H. 16b.)

dim of our scholars." The reason for this, as given in the Talmud, is that different texts for a congregational *Modim* response had been suggested by several scholars. R. Papa suggested that a composite of the various texts be recited by the congregation (Sotah 40a). The composite prayer is therefore known as *Modim de-Rab-banan.*

The last phrase of this response is *al sheanahnu modim lakh* ("in that we thank Thee"). Rashi offers this explanation for this seemingly superfluous phrase: "We acknowledge God as the God of all mankind, the Creator of the world. We offer thanks for our life and for our sustenance and pray that we may be privileged to worship God in the Temple courts of Jerusalem. In conclusion, we thank God, 'that He has put it into our hearts to acknowledge Him and to be close to Him.' "

שִׂים שָׁלוֹם

Grant peace, well-being, blessing and grace to us and unto all Israel, Thy people

Shalom in the liturgy

This prayer follows the priestly, threefold benediction: "The Lord bless thee, and keep thee; The Lord make His face to shine upon thee, and be gracious unto thee; The Lord turn His face unto thee and give thee peace." The Talmud (Meg. 18a) tells us that *Sim Shalom* is recited in fulfillment of the verse: "So shall they put My name upon the children of Israel, and I will bless them" (Num. 6:27).

It is an interesting coincidence that just as *Adonai* occurs three times in the priestly benediction, so the name of Israel is mentioned three times in *Sim Shalom.* During the Days of Awe there is interpolated into *Sim Shalom* the prayer *Besefer Hayyim:* "In the book of life, blessing, peace . . . may we be remembered and inscribed before Thee, we and all Thy people, the house of Israel. . . ." The concluding blessing then is *Barukh attah . . . oseh hashalom* ("Blessed art Thou . . . who makes peace"), instead of, *Barukh attah . . . hamevarekh et ammo yisrael bashalom* ("Blessed art Thou . . . who blesses His people Israel with peace"). The Sephardic rite uses this longer form, which is already mentioned in the Talmud (Meg. 18a), all during the year, including the Days of Awe. The substitution of the shorter form, *Oseh Hashalom,* in most other rites, is due to the fact that this form was used in Palestine. Since the interpolated *Besefer Hayyim* also originated in Palestine where such interpolations were encouraged (see pages 19-20), the entire text was taken over, including the *Oseh Hashalom.*

The frequency of the word *shalom* as a liturgical conclusion occasioned this comment by Rabbi Levi:

Great is peace, for all the blessings and supplications we invoke before God conclude with *shalom.* The (evening) *Shema* is concluded with "He who spreads a canopy of peace," the priestly benediction closes with *shalom,* and the *Tefillah* concludes with *oseh hashalom* (He who makes peace) (*Leviticus Rabbah,* 9:9).

The "Days of Awe" as days of hope and joy: Why *Hallel* is not recited on Rosh Hashanah

Rosh Hashanah is not only a holy day, it is also the New Moon of Tishre. Yet *Hallel* is not said as on other holidays and New Moons. The reason for this is given as follows:

The ministering angels said to the Holy One, blessed is He, "O Master of the universe, why does not Israel sing songs of *Hallel* on Rosh Hashanah and Yom Kippur?" He answered them: "Is it proper for Israel to sing joyful praises when the King sits in judgment with the books of life and death open before Him?" (R. H. 32b)

This reflects the solemnity with which the Days of Awe are invested. But they are by no means days of sadness. Man has the assurance of forgiveness if he but takes the initiative to open—even ever so little—the door of repentance. God then prepares for him a broad entrance into a life of peace (*Song of Songs Rabbah,* 5).

In the same spirit, the white garments worn on the High Holy Days are said to be symbolic of the assurance that God's forgiveness would follow sincere repentance:

What a wonderful people is Israel! It is customary that when a man is up for trial, he dresses in black and lets his beard grow untrimmed, for he does not know how the trial will end. But not such is the case with Israel. On the day when they are being tried, they dress in white, cover themselves in white, trim their beards, and even partake plentifully of food and drink, knowing that God will perform miracles for them (TP R. H. 57b).

Here again, we have an illustration of Judaism's estimate of man's capacity to mend his ways. Repentance is readily available as an effective means of moral purification and of reconciliation with God. The belief that human nature is incorrigible is unacceptable to Judaism. Moral disease is not malignant and incurable. The psalmist expresses belief in the possibility of self-renewal when he prays: "Create me a clean heart, O God and renew a steadfast spirit within me" (Ps. 51:12).

An eventful Rosh Hashanah celebration is portrayed in the Book of Nehemiah, where we are told that on the first day of the seventh month (Rosh Hashanah of 458 B.C.E.) the people were gathered before Ezra, Nehemiah, the priests and the Levites, and the tribal leaders of the community. From a raised platform Ezra read to the people the "Book of God's Torah." With the guidance of the Levites, the people heard the Law read distinctly and gave it their close attention (Neh. 8:8). Upon realizing how derelict they had been in their duties to God, the people wept in deep remorse. Then Nehemiah said to them:

This day is holy to the Lord your God; mourn not, nor weep . . . go your way, eat the fat and drink the sweet, and send portions unto him for whom nothing is prepared; for this day is holy to our Lord; neither be ye grieved; for the joy of the Lord is your strength (Neh. 8:9-10).

אָבִינוּ מַלְכֵּנוּ

Our Father, our King, be Thou gracious to us and answer us for we are unworthy

Avinu Malkenu is an expansion of a brief supplication offered by Rabbi Akiba on public fast days. He prayed as follows:

Our Father, our King we have no King but Thee. Our Father our King, for Thine own sake have compassion upon us (Taan. 25b).

The same spirit pervades the much expanded version of *Avinu Malkenu* used during the Days of Awe. As in Akiba's original version, we avow our own lack of meritorious deeds and present as our credentials the merit of our ancestors and of the martyrs who died for the Sanctification of the Name. For their sake, we ask to be spared the chastisements warranted by our sins.

Why *Avinu Malkenu* is not recited on Sabbaths

Sabbath is a day when prayer for relief from personal anxieties is regarded as inconsistent with the spirit of the day (TP Shab. 15b). Hence, the *Amidah* prayers of the Sabbath do not refer to such mundane concerns as the need for health and sustenance. When a prayer for the sick is recited on Sabbath, the concluding formula is: "Because today is Sabbath, we may not offer personal supplications but may healing come very soon." Because *Avinu Malkenu* originated as a prayer for rain to be recited on fast days, and because it contains many references to personal anxieties and needs, it is not recited when Rosh Hashanah or Yom Kippur occur on a Sabbath.

THE READING OF THE TORAH

"And they went three days in the wilderness, and found no water" (Exod. 15:22). Those who interpreted the Torah metaphorically said that here "water" refers to the Torah. That the Torah is compared to water is evident from the verse, "Ho, everyone that thirsteth, come ye for water" (Isa. 55:1). "And they went three days without water" informs us that the Israelites, after going three days without water (i.e., without Torah) had lost their courage. It was then enacted that the Torah should be read weekly on Sabbaths and also on Mondays and Thursdays, so that the people would never again be deprived of the waters of the Torah for a period of three days (B. K. 82a).

From this talmudic passage, we see that the origin of the public reading of the Torah was ascribed to Moses. Another tradition credited Ezra (458 B.C.E.) with having instituted the reading of the Torah on Mondays and Thursdays, the marketing days when villagers would

come to the towns and could therefore attend the synagogue service. To Ezra they also ascribed the regulation
that every Monday and Thursday a minimum of ten
verses are to be read from the Torah and that three
people should then be called to the scroll (B.K. 82a).
The number of people given an *aliyah** varies with the
relative importance of the occasion. Three are called up
on Mondays and Thursdays, four on fast days and on
the intermediate days of Passover and Sukkot, five on
holidays (including Rosh Hashanah, six on Yom Kippur,
and seven on Sabbath (Meg. 22b). When a holiday falls
on Sabbath, the Torah portion is divided into seven
aliyot. Originally the person called to the first *aliyah* recited the opening blessing over the Torah, and the one
called up for the last *aliyah* recited the concluding blessing (Mishnah Meg. 4:2). In Amoraic times it was enacted
that the blessings be recited before and after each
aliyah so that those arriving during the Torah reading
and those leaving before its conclusion could hear both
blessings (Meg. 21b). It is, however, considered irrev-
erent for a person to leave the synagogue during the
reading of the Torah, except between *aliyot* (Ber. 8a).

The first blessing over the Torah may be recited with
the scroll unrolled, but the Torah scroll must be rolled
up before the second blessing is recited to indicate that
the blessings are not part of the text of the Torah (Meg.
32a).

In Palestine the Torah portion was read in a triennial
cycle (Meg. 29b). This practice was no longer widespread
in the days of Maimonides (*Mishneh Torah, Hilkhot
Tefillah,* 13). The portions to be read on holidays and
other special occasions are prescribed in the Mishnah
(Mishnah Meg. 3:4-6). There the portion prescribed for
Rosh Hashanah is Leviticus 23:23-41. Since Rosh Hashanah was observed for only one day in Palestine, the
Mishnah makes no reference to a reading for the second
day. In the *Tosefta* (Meg. 3:6), Genesis 21:1-34 is mentioned as the portion for Rosh Hashanah, according to
another opinion. The Babylonian Talmud rules that

* *Aliyah* (plural: *aliyot*). A person who is "called up" to the raised
platform (*bimah*) on which there is placed the lectern (*shulhan*)
from which the Torah is read is honored with an *aliyah* (lit. "a
going up").

"since we now observe Rosh Hashanah for two days" the twenty-first chapter of Genesis should be read on the first day, and the twenty-second chapter on the second day (Meg. 31a). This practice obtains today.

THE READING OF THE *HAFTARAH*

Haftarah literally means "conclusion." It denotes a selection from the Prophets which is read as a conclusion to the reading of the Torah. A *Haftarah* is read on Sabbath, on all holidays, on the Ninth of Ab, and at the *Minhah* service on all fast days.

The Talmud, which traces the institution of the reading of the Torah to Moses and Ezra (see pp. 119-20), offers no theory regarding the origin of the *Haftarah* reading. But the Mishnah already refers to it as a familiar and long-established custom (Mishnah Meg. 4:4); and the New Testament speaks of the reading of the "law and the prophets" (Acts 13:15), that is, the Torah and the *Haftarah*. The Talmud requires that the theme of the *Haftarah* must be relevant to that of the *Sidrah* (Meg. 29b). This requirement may account for the theory advanced by Abudraham (Spain, 1340 C.E.), in which he says that the *Haftarah* was introduced during the period 160-165 B.C.E. when Antiochus prohibited the reading of the Torah; and that the *Haftarah*, consisting of a selection from the Prophets with a content corresponding to that of the Torah portion, was then substituted and later continued as a permanent part of the service. While Abudraham's theory is not at all convincing, we may safely assume that by the first century C.E. the *Haftarah* was an accepted part of the synagogue service. The Talmud speaks of twenty-one verses—three for each of the seven *aliyot* required on Sabbaths—as the minimum requirement for a *Haftarah* (Meg. 23a). Actually there are *Haftarah* selections of less than twenty-one verses, such as the ten-verse *Haftarah* of the *Sidrah Ekev*, consisting of Isaiah 54:1-10. In such cases the reason given for the brevity is that the succeeding verses deal with a different theme (Meg. 23a).

The *Maftir*, the person who is called to read the prophetic portion, is first required to read (or have someone read for him) the concluding verses of the *Sidrah*. On holidays, he recites the blessings over the prescribed reading from the second scroll* before reciting the *Haftarah*. This is done as a sign of "respect for the Torah," which enjoys a sanctity higher than that of the prophetic books. The Mishnah provides that supplementary honors be conferred on the *Maftir*, such as leading in the reading of the *Shema* and the *Tefillah* (Mishnah Meg. 4:5). The reason for this is that by itself the reading of the *Haftarah* was originally not considered a distinction comparable to that of being called to the Torah for one of the prescribed *aliyot* (Rashi, Meg. 23a). Because the *Maftir* is called to the Torah after the prescribed number of *aliyot* has been completed, the *Hatzi Kaddish* is recited before his brief Torah portion is read to mark the official end of the prescribed Torah reading.

The blessings of the *Haftarah* are five in number: one before, and four after the reading of the *Haftarah*. They are first mentioned in Tractate Soferim 9:9-14. Abudraham says that these five blessings are to remind us of the Five Books of Moses. He also comments that with the first two blessings recited by the *Maftir* over the Torah portion, we have a total of seven blessings corresponding to the seven *aliyot*. The content of these blessings is as follows:

1. Gratitude for the Torah and the Prophets.
2. The trustworthiness of God's word as spoken by the prophets.
3. Prayer for Zion's restoration and for the rehabilitation of her exiled children.
4. Prayer for the Messianic Era and for renewal of the rule of the dynasty of David.
5. Gratitude for the gifts of the Sabbath and the particular holiday.

Cantillation

The Torah and *Haftarah* are rendered as a chant, and the accents in the printed texts, known as *teamim*, indicate the intonation, the melody, and the mode of the ren-

---

* For our discussion of the second scroll, see pp. 133-34.

dition. There are references in the Talmud to the use
of chironomy by the reader as a means of indicating the
melody (Ber. 62a, *see* Rashi on *Taame Torah, ad locum*).
To this day, Yemenite readers indicate with their fingers
the movements of the cantillation melody. The cantillation system was perfected in the 9th century by Aaron
ben Asher of Tiberias, hence it is known as the "Tiberian
system." The music of the cantillation is not one of melo-
dies but of modes, in which the octave runs through a
diatonic scale. While the accents indicate the rising, the
falling, and the carving of the melody, the mode of the
cantillation varies. The notes are so arranged that the
chant accentuates the meaning as well as the rhythm of
the text. The special mode of the High Holy Day Torah
cantillation and its high-pitched tone induce a mood of
utter confidence and a feeling of high solemnity, but the
Haftarah cantillation on the High Holy Days is the same
as that used all during the year.

SERVICE FOR TAKING OUT
THE TORAH

אֵין כָּמוֹךָ

There is none like unto Thee among the mighty,
  O Lord.
Thy Kingship is an everlasting Kingship.
The Lord will give strength to His people;
The Lord will bless His people with peace.

The verses which are recited as a prelude to the opening
of the ark are mentioned in Tractate Soferim (14:8-14).
The first three verses, celebrating the Kingship of God,
lead to the fourth verse: "The Lord will give strength to
His people, the Lord will bless His people with peace."
The latter passage is associated with the giving of the
Torah in this description of the revelation at Sinai:

Rabbi Eleazar of Modin said: "When the Holy One, blessed
is He, appeared to give the Torah to Israel, the earth shook
and the mountains quaked, and all the sons of the mighty
(*bene elim*) trembled in their palaces. . . . The kings of the
world came to Balaam saying: 'What is this uproar that we

heard? Is a flood coming to destroy the earth?' He answered:
'The Holy One, blessed is He, swore long ago that he would
never again bring a flood upon the world for after the flood,
God reigned as King forever' (Ps. 29:10). He thus assured
them that God was going to bring neither a flood of water
nor a flood of fire. 'What then is the tumultuous noise that we
hear?' they asked. Balaam answered: 'God possesses in His
storehouse a priceless treasure, the Torah, which he is about
to present to His people, as it is said *The Lord will give
strength* [i.e., the Torah] *to His people* (Ps. 29:11). As soon as
the kings heard this, they recited the benediction, *The Lord
will bless His people with peace"* (Zeb. 116a).

וַיְהִי בִּנְסֹעַ הָאָרֹן . . . כִּי מִצִּיּוֹן תֵּצֵא תוֹרָה

And it came to pass, when the ark set forward,
that Moses said, "Rise up, O Lord, and let
Thine enemies be scattered"   Numbers 10:35
For out of Zion shall go forth Torah, And the
word of the Lord from Jerusalem
                                        Isaiah 2:3

The juxtaposition of these two biblical passages, one
from the Torah and one from the Book of Isaiah, can
serve to symbolize for us the manner in which the Jewish
liturgy fuses an early and a later period of biblical religion into a unitary motif of universal peace. The passage
from the Torah reflects a time when the ark of the
covenant was carried by the Levites as an assurance of
God's protection of His people against their enemies.
This martial declaration is followed by the verse in
which the Torah is associated with an inspiring vision
of enduring peace among all the peoples of the earth:

And it shall come to pass in the end of days, that the mountain of the Lord's house shall be established as the top of the
mountains, and shall be exalted above the hills; and all nations shall flow to it. And many peoples shall go and say:
"Come ye, and let us go up to the mountain of the Lord, to
the house of the God of Jacob; and He will teach us of His
ways, and we will walk in His paths." *For out of Zion shall go
forth the Torah, and the word of the Lord from Jerusalem.*
And He shall judge between the nations, and shall decide for
many peoples; and they shall beat their swords into plowshares;

and their spears into pruning-hooks; nation shall not lift up sword against nation, neither shall they learn war any more.

Isaiah 2:2-5

This exalted vision of peace and justice is also found in Micah 4:1-5. It is uncertain whether Isaiah or Micah or an earlier prophet was the author.

Out of Zion shall go forth the Torah

In this passage, the word *Torah* does not refer to a book, but to divine guidance in situations that threaten to undermine peace between peoples.

Commenting on this passage, Julius A. Bewer surmises that Isaiah most likely spoke this prophecy in his old age after the signal deliverance of Jerusalem from the invading Assyrians in 701 B.C.E. It was then that the prophet looked forward with renewed faith into the future when God would arbitrate among the nations, resolve all discord between them, and bring universal peace. Nations would then go to Zion, because from Zion there would go forth Torah. Professor Bewer makes the further observation that nothing is said here of the nations rendering to God sacrifices and prayers. The nations would come to Jerusalem because it is the seat of moral instruction and guidance in the ways of the Lord. There is no hint of a political submission to Judah, or of confederation with it. All nations would retain their freedom and autonomy.

The recitation of this verse from Isaiah's arresting vision of a world at peace can serve for us as a symbol of the wider implications of the restoration of an autonomous Jewish community in the Holy Land. "Out of Zion shall go forth the Torah." By Torah we do not mean abstract theological and philosophical teachings; rather, we express the belief that an autonomous *Eretz Yisrael* will, in increasing measure, become a laboratory for experiment into the baffling problems of human society and for the cultivation of standards which will attempt to concretize and fulfill the ideal aspirations of the Torah.

ה' ה' אֵל רַחוּם וְחַנּוּן

The Lord, the Lord, God, merciful and gracious, long-suffering, and abundant in goodness and truth; keeping mercy unto the thousandth generation, forgiving iniquity

Exodus 34:6-7

The Thirteen Attributes

These verses, from which the concept of the Thirteen Attributes of God is derived, are recited at this point on all holidays except when a holiday falls on a Sabbath. The petitionary tone of these verses, and of the personal prayer which follows, is deemed to be out of tune with the Sabbath, when man is to enjoy a respite from the mundane.

The custom of reciting the Thirteen Attributes at this point before the open ark originated in the Middle Ages under the influence of the Kabbalistic school of Isaac Luria (1534-1572).

The concluding words of the biblical passages which comprise the Thirteen Attributes, "but that will by no means clear the guilty" (Exod. 34:7), are omitted to underscore the predominance of the quality of mercy (*Middat Harahamim*) over that of strict justice (*Middat Hadin*).

The efficacy of the recital of the Thirteen Attributes is affirmed in the following comment:

And the Lord passed before him and said: "The Lord, the Lord, God, merciful and gracious. . . ." Rabbi Yohanan said: "Were it not so stated in the Torah, one could not [because of its bold anthropomorphism] say this: The Holy One, blessed is He, wrapped Himself in a *tallit* like one who leads the congregation in prayer, showed Moses this order of prayer (the Thirteen Attributes) and said to him: 'Whenever Israel sins, let them recite this same order of prayer and I shall forgive them'" (R. H. 17b).

The efficacy of imploring God by invoking the Thirteen Attributes is also affirmed by Rabbi Judah, who remarked "A covenant has been established (between God and Israel) that whenever the Thirteen Attributes are invoked, that prayer will not be in vain" (R.H. 17b).

On the exact order of the Thirteen Attributes there were differences of opinion among the Geonic interpreters of the Talmud. The enumeration suggested by Rabbenu Tam (France, 1100-1171) is as follows:

1. *Adonai:* The Lord is merciful before one has sinned.
2. *Adonai:* The Lord is also merciful to the repentant sinner.
3. *El:* He is all-powerful
4. *rahum:* He is compassionate
5. *vehannun:* He is gracious
6. *erekh appayyim:* He is slow to anger
7. *verav hesed:* He is abounding in kindness
8. *veemet:* And in truth
9. *notzer hesed laalafim:* Maintaining kindness to the thousandth generation
10. *nose avon:* Forgiving sins committed with premeditation
11. *vafesha:* And sins committed in rebellion
12. *vehataah:* As well as those committed unwittingly
13. *venakkeh:* And acquitting the penitent.

(Tosefot, R. H. 17b)

שְׁמַע יִשְׂרָאֵל

אֶחָד אֱלֹהֵינוּ

גַּדְּלוּ לַה׳ אִתִּי

Hear O Israel . . . One is our God . . . Extol the Lord with me. . . .

After the scrolls have been taken out of the ark, the reader leads in the responsive chanting of these lines. Then the Torah procession takes place with the chanting of, "Thine, O Lord, is the greatness, and the power, and the glory, and the victory, and the majesty . . ." This verse is appropriately chosen from the prayer of thanksgiving offered by David in joyful celebration of the generous contributions of money and matériel given by all segments of the people toward the building of the First Temple (I Chron. 29:11).

While the Torah is being prepared for the reader, the congregation recites *Al Hakol* ("Above all may the name of God be glorified"), a Geonic *piyyut* which reads like a Hebrew version of the *Kaddish,* and which is mentioned in Tractate Soferim (14:12). It implores God to manifest

His power before all mankind through Israel's redemption and through His return to Zion, the earthly seat of His glory. *Av Harahamim* ("Father of mercy"), a later addition to this prayer, refers to Israel as the people who have been carried (*amusim*) and sustained (*nesuim*) by God, and with whose patriarchs (*etanim*) He had established a covenant assuring their survival through perilous times and endowing them with the will to resist the evil impulse.

וְזֹאת הַתּוֹרָה אֲשֶׁר שָׂם מֹשֶׁה

This is the Torah which Moses set before the children of Israel at the commandment of the Lord by the hand of Moses

This is said by the congregation as the Torah is raised and as the writing is shown to the congregation. It is a conflation of a verse from the Book of Deuteronomy with the first and last part of a verse from the Book of Numbers. The complete texts are as follows:

1. And this is the Torah which Moses set before the children of Israel (Deut. 4:44).
2. At the commandment of the Lord they encamped, and at the commandment of the Lord they journeyed; they kept the charge of the Lord, at the commandment of the Lord by the hand of Moses (Num. 9:23).

The conflation of these two verses must have come about when, for the sake of brevity, an edition of the Prayer Book indicated the longer verse from Numbers through its opening and closing words: "At the commandment of the Lord" (*al pi adonai*) . . . "by the hand of Moses" (*beyad Moshe*). In the edition of the Prayer Book which he edited, Rabbi Max D. Klein points out that editions of the Siddur of the Gaon of Vilna contain the full text of the verse from Numbers.

TORAH READING FROM
THE FIRST SCROLL: FIRST DAY OF
ROSH HASHANAH

Genesis, Chapter 21

God "remembers" man. This, the major motif of Rosh Hashanah, means that God takes cognizance of our prayers even as He remembered Sarah. Tradition has it that it was on Rosh Hashanah that Sarah, Rachel, and Hannah were each "remembered" and blessed with child (R.H. 10b). The blessings of parenthood, and more particularly of motherhood, are celebrated in this Torah reading, as well as in the corresponding prophetic portion.

On the eighth day after his birth, Isaac is brought into the covenant. There is a great celebration when he is weaned. Sarah, concerned about the influence of Ishmael on Isaac, demands that he and his mother, Hagar, be banished. This demand appears to us to be unreasonable; the biblical account must, however, be read and understood in the context of a society in which a concubine and her children expected and enjoyed only limited prerogatives.

The account of Hagar's tender motherly feelings is so masterfully presented that she elicits our full sympathy, and we feel relieved as we read that Ishmael's separation from Isaac was in the end not as tragic as it originally portended to be.

The chapter closes with an explanation of the origin of the name of the city of Beer-sheba. At a well (Hebrew, *beer*) which Abraham's servants had dug and which the servants of Abimelech, the Philistine king, had expropriated, Abraham and Abimelech swore (Hebrew: *sheva*) that peace would always reign between them. Having regained possession of Beer-sheba, Abraham planted a tamarisk tree at the place and there offered worship to "the Lord, the everlasting God."

Comments on the text (Genesis, Chapter 21)

"as He had said" (21:1)

This refers to the promise that had been made to Abraham, "And he said, I will certainly return unto thee . . . and, lo, Sarah, thy wife, shall have a son" (Gen. 18:10).

"Who would have said unto Abraham" (21:7)

The American-Jewish Bible scholar, Arnold B. Ehrlich (d. 1919), suggests that this question implies the following query of astonishment: "Who can properly express what has happened to Abraham! Not only has Sarah borne him a child, but she herself, despite her advanced age, nurses the child."

"Cast out this bondwoman and her son" (21:10)

The Bible does not hesitate to expose the human weaknesses of its saints, even as it often commends the virtues of its sinners. Here Sarah is portrayed as Hagar's harsh mistress. At the same time, the narrative depicts the separation of Ishmael from Isaac as a step in the unfolding of the providentially planned destiny of Isaac and his descendants.

"And the thing was very grievous in Abraham's sight" (21:11)

Torn between conflicting loves and loyalties, Abraham is told to comply with Sarah's demands, for the fulfillment of the covenant depends upon Isaac.

"For in Isaac shall thy seed be called to thee" (21:12)

Every person and every event in the Torah is related to the main theme of the Bible—that the descendants of Abraham would become God's chosen people, through whom mankind would come to know God and His moral law. Through the descendants of Isaac, the covenant made with Abraham would be realized.

A recurrent theme of the early biblical narratives is the rejection of the older brother (whose claim to distinction is based purely on the accident of primogeniture) in favor of the younger brother. This theme is apparent in the accounts of the preference of Isaac over Ishmael, Jacob over Esau, Judah over Reuben, and Ephraim over

Manasseh. This can suggest to us that the claim of personal worth is higher than that of prior birth.

"bread and a bottle of water" (21:14)

There is no implication in the narrative that the amount of food given her was insufficient. Hagar exhausted her supply of water because she lost her way in the wilderness of Beer-sheba.

"and she cast the child" (21:15)

The meaning of the Hebrew text is that she abandoned the child (Ehrlich).

"Let me not look upon the death of the child" (21:16)

No reference is made to Hagar's lack of food and drink. True to her motherly instincts, she is oblivious of her own needs; her sole concern is for her child.

"God heard the voice of the lad" (21:17)

There seems to be at this juncture a contradiction or, at least, a lapse in the narrative. We are first told that Hagar was crying, and here we are told that God heard the "voice of the lad." This is an example of the literary craftsmanship of the narrative. The implication is that the mother cried only because she heard her child crying. The angel comforted her with the news that God had heard the child's cries—the same cries which had moved her to tears.

"and hold him fast by thy hand" (21:18)

You need not abandon him to starvation, for there is a future in store for him. (Ehrlich).

"and [he] became an archer" (21:20)

This is perhaps intended to point out the contrast between the warlike Ishmael and the pastoral Isaac.

Rabbinic comments on the text

"as He had said" (21:1)

"He had said" can also be read to refer not to God, but to Abraham. Abraham said prayers for the recovery of Abimelech, and he also prayed for the king's wives, who had been afflicted with childlessness (Gen. 20:17). As a reward for his concern for others, the blessings of parenthood were also conferred on him. He who prays for his fellow man and is also in need of similar help, is answered first (B. K. 92a).

"And Abraham made a great feast" (21:8)

The feast was great because the "Great One" of the universe was there. The Divine Presence rejoiced in the happiness that had come to Abraham and Sarah (*Gen. Rabbah*, 53:10).

"making sport" (21:9)

Ishmael showed traits which anticipated his submission to the three sins severely condemned by the Torah: idolatry, unchastity, and bloodshed (*Tosefta Sotah*, 6:6) .

"for God hath heard the voice of the lad where he is" (21:17)

Ishmael's conduct was beyond reproach "where he is." God judges man not on the basis of some future eventuality, but according to his present deserts (R. H. 16b).

"Abraham reproved Abimelech" (21:25)

No friend is sincere if he withholds corrective rebuke. "Better is open rebuke than love that is hidden" (Prov. 29:5). Abraham's heart-to-heart conversation with Abimelech led to a peaceful settlement of their difficulties (*Gen. Rabbah*, 54:3).

"these seven ewe-lambs" (21:29)

The seven lambs were reminders of the "seven laws of the sons of Noah" which comprise the basic moral code binding on all mankind (*Midrash Hagadol, Vayyera*).

A share in the world to come is assured to the righteous and pious of all nations who abide by these seven laws:

1. Not to worship idols
2. Not to blaspheme the name of God
3. Not to commit murder
4. Not to steal
5. Not to commit adultery
6. To establish courts of justice
7. Not to eat the flesh torn from the limb of a living animal
(Sanh. 56b)

"And Abraham planted a tamarisk tree" (21:33)

The letters אשל forming the name of this tree, also form the word שאל "to ask." Abraham's hospitality was so sincere that he anticipated what his guests would ask of him. He cheerfully offered wayfarers the hospitality symbolized by these three letters: 1) אכילה (food); 2) שתיה (drink); 3) לויה (escorting them in the direction of their destination); or לינה (lodging).

"and [he] *called there on the name of the Lord, the Everlasting God"* (21:33)

With a change of vowels, "and he called" can be read "and he influenced others to call on the name of the Lord." When his guests would rise to thank him, Abraham would say: "You owe thanks not to me, but to the King of the Universe of whose bounty you have partaken" (Sotah 10b).

TORAH READING FROM THE SECOND SCROLL: FIRST AND SECOND DAYS OF ROSH HASHANAH

Numbers, Chapter 29:1-6

The reading from the second scroll consists of the Torah passage Numbers 29:1-6. Nowhere in the Talmud is a reading from a second scroll prescribed for Rosh Hashanah. The first mention of this practice is in the *Seder of R. Amram* (9th century C.E.). The talmudist, Mordecai ben Hillel (13th century C.E.), suggests that a sanction for this reading from the second scroll might be discerned in this talmudic statement: "After the destruction of the Temple, the act of reading the Torah portion describing the sacrifices prescribed for the particular day was accounted to the people as if the sacrifices had actually been offered . . ." (Taan. 27b).

Where only one scroll is available, the second portion is read from the same scroll. But it is a rule that one must avoid a tedious unrolling of a scroll from one portion to another portion "out of respect for the congregation" (Yoma 70a). Rashi (*ibid.*) explains the passage to mean that the congregation would have to wait in silence while the scroll is being rolled to the proper passage. For this reason a second scroll is taken out. That the reading of the portion dealing with the sacrifices of the day is not a prescribed one can be seen from the fact that it is only a *Maftir* portion and is not reckoned among the number of *aliyot* prescribed for the Torah reading either on Rosh Hashanah, Yom Kippur, or the Festivals.•

In the instructions for the sacrifices offered on all other holidays and festivals, the term used is *vehikravtem olah* "and you shall offer a burnt offering." But in prescribing the burnt offering for Rosh Hashanah, the Torah uses the term *veasitem olah* "and you shall make a burnt offering." This variation inspires the comment that on Rosh Hashanah it is man's opportunity to become spiritually renewed: "On this day I shall transform you into new persons" (TP R. H. 59c).

The Hebrew language has no exact equivalent for the term New Year. Rosh Hashanah means literally, the beginning of the year. In a sense, the year is not new. Not the year, but each individual must become as new. Life can be a progress and unfolding of moral and intellectual growth, or it can be purposeless. The choice is man's, but it is for God to judge that choice—to approve it, or to rebuke it. Man can become a "new personality" if he remembers the psalmist's prayer, "So teach us to number our days that we may get us a heart of wisdom" (Ps. 90:12), and if he considers each day a fresh occasion on which to mature his judgment and to refine his sensibilities.

HAFTARAH: FIRST DAY OF ROSH HASHANAH

I Samuel, Chapters 1—2:10

This *Haftarah* was chosen because of the resemblance of its theme to that of the Torah reading. God "remembered" Hannah even as he had "remembered" Sarah. The childless Hannah is at last blessed with the child for

• Saul Lieberman, *Tosefta Ki-Fshutah, Moed* (New York: The Jewish Theological Seminary of America, 1962), p. 1171.

which she had so fervently prayed. Elkanah's love for Hannah is touchingly expressed when he says to her: "Am not I better to thee than ten sons?" (1:8) The psalm-like prayer of thanksgiving, with which the *Haftarah* concludes, is attributed to Hannah, because of the verse: "While the barren hath borne seven, she that had many children hath languished" (2:5). Particularly noteworthy is the reference made in this *Haftarah* to a custom of annual family pilgrimages to Shiloh where the ark was housed prior to David's selection of Jerusalem as the site of the Temple.

Comments on the text (I Samuel, Chapters 1—2:10)

"year to year" (1:3)

This would indicate that entire families would make yearly pilgrimages to the sanctuary.

"And it came to pass upon a day" (1:4)

For the clarification of the narrative sequence of these verses, Ehrlich's free rendering is suggested:

One day, Elkanah offered a sacrifice—his had been the practice to give portions to his wife Peninah and to all her sons and daughters, but to Hannah he would give a double portion because he preferred Hannah, though the Lord had made her childless. Her rival would then taunt her to provoke her, in that the Lord had made her childless. This happened every year. Whenever she would go up to the sanctuary of the Lord she would provoke her. One year on one such day, when Hannah cried and would not eat, her husband Elkanah said to her:

"but unto Hannah he gave a double portion" (1:5)

The Septuagint translation implies that the original reading may have been: "to Hannah he would give only one portion, but he loved Hannah, though the Lord had shut her womb."

"am not I better to thee than ten sons?" (1:8)

This means, "Am I not more precious to you than ten sons?" The number ten is mentioned only for stylistic emphasis.

"and there shall no razor come upon his head" (1:11)

The word for razor is *morah,* and the text seems to have been read differently by the *Targum Jonathan* which translates here: *umarvat enosh lo tehe alohi* ("he will not be under the authority of any human being.")

"How long wilt thou be drunken?" (1:14)

This means, "How long will you do things that are done by drunkards?" (Ehrlich)

"Let thy servant find favor in thy sight" (1:18)

In the Hebrew idiom this is a gracious way of saying "Thank you."

"and there abide for ever" (1:22)

Since she had made that vow, she would have to leave Samuel at the sanctuary even before he was weaned, once she brought him there. For this reason she did not go on a pilgrimage until the child was weaned.

"only the Lord establish His word" (1:23)

Elkanah was fearful lest Hannah's remaining at home be considered a violation of her vow, thereby bringing possible harm to the child.

"and the child was young" (1:24)

Though he was already more or less self-reliant (this is what "weaned" means here), he was still of a very tender age (Ehrlich).

Rabbinic comments on the text (I Samuel, Chapters 1—2:10)

"And this man went up" (1:3)

He "went up" means that he rose continually in the esteem of his fellow men, ever enlarging his sphere of influence. He first became distinguished in his home life, then in his neighborhood, then in his town, and then in his service to all Israel. His reputation, matched by his character, was justly merited (*Yalkut Samuel,* 77).

"to worship and to sacrifice" (1:3)

Elkanah influenced people to right action by example rather than by exhortation. On the pilgrimages to Shiloh, he would

be accompanied by his immediate family and by other rela-
tives. They would lodge in the main square of a city, and thus
strangers would be inspired to join them. Each year Elkanah
selected another road, so that he might reach people of different localities. God said to him: "You have conferred merit on
Israel, having inspired many to observe the *Mitzvot*. You will
therefore be blessed with a son who will likewise confer merit
on Israel and train them to observe the *Mitzvot*" (*Yalkut
Samuel*, 77).

"but wilt give unto Thy handmaid a manchild" (1:11)

According to Rabbi Dimi, this means that Hannah prayed for
a child that would not be conspicuous among his fellow men.
She wanted a child of average capacities, neither abnormally
clever nor stupid, nor abnormally tall nor short (Ber. 31b). Another interpretation, however, derives an opposite lesson. She
wanted a "manchild"—one who would gain renown among wise
men and men of understanding—a man with prophetic gifts
(*Midrash Samuel*, 2:7).

"Now Hannah, she spoke in her heart (al libbah)" (1:13)

The Hebrew text implies that she was speaking about that
which was "above" her heart. Hannah addressed her prayer to
God in rather bold language when she said, "Lord of the universe, hast Thou created anything in vain? . . . Didst Thou
not create these breasts above my heart that I might give suck
to a child? O grant me a son . . . for mortal man eats, drinks,
propagates his kind, and dies. As I belong to mortal mankind,
let me do my part in perpetuating mankind" (Ber. 31b).

Rabbi Hamnunah remarked (Ber. 31a-b) that many important
laws concerning propriety in prayer and in human relations
can be derived from this verse and from those that follow.
Among the lessons derived from the description of Hannah's
manner of praying are the following:

"Now Hannah, she spoke in her heart" (1:13)

True prayer comes from the heart. Prayer can therefore be
defined as: *avodah shebalev*—worship that emanates from the
heart.

"only her lips moved" (1:13)

A feeling embedded in the heart clamors for expression; hence,
one who prays should speak his prayer with his lips.

"but her voice could not be heard" (1:13)

Loud prayer is to be avoided since it is disturbing to other worshipers.

"Eli thought she had been drunken" (1:13)

He who imbibes strong drink is forbidden to lead in prayer.

"How long wilt thou be drunken?" (1:14)

If you suspect your fellow-man of unbecoming conduct—as did Eli the High Priest, of Hannah—tell him of your suspicion" (Ber. 31b). He might either prove your suspicion to be wrong or be moved to mend his ways. We tend to be critical of one another before strangers and to refrain from direct rebuke. The verse, "Thou shalt love thy neighbor as thyself" (Lev. 19:18) is preceded by the verse, "Thou shalt not hate thy brother in thy heart; thou shalt surely rebuke thy neighbor."

"No, my lord" (1:15)

A person who knows that he is wrongly suspected of unbecoming conduct should take steps to correct the misapprehension (Ber. 31b).

"Go in peace, and the God of Israel grant thy petition" (1:17)

First the High Priest asked forgiveness of Hannah for having wrongly suspected her of impropriety, then he gave her his blessing (Ber. 31b).

"Because I rejoice in Thy salvation [help]" (2:1)

Thy help seems to imply that *God* is helped. Does God need help? Yes. God is victorious when the righteous triumph. Likewise the Divine Presence "suffers" when the righteous suffer. As the psalmist says, "I will be with him in trouble" (Ps. 91:15). But when Israel rejoices, God rejoices (*Midrash Samuel,* 4:4).

"there is none beside Thee" (2:2)

The letters of the word *biltekha,* when rearranged, spell the word *leballotekha* which means, "none outlives Thee" (Meg. 14a).

"Neither is there any rock like our God" (2:2)

The word for rock is *tzur,* and this suggests the word *tzayyar* (artist). There is no artist like God. A human being paints a picture on a wall, but he cannot breathe life into it and give it functioning organs. But God draws a picture within a picture (i.e., the embryo in the womb of the mother) and endows it with life and functioning organs (Meg. 14a).

"For the pillars of the earth are the Lord's And He hath set the world upon them" (2:8)

The "pillars of the earth" are the patriarchs. God desired to establish the world on firm foundations, but found no suitable means of doing so before the patriarchs arose. He was like a king who sought to build a city on a site. When he came to lay the foundations, water welled forth from the deep. He chose another site but again water undermined the foundations. Finally, he came to a place where he found a large rock; then he said, "On this rock I will found the city." Likewise, in the beginning, the world was full of water. God wished to establish the world, but the wicked would not allow Him . . . When the patriarchs came and proved themselves righteous, God said "On them will I establish my world" (*Exod. Rabbah,* 15:7).

TORAH READING FROM FIRST SCROLL: SECOND DAY OF ROSH HASHANAH

Genesis, Chapter 22

Though this is the only place in the Bible where the *Akedah* (the Binding of Isaac) is mentioned, this narrative has made an indelible impression on the Jewish consciousness. When, in our prayers, we admit our own lack of merit and seek the mercy of God, we do so by recalling our descent from Abraham and Isaac—from the father who was willing to sacrifice his son at God's asking, and from the son who stood ready to be sacrificed. Before irrelevant moral and philosophic objections are raised to Abraham's conduct, let it be recalled that the *Akedah* reflects a society where a father had unlimited authority over the life of his child. In such a society it was possible for Reuben to say to his father, "Thou shalt slay my two sons, if I bring him [Benjamin] not to thee" (Gen. 42:37).

But our Torah Reading does not for a moment condone child sacrifice. The account of the *Akedah* begins with the clear statement that God *tested* Abraham. In that test Abraham was called on to demonstrate his complete devotion to God by his readiness to give up the son for whom he had waited so long.

In biblical religion, the practice of child sacrifice is condemned as an affront to the sanctity of God's name (Lev. 20:1-5). The offering of the first-born as a sacrifice, a widespread practice in primitive religion, is in the Torah transformed into the rite of the redemption of the first-born, to serve as a reminder of the intervention of God in the redemption of Israel from Egyptian bondage (Exod. 13:12-15). It took centuries to uproot the pagan practice of human sacrifice. Ahaz, king of Judah "made his son to pass through the fire, according to the abominations of the heathen, whom the Lord cast out from before the children of Israel" (II Kings 16:3). King Manasseh did likewise (II Kings 21:6). Child sacrifice is also reported to have been practiced in the Northern Kingdom of Israel (II Kings 17:17). A grim reminder of this practice is the word *gehenna* derived from *Ge ben-Hinnom* (the Valley of ben-Hinnom) to the Southwest of Jerusalem, where an altar had been erected to the idol Moloch to whom children were sacrificed (II Kings 23:10). That the God of Israel reviled human sacrifice and counselled a different way to serve Him is expressed with eloquence by Micah:

> "Wherewith shall I come before the Lord . . .
> Shall I give my first-born for my transgression,
> The fruit of my body for the sin of my soul?
> It hath been told thee, O man, what is good,
> And what the Lord doth require of thee:
> Only to do justly, and to love mercy, and to
>   walk humbly with thy God"
>
> Micah 6:6, 8.

It was in rabbinic times, when child sacrifice was no longer practiced even among the pagan neighbors of Israel, that the theme of the *Akedah* proved to be particularly significant. Out of a sense of utter humility before God, a contrast was drawn between the self-sacrificing devotion of Abraham and Isaac, and the inconstancy of the faith and practice of the average person. It was from this impulse that the doctrine of *Zekhut Avot* (Merit of the Fathers) was developed to encourage the people in the expectation that their prayers would be heard in spite of their deficiency. The doctrine avowed that while the descendants of Abraham and Isaac may have fallen far short of what God demands of them, they can invoke His mercy and secure His forgiveness because of the "merit" established for them by Abraham and Isaac in having met the test of the *Akedah*. Indeed, the *Akedah* is so dominant a theme in the liturgy of Rosh Hashanah that Rabbi Abbahu makes the observation that when, on Rosh Hashanah, we blow the ram's horn, reminiscent of the ram that Abraham used as a substitute for Isaac (Gen. 22:13), God accounts it as if each worshiper had actually bound himself on the altar as a willing martyr to God (R.H. 16a).

In a comprehensive monograph, Dr. Shalom Spiegel shows how midrashic fancy often went so far as to entertain the startling assumption that Isaac had actually been slaughtered and then restored to life. But in the mainstream of Jewish tradition, the accent was placed not on vicarious atonement, but on the unconditional love for God which the *Akedah* typified.

In the Torah account and in the rabbinic traditions based on the account, the *Akedah*'s impact on the Jewish consciousness was that of a vivid, quasi-personal experience. Abraham and Isaac met the test of loyalty by their readiness to offer God unconditional sacrifice. To the Jewish people—a people used to martyrdom and heroism —the *Akedah* demonstrated how its patriarchal forebears conducted themselves when confronted by a supreme test of their devotion to God.

Comments on the text (Genesis, Chapter 22)

"after these things [happenings]" (22:1)

After Ishmael had been sent away, as described in the preceding chapter, Isaac was the only one through whom God's covenant could be fulfilled. It was then that Abraham's trust in God was to be subjected to a most critical test.

"God did prove [test] Abraham" (22:1)

Constancy of character is tested whenever a crisis occurs and a decision is called for. We readily sustain our principles when no sacrifice is entailed. But too often we rationalize their abandonment when the situation calls for heroic disregard of immediate personal comfort or interest. The Hebrew word for such crucial tests of character is *nissayon,* and one of the prayers in the early part of the daily morning service contains the supplication: "Do not, O Lord, put me to test (*nissayon*)." Furthermore, the modern Hebrew word for "experience" is *nissayon,* suggesting that in every experience man is subjected to the test of his principles.

"Here am I" (22:1)

Abraham thus expresses his unconditional readiness to obey.

"Take now thy son, thine only son" (22:2)

Isaac was more precious to Abraham than his own life, for he represented the fulfillment of the covenant which God had made with him. God Himself had assured Abraham, "In Isaac shall thy seed be called to thee" (Gen. 21:12). The sacrifice of Isaac meant the blasting of Abraham's hopes for the future. Yet Abraham asks no question. The trust which he evinces reminds us of Job's declaration, "Though He slay me, yet will I trust in Him" (Job 13:15).

"Abraham rose early in the morning" (22:3)

He did not reply to God. He proceeded to obey. In the face of what was being demanded of him, silence was the eloquent companion of obedience. His silence here contrasts sharply with his bold plea for justice on behalf of the Sodomites:

And Abraham drew near, and said: "Wilt Thou indeed sweep away the righteous with the wicked? . . . That be far from Thee to do after this manner to slay the righteous with the wicked . . . shall not the Judge of all the earth do justly?" (Gen. 18:23-25).

"On the third day" (22:4)

His obedience was not a matter of impulsive compliance. There ensued three long days, during which he could consider and reconsider what he was about to do.

"Abide ye here with the ass" (22:5)

Abraham knew that his young servants could not bear to witness that which he was determined to do. Although he would suffer, he had no cause to give his servants suffering.

"and they went both of them together" (22:68)

The Torah's account is masterfully textured. The wood for the sacrifice is being carried by Isaac, the knife and the fire by Abraham. Isaac does not suspect the intentions of his father. In asking, "Where is the lamb for a burnt offering," he reveals a childlike innocence. Thus the narrative accentuates the inner torment that Abraham was experiencing. (See, however, in the section, "Selected rabbinic comments," which follows, how the Rabbis interpret this same passage as evidence of Isaac's willingness to be sacrificed.)

"Milcah, she also hath borne children" (22:20)

The purpose of this section is to establish the genealogy of Rebecca, who was to become the wife of Isaac. The Bible deals with two main "heroes"—God and Israel. In the biblical conception, God commissioned Israel to serve as the pre-eminent recipient of His demands. Hence every detail in the genealogy of this people and in the life of its major and minor personalities is considered to be relevant.

Selected rabbinic comments (Genesis, Chapter 22)

"God did prove [test]" (22:1)

Abraham was subjected to one test after another. Tested ten times, he maintained the constancy of his faith (Ab. 5:4).

A potter does not venture to test a defective earthen flask by striking it. One such blow might shatter it. But he does not hesitate to so test a flask that has been properly hardened. No matter how often he strikes it, it does not crack. So, the Holy One, blessed is He, tests the righteous and not the wicked (*Gen. Rabbah,* 51:1-2).

"upon one of the mountains which I will tell thee of" (22:2)

God tests the faith of the righteous in that he reveals to them only at a later time the ultimate meaning of the trials to which they are subjected (*Gen. Rabbah,* 55:7).

"and saddled his ass" (22:3)

Though Abraham had servants, he himself saddled his animal, being so zealous in his love for God. True love never calculates the effort demanded by duty. Likewise, unmitigated hatred knows no restraints. When Balaam, in his hostility toward Israel, set out on a journey with the intent to curse them, he rose early in the morning and he himself saddled his ass (Num. 22:21). He did not ask one of his many servants to do this, for his excessive zeal for evil was nourished by his hatred (*Gen. Rabbah*, 56:21).

Those intent upon evil usually pursue their designs with vigorous persistence. The champions of the good are often not so diligent. They improvise and procrastinate. This is perhaps so because too often their conviction, instead of being a spur to conscientious action, induces in them a sense of self-righteous indolence.

"On the third day" (22:4)

The place was really close by and did not require a three day journey. But Abraham's and Isaac's journey was prolonged because of what happened as they were headed for the place. First, Satan appeared to Abraham in the figure of an old man and argued with him that he should not snuff out the life of the child that God had given him in his old age. Abraham did not allow these words to dissuade him from obeying God's command. Then Satan came to Isaac in the form of a young man and warned him of his father's intent to put an end to his young life. Isaac told his father about this, and after Abraham had convinced Isaac not to give heed to Satan's words, he rebuked Satan for his vicious designs. Seeing that no arguments could dissuade them, Satan transformed himself into a brook of stormy waters. As they entered the waters, they became deeper and more turbulent. Abraham again rebuked Satan and prayed to God to spare their lives, so that he and Isaac might proceed to obey His command (*Tanhuma Vayyera*).

"upon [above] *the wood"* (22:9)

"Above" alludes to the angels in heaven who broke out into weeping protest saying: "It is not just that Abraham, who showed such warm hospitality to strangers and with whom God made an everlasting covenant, should be asked to do so inhuman a thing as to slaughter his own son" (*Tanhuma Vayyera*).

"behind him a ram (ayil ahar)" (22:13)

The Hebrew seems to say: "a ram afterwards." Abraham saw
with his mind's eye the shape of things to come. First the ram
was entangled in a tree and when it extricated itself, it was
caught in a bush. Then it was ensnared in a thicket. This
foreshadowed the destiny of Israel. This people would be entangled in their failings, and as a consequence, would fall into
the clutches of one tyrannical power after another, but in the
end (*ahar*) they would hear the ram's horn sounding their
liberation (*TP Taan.* 65a).

"Abraham went and took the ram" (22:13)

Not a particle of the ram went to waste. Its ashes later became
the foundation of the altar on which atonement was made for
Israel. Out of its sinews were made the strings of David's harp,
and out of its skin, Elijah made his girdle. One of its horns
was sounded at the giving of the Torah at Mt. Sinai, and the
other will be sounded at the "end of days" proclaiming a new
era of liberation for Israel and the world (*Pirke R. Eliezer,* 31).

The psalmist says "Ascribe unto the Lord, O ye sons of might
(*bene elim*), Ascribe unto the Lord glory . . ." (Ps. 29:1). Who
are the *bene elim?* Read not *bene elim* but *bene ilmim,* the sons
of the dumb and the deaf (i.e., the sons of Israel). They could
remonstrate with the Holy One, blessed is He, but they refrain
from doing so, and they suffer the yoke of the nations for the
sanctification of His Name.

Bene elim also means: sons of rams. Again this refers to the
children of Israel who are slain like *elim,* rams. Abraham said:
"I slay"; Isaac said: "I am ready to be slain" (*Midrash Tehillim,*
ed. Buber, p. 232).

"The Lord is seen" [*Adonai yireh*] (22:14)

This means: "May the Lord be mindful." Abraham prayed that
the Lord would be mindful of his unquestioning obedience,
and that the merit of his unwavering faith would win forgiveness for his descendants. Said Abraham, "O God, when Thou
didst ask for the sacrifice of Isaac, I might have retorted: "Lord
of the Universe, a little while ago Thou didst assure me, 'In
Isaac shall thy seed be called to thee' and now Thou sayest:
'Take thy son . . . and offer him.' But I restrained myself and
said nothing." God then assured him that on Rosh Hashanah,
whenever his descendants would sound the *shofar,* He will bear
in mind Abraham's unquestioning faith and forgive Israel's
sins (*Tanhuma Vayyera*).

Abraham asked for no other reward than the assurance that his sacrificial devotion would benefit his descendants. Such an attitude motivates the selfless and courageous action of all true idealists. They have a vision of the Promised Land of the future and are content with the knowledge that generations yet unborn will be helped by their life, sacrifices, and labors.

"Abraham returned unto his young men" (22:19)

And where was Isaac? Why did he not return? Abraham sent him to the academy of Shem to study Torah, for he said; "All the spiritual delights that have come to me in my lifetime were the outcome of the study of Torah and the practice of *Mitzvot;* therefore I do not want these to depart from my seed" *(Gen. Rabbah,* 56:11).

After completion of the reading of the Torah portion from the First Scroll, Numbers 29:1-6 is then read from the Second Scroll as on the first day of Rosh Hashanah. For our discussion of this reading, see pp. 133-34.

HAFTARAH: SECOND DAY OF ROSH HASHANAH

Jeremiah, Chapter 31:1-20

The prophetic reading for the second day of Rosh Hashanah corresponds in some ways to the contents of the Torah portion. In the Torah reading, Abraham is told to offer up "thy son, thine only son, whom thou lovest." In this *Haftarah,* God calls Ephraim (Israel) "a darling son unto me . . . for as often as I speak of him, I do earnestly remember him still" (Jer. 31:20). Abudraham (Spain, 14th century) calls attention to the words, *zakhor ezkerenu* ("I shall remember him") in this verse, as being especially appropriate for Rosh Hashanah, which is *Yom Hazikkaron* (The Day of Remembrance).

Here Jeremiah envisions the restoration of the Northern Kingdom of Israel, which had been destroyed by the Assyrians in 722 B.C.E. He predicts the reunion of the two kingdoms of Judah and Israel around the central sanctuary at Mt. Zion, and depicts a touching reconciliation of God with Ephraim (Israel) who, being to God the child of His delight, elicits His tender and merciful consideration. The sequence of the chapter is as follows: God says: The people who escaped from the sword have found favor in the wilderness (vs. 1). In the distant past, the Lord revealed Himself to Israel and declared His everlasting love for His people. Therefore, He now extends grace to those of the Northern Kingdom who survived (vss. 2-3). The "maiden of Israel" will yet be restored to the hills of Samaria. Their vineyards will again be planted, and the vintage will be celebrated in joyous manner (vss. 4-5). On Ephraim's heights, watchmen will sound the call for pilgrims to wend their way to Zion, there, with a reunited people, to worship the Lord in His Temple (vs. 6). Among the nations the news will go forth that God is reclaiming the remnant of Israel. He is gathering them from the most distant places and bringing back even the young and the handicapped among them, on safe roads on which there will be no danger of stumbling. God is a father to Ephraim and, like a father's love for a child, His love for Israel is abiding and, therefore, a reconciliation must ensue (vss. 6-8). The glad news will be proclaimed of God's reconciliation with His people, and of His gathering them and guarding them as a shepherd guards his flock (vss. 9-11). With the return of security and prosperity, the sorrows of the past will be forgotten, and a joyful people—young and old together—satiated with God's bounty, will, on Zion's heights, bring to God offerings of gratitude (vss. 12-13). The prophet now addresses Rachel, the matriarch of the people of the Northern Kingdom of Israel. From her tomb at Ramah, on the roadside, she had mournfully seen her children go into exile. He bids her dry her tears, for she would yet see her children return to their homeland by the very road through which they had fled (vss. 14-16). That the exiles would return by the same road is more clearly indicated in a later verse of the same chapter, not included in the *Haftarah* reading:

> Set thee up waymarks,
> Make thee guide-posts;
> Set thy heart toward the highway,
> Even the way by which thou wentest;
> Return O maiden of Israel, return to these thy cities.
>
> Jeremiah 31:21

God hears the remorseful soliloquy of His repentant people, as it evinces a deep sense of shame for its sinful conduct in the past (vss. 17-18). Moved to compassion by His fatherly feelings, God resolves to "remember" Ephraim and to extend to him again His fatherly love. God's compassion for Israel is that of a father for a child. Whenever He would disown Israel, His thoughts still dwelt on him. Because His heart yearns for him, He will receive him back in love (vss. 19-20).

יְקוּם פֻּרְקָן

[Heavenly Father] we invoke Thy divine aid upon the scholars and teachers

This Aramaic prayer is recited in the Ashkenazic rite immediately after the reading of the *Haftarah*, when Rosh Hashanah occurs on a Sabbath.

Composed in the eleventh century C.E., it is a touching supplication on behalf of the scholars and students of the Palestinian and Babylonian academies, which were then in danger of closing down because of diminishing support from communities the world over.

Yekum Purkan is followed by a shorter prayer beginning with the same opening words, beseeching the security and welfare of "this entire holy congregation . . . and all other congregations" and praying that their children" may not neglect the words of the Torah and that the study of the Torah may never cease among them."

Scholars assume that the two *Yekum Purkan* prayers were originally one prayer for the welfare of the exilarch and the heads of the academies in Palestine and Babylonia, as well as for that of congregations in lands near and distant that supported the academies. Later, the one prayer became two prayers, each beginning with the words *Yekum Purkan*. The earliest appearance of the two as separate prayers is in a manuscript dated 1318.*

* Israel Davidson, *Theasaurus of Mediaeval Hebrew Poetry,* Vol. 2, p. 424.

THE SOUNDING OF THE *SHOFAR*

The *shofar*'s sound of hope

The Torah designates the first day of the seventh month as "a day of blowing the horn" (Num. 29:1). The sounding of the *shofar* occurs at two points in the service—after the reading of the Torah, and during the *Musaf Amidah.*

Among ancient peoples, the celebration of a new year was marked by the creation of shrieking, deafening noises, whose purpose was to frighten off evil spirits and demons. The *shofar,* however, is sounded not to drive off evil spirits, but to bring men closer to God, and to invoke His merciful remembrance of them (Num. 10:10). It is God (*Elohim*) "who is gone up . . . amidst the sound of the horn (*teruah*)"; it is the Lord (*Adonai*) who manifests Himself with the sound of the *shofar* (Ps. 47:6). This verse is said by the rabbis to inform us that at first God ascends and sits on the throne of severe judgment, but when the people of Israel take the *shofar* and sound it, He leaves the throne of judgment and sits on the throne of mercy (*Leviticus Rabbah,* 29:1). The Bible verses in the *Musaf Amidah* which accompany the sounding of the *shofar* enlarge on the *shofar's* message of redemption. They celebrate the "coronation of God" (*Malkhuyot*) as sole Sovereign over our lives and avow that, as our Judge and Arbiter of our destiny, He will "remember" us (*Zikhronot*) with merciful consideration; and, as Lawgiver and Redeemer, He will bring us to messianic redemption (*Shofarot*). To avoid a despairing interpretation of the *shofar* sounds, the Mishnah forbids the inclusion of any biblical verses expressing forebodings of punitive chastisement among the ten verses which are to accompany each of the three sets of *shofar* sounds (Mishnah R.H. 4:6). The hopeful import of the *shofar* sounds is the burden of this midrashic comment:

R. Josiah said: "It is written: 'Happy is the people that know the joyful shout (sound of the trumpet)' (Ps. 89:16). Do not the other nations of the world know how to sound the trumpet? What a multitude of horns, sirens and trumpets they have, and yet we say 'Happy is the people that know the joyful shout (sound of the trumpet).' Therefore, this can only mean that this is the people that knows how to win over their Creator with the *shofar blasts*" (*Leviticus Rabbah*, 29:4).

"Destroy Satan"

It is the genius of Judaism to draw on elements of popular folklore and fancy for moral instruction. Among the people there persisted vestiges of a primitive belief that the sounding of the *shofar* was intended to expel evil spirits. This may account for Rabbi Isaac's explanation that the purpose of blowing the *shofar* twice during the Rosh Hashanah service is to confound and confute Satan (R.H. 16b). Rabbi Isaac's comment is reflected in the later practice of reciting, before the first series of *shofar* sounds, six biblical verses which form an acrostic of the words: *kera satan* (destroy Satan).

Rabbinic folklore tends to strip Satan of any autonomous power, to make him, rather, the hypostasis of those impulses within man which divert him from the path of duty. The numerical value of the Hebrew letters *hasatan* (the Satan) is 364. This prompts the observation that for 364 days during the year (Yom Kippur being the exception), Satan exercises his prerogative of corrupting and then accusing man (Yoma 20a). As man's invisible but implacable enemy, Satan is equated with the evil impulse and with death itself (B. B. 16a). While Abraham and Isaac were on their way to the *Akedah,* as noted earlier (p. 144), Satan tries to discourage and dissuade them from obedience to God's bidding. He attempts to deter Israel from receiving the Torah (Shab. 89a), and later creates the state of panic which induced Israel to worship the golden calf (*ibid.*).

The identification of Satan with the evil impulse can serve as a useful reminder of the all too frequent human tendency of rationalizing sinful conduct into saintly behavior, of postponing the performance of a momentous duty for the sake of a distracting pastime, of seeking the line of least resistance in situations that call for tenacity and courage. *Kera Satan* can symbolize for us the need to wage war against the evil in ourselves.

Why the *shofar* is not sounded on the Sabbath

The Mishnah (R.H. 4:1) informs us that when Rosh Hashanah fell on a Sabbath, the *shofar* was sounded in the Temple area, but it was not sounded in other parts

of Jerusalem, or in any other place or country (Mishnah
R.H. 4:1). The Palestinian Talmud (TP R.H. 29b) gives
a biblical basis for this, as it calls attention to the fact
that in one passage (Num. 29:1), the Torah designates
Rosh Hashanah as "a day of blowing the horn" (*Yom
Teruah*), while in another, it characterizes it as "a solemn
rest unto you, a memorial proclaimed with the blast of
horns" (Lev. 23:24). The latter verse is taken to imply that
on Sabbaths the *shofar* is not sounded outside the Temple area. The Babylonian Talmud finds as a basis for this
prohibition the rabbinical interdiction (*gezerah*) lest on
a Sabbath one be tempted to carry the *shofar* to an "ex-
pert" for practice instruction. The violation of a rabbinical interdiction being only a *shevut* (a minor Sabbath
infraction), it did not apply to the Temple area (R.H.
29b). In his desire to assert and demonstrate the authority
of the *Bet Din* at Yavneh and of that of similar courts,
Rabbi Yohanan ben Zakkai (1st century C.E.) ruled that
the *shofar* should be sounded on Sabbaths wherever there
existed a central *Bet Din* (Mishnah R.H. 4:1).

Tekiah, Shevarim, Teruah

The Bible refers to two kinds of trumpet sounds: *tekiah*
and *teruah* (Num. 10:6-8), and the Mishnah identifies
the *tekiah* as a long blast, and the *teruah* as a *yevavah,* a
wavering blast. It proceeds to prescribe three sets of *shofar* sounds, each set consisting of a *tekiah,* a *teruah,* and a
tekiah thrice repeated (Mishnah R.H. 4:9).

In the third century, doubt arose as to the exact nature
of the *teruah*. Some said that it was like a moaning sound
(*genuhe ganah*), and others said it was like an outcry
(*yelule yalal*). The first opinion would call for *shevarim*
(literally: broken sounds), while the second would call
for what we designate as a *teruah* sound, a tremolo of
nine staccato notes. Rabbi Abbahu of Caesarea reconciled
these differences by having the first set of sounds include
both *shevarim* and *teruah* as follows:

> *Tekiah, shevarim teruah, tekiah.*

The two other sets consist of the following order:

> *Tekiah, shevarim, tekiah.*
> *Tekiah, teruah tekiah.*

(R. H. 34a).

Why there are two series of *shofar* soundings

A passage in the Palestinian Talmud makes cursory allusion to an incident which was said to account for the transfer of the sounding of the *shofar* from the *Shaharit Amidah* to that of the *Musaf*. We are informed that on one occasion when, as was the original practice, the *shofar* was sounded during the *Shaharit,* the "enemy" (the Romans) suspected the early morning trumpet sounds to be a call to rebellion. The Jews were therefore attacked and slain. It was then decided to delay the sounding of the *shofar* until the *Musaf*. By then there could be no suspicion of rebellion, "For when the enemy noticed that first the Jews read the *Shema* and then recited the *Shaharit Amidah,* and then read the Torah, and then they sounded the *shofar* during the *Musaf Amidah,* they realized that the Jews were just observing their religious rites" (TP R.H. 59c). While the period during which this incident took place has not been dated exactly, it must have occurred prior to the Hadrianic persecutions of 132-135 C.E., since, during Hadrian's reign, the practice of Judaism was entirely forbidden.

The Mishnah refers to the *shofar* service during the *Musaf* as an established practice. It rules that the reader of the *Musaf Amidah* must prompt the person who sounds the *shofar,* in the prescribed sequence of the *shofar* notes (Mishnah R.H. 4:7).

The Rosh Hashanah liturgy calls for the *shofar* to be sounded at two points in the service: immediately after the reading of the Torah, and during the *Musaf Amidah*. The first series of *shofar* sounds is designated as *tekiot meyushav* (*shofar* sounds heard while sitting), and the second series as *tekiot meummad* (*shofar* sounds heard while standing). The first *shofar* service—the *tekiot meyushav*—opens with the blessings occasioned by the *mitzvah* of "hearing the sounding of the *shofar*." It takes place immediately after the reading of the Torah, because by then the entire congregation has already arrived at the synagogue. It is called *tekiot meyushav,* though in conformance with the rule that one stand during the performance of a *mitzvah,* the congregation rises, to distinguish it from the second series of *shofar* sounds which takes place at the *Musaf Amidah,* during the entire course of which the congregation is standing.

The symbolism of the *shofar*

Maimonides offers as the rationale for the sounding of the *shofar* the fact that this rite is ordained in the Torah. But he proceeds to suggest that, in addition, there is this exhortation that we can discern in the *shofar* sounds:

Awake, ye sleepers from your slumber, and rouse you from your lethargy. Scrutinize your deeds and return in repentance. Remember your Creator, ye who forget eternal truth in the trifles of the hour, who go astray all your year after vain illusions which can neither profit nor deliver. Look well into your souls and mend your ways and your actions; let each one of you forsake his evil path and his unworthy purpose, and return to God, so that He may have mercy upon you (*Hilkhot Teshubah*, 3:4).

What we often seek are trivialities, vain and illusory things which yield neither profit nor give satisfaction. Too often we are asleep to true and enduring values, and pursue the false values of fame and fortune, spiraling success, and spinning pleasure. These illusionary pursuits induce a state of mind in which, to use a rabbinic phrase, "we are asleep to the *Mitzvot*." We need to be shocked into wakefulness and to be aroused from moral stupor. The *shofar* calls us to awaken ourselves, to become alert once more to real and authentic possibilities, to make of our life an expedition through the vast continents of the mind and an exploration of the beauty and sublimity of Creation.

"A prayer without words"

Professor Saul Lieberman characterizes the *shofar* sounds as "a prayer without words." The sounds induce in us a range of emotions that surge in the heart, of thoughts that race through the mind. We think of the situation of man, "his works and his ways, his thoughts and his schemes," as the introduction to the *Zikhronot* expresses it; we are awakened by the awesome *tekiah* sound to the multiple dangers that threaten human life and make it so precarious. The weird, plaintive *shevarim-teruah* notes which follow serve to remind us that the fears that we fear often come upon us, that human life is frequently the bearer of tragedy and frustration. But not for long are we allowed to wander in despondency. We are lifted to the heights of a bright hope as we hear the *tekiah gedolah*, the prolonged concluding blast. This hope is one of redemption—the redemption of man from the inner and outer "drives" that threaten to efface the divine image in which he is made, the redemption of Israel from the yoke of exile, and the liberation of all mankind from exploitation and tyranny.

לַמְנַצֵּחַ לִבְנֵי קֹרַח מִזְמוֹר

God is gone up amidst shouting (*teruah*), The Lord amidst the sound of the horn . . . God reigneth over the nations. God sitteth upon His holy throne

(Psalm 47:6-10)

God reigns over the nations

This psalm is an appropriate introduction to the sounding of the *shofar*, and may have even originated as a psalm for the New Year. It underscores the awesome majesty of God whom all the peoples are destined to acclaim.

God sits as King on His throne while the "princes of the peoples are gathered, the people of the God of Abraham." Some Bible scholars see in the phrase "the people of the God of Abraham" a reference to all mankind, since Abraham was the (spiritual) father of a "multitude of peoples." A similar insight is suggested in the Midrash.

Selected rabbinic comments

"God [Elohim] *is gone up amidst shouting, the Lord* [Adonai] *amidst the sound of the horn* [shofar]"

Basing his interpretation on the use of *Elohim* (associated in rabbinic teaching with the Attribute of Justice) in the first part of the verse, and *Adonai* (associated with the Attribute of Mercy) in the second, Rabbi Judah ben Nahman said: "When the Holy One, blessed is He, ascends the judgment throne on Rosh Hashanah, He first sits on the throne of stern judgment. But when Israel takes the *shofar* and sounds it before Him, He rises from the throne of stern judgment and ascends the throne of mercy and extends compassion to His people (*Leviticus Rabbah*, 29:3).

"O clap your hands, all ye peoples"

When will all the nations rejoice? "When the righteous are increased, the people rejoice; but when the wicked beareth rule, the people sigh" (Prov. 29:2). When the wicked rule the world, men groan under the weight of oppression. They dare not walk with erect and dignified posture. God sympathizes with those who suffer from man's brutality toward man. But when the tyrant's rule is smashed, all the peoples clap their hands for joy. The entire world is then at peace, as God's sovereignty replaces man's tyranny (*Midrash Tehillim,* 47:1).

"The people of the God of Abraham"

Why not also "the God of Isaac and Jacob?" Because Abraham symbolizes all mankind, he having been the first to abandon idolatry (Suk. 49b).

SERVICE FOR RETURNING THE TORAH

אַשְׁרֵי יוֹשְׁבֵי בֵיתָךְ

Happy are they that dwell in Thy house

Rabbi Abina declared that one who recites *Tehillah le-David* (Ps. 145) thrice daily "is assured of being admitted to the world to come" (Ber. 4b). In the Talmud's explanation of Rabbi Abina's statement, the psalm is identified as *Ashre,* indicating that already in Amoraic times, two verses: "Happy (*ashre*) are they that dwell in Thy house" (Ps. 84:5) and "Happy (*ashre*) is the people that is in such a case, Yea, happy (*ashre*) is the people whose God is the Lord" (Ps. 144:15), were prefixed to *Tehillah le-David.* As the word *ashre* occurs three times in these verses, they may have been added to serve as a reminder of Rabbi Abina's statement. In the daily liturgy, *Ashre* is recited three times: in the *Pesuke de-Zimra* section of the morning service (see p. 38), in the *Kedushah de-Sidra* before *Uva Letziyyon* (see p. 62), and in the *Minhah* service. The reason given in the Talmud for the importance of Psalm 145 is that in addition to its alphabetical structure, it speaks of God's bountiful kindness to all the living: "Thou openest Thy hand and satisfiest every living thing with favor" (vs. 16). A Genizah fragment of the late Geonic period, edited by Louis Ginzberg,* offers additional reasons for the importance of *Ashre*. Among them are the following: 1. The superscription of this psalm opens with *tehillah* (praise), and so does its last verse begin with *tehillat Adonai* ("the praise of the Lord"); 2. The first verse: "I will extol Thee, my God, O King (*hamelekh*); and I will bless (*vaavorkha*) Thy name (*shemekha*) for ever (*leolam*) and ever," alludes to the four required elements of the blessing formula: *berakhah, shem, olam,* and *malkhut* (the praise of God, the mention of His name, His eternity and His Kingship).

In a detailed study of the structure of Psalm 145, Leon J. Liebreich** points out that the root *barekh* (to praise) occurs at the beginning of Psalm 145 in the first verse: "And I shall praise Thy name for ever and ever"; in the middle of the psalm, in verse 10: "And Thy saints shall praise Thee"; and at the end of the psalm, in verse 21: "And let all flesh bless His holy name for ever and ever." Liebreich shows how these verses are patterned in a progression of ideas. In the opening verse the poet alone praises the Lord, in the middle verse only the select saintly ones praise Him, and in the final verse the hope is expressed that "all flesh" may praise Him. Furthermore, the psalm is structured on the word-chain plan, with certain key words being repeated at strategic points. An outstanding example of this is the tenfold occurrence of the word *kol* (all) in verses 14-20, as a means of accentuating God's all-encompassing love and justice.

"And we will bless the Lord . . . Hallelujah"

The verse "And we will bless the Lord from this time forth and for ever, *hallelujah*" (Ps. 115:18) is attached to the conclusion of *Ashre* to make it conform to the succeeding psalms of the *Pesuke de-Zimra,* each of which ends with *hallelujah*.

יְהַלְלוּ אֶת שֵׁם ה'

Praise the name of the Lord

The appropriateness of this verse (Ps. 148:13) for the recessional with the Torah is clearly demonstrated when

* Ginzberg, *Ginze Schechter,* I, 301.
** *Hebrew Union College Annual,* XXVII, 187-191.

we bear in mind the verse which precedes it: "Both young
men and maidens, old men and children; let them praise
the name of the Lord, for His Name alone is exalted."

הָבוּ לַה׳ בְּנֵי אֵלִים

**Ascribe unto the Lord, O ye sons of might,
Ascribe unto the Lord glory and strength**

One tradition has it that the Torah was given on a Sabbath (Shab. 86b). The Midrash notes that in the account
of the revelation at Sinai, the word *kol* (voice) occurs
seven times (*Yalkut Tehillim*, 443). Since this is also the
case in Psalm 29 where *kol Adonai* (the voice of the Lord)
occurs seven times, the Rabbis saw in this psalm a description of the sinaitic revelation, even as they found in
its sevenfold reference to *kol* an intimation of the seven
blessings of the Sabbath *Amidah* (TP Ber. 8a). The
selection of this psalm for the Torah recessional on Sabbath mornings, which dates from the twelfth century,
may have been prompted by these considerations.

לַה׳ הָאָרֶץ וּמְלוֹאָהּ

The earth is the Lord's, and the fulness thereof

On other days than the Sabbath, Psalm 24 is read during
the Torah recessional. The psalm is associated with the
ark of the Torah in this charming talmudic legend:

When the ark was about to be brought into the Holy of Holies,
the door of the sacred chamber locked itself and it was impossible to open it. Solomon said: "Lift up your heads O ye gates,
And be ye lifted up, ye everlasting doors, that the King of glory
may come in" (24:7). And he also recited the succeeding verses
of this psalm. But all was of no avail until he pronounced the
words "O Lord turn not away the face of Thine anointed; remember the good deeds of David Thy servant" (II Chronicles
6:42). Then the doors opened (Shab. 30a).

וּבְנֻחֹה יֹאמַר

And when the ark rested

The mosaic of verses read before the closing of the ark
affords a review of the role of the ark in the remote past,

even as it ends with a plea for the renewal of Israel's glory.

The Torah relates: "When it [the ark] rested [during the Israelites' travels in the wilderness of Sinai], he [Moses] said: 'Return, O Lord, unto the ten thousands of the families of Israel' " (Num. 10:36). The three verses which follow this passage (Ps. 132:8-10) are also associated with the ark. The next three verses: *Ki lekah tov natati lakhem* ("For I give you good doctrine"), *Etz hayyim hi* ("She is a tree of life"), and *Derakheha darkhe noam* ("Her ways are ways of pleasantness") from Proverbs 4:2, 3:18,17 respectively, also praise the grandeur of the Torah.

The concluding verse, *Hashivenu Adonai elekha* ("Turn Thou us unto Thee, O Lord") from the Book of Lamentations (5:21), is a plea for the future, when a penitent and regenerated people will be restored to its former glory.

THE *MUSAF AMIDAH:* ROSH HASHANAH

The theme of the *Musaf Amidah*

A unity of religious concept binds together the seemingly disparate parts of the *Amidah*. From its opening words of praise to the God of Abraham, Isaac, and Jacob, to the closing supplication that we be inscribed in the "Book of Life, Blessing and Peace," Judaism's doctrine of man is underscored. The rabbinic conception of man's nature avoids both extremes—the one which is radically pessimistic, and the other which is naively unrealistic. The former would announce man's depravity, his inability, by any effort of his own, to extricate himself from the perversity of which he is capable. The other is an exaggerated avowal of man's natural goodness, nay, even innocence! Judaism reckons with the corrupting tendencies in man. Yet, however much it has suffered from the historical exhibition of these tendencies, it maintains its faith in man as a creature capable of reaching a high level of moral achievement. With its twin concept of *yetzer hara,* "the evil impulse," and *yetzer tov,* "the good impulse," Judaism conceives of man as a creature in whom two personalities, both capable of actualization, are concealed—a brute and a saint. Every person is obligated to restrain the brute and to educate the saint within him. This internal tension is described by the Rabbis when they affirm: "It is man's duty to arouse the good *yetzer* over the evil *yetzer*" (Ber. 5a). It is worthy of note that in this passage and in almost every other talmudic reference to man's twin impulses, the evil impulse is referred to as *yetzer hara*, "the evil impulse," while the good impulse is referred to without the definite article as *yetzer tov*, "*a* good impulse." The probable reason is that the evil impulse is identified as the tendency to evil already mentioned in the Torah: "the imagination (*yetzer*) of man's heart is evil (*ra*) from his youth" (Gen. 8:21), while *yetzer tov* is a parallel concept introduced by the Rabbis to identify the good impulse which functions as an antidote to the *yetzer hara*.

The juxtaposition of *the* evil impulse and *a* good impulse can also serve to symbolize for us a basic fact in human nature. The *yetzer hara*, the evil impulse, is ever active. Unless it is sublimated and redirected, it can take full possession of a person and lead him to the merciless treatment of others. On the other hand, the good impulse is more potential than actual. It needs to be consciously and persistently activated. This is the abiding lesson suggested to us in the rabbinic passage just cited—calling on man always to arouse a good impulse over the evil impulse.

Our liturgy is inspired by the belief that man is held accountable for the mastery of his evil drives, and for calling into action the potential good within him. This belief defines man as a morally responsible being, standing under God's judgment. Such a conception expresses a more profound respect for our person than one which would absolve us by attributing man's conduct to hereditary and environmental influences beyond his control. The belief that he is morally irresponsible tends to make a person indeed irresponsible, even as the belief that he is accountable for his conduct can serve to heighten his moral sensitivity.

Weary idealists and misanthropes may wonder whether the struggle for human perfection is worth the effort. What can one person accomplish in a vast universe, of which he is but a tiny particle? Against such debilitating speculation, the threefold division of the *Musaf* into the *Malkhuyot,* the *Zikhronot,* and the *Shofarot* suggests some measure of response. Man's brief existence is given perspective and significance, juxtaposed as it is to God's eternity. As God's creatures, we are to acknowledge His sovereignty over the whole universe; as His children we are to see in history the unfolding of His purpose; and as His servants we are to listen to the *shofar* sounds which reassure us of the coming fulfillment of Israel's and the world's redemption. Broad is the vision, deep is the conviction, and deathless is the spirit of the people that expresses all this in the prayers of its liturgy!

ORDER OF THE *MUSAF AMIDAH:*
ROSH HASHANAH

The unique features of this *Musaf Amidah* are first, that it contains nine blessings instead of the usual seven; and second, that it includes three sets of ten verses each: the *Malkhuyot* (Kingship verses), the *Zikhronot* (Remembrance verses), and *Shofarot* (*Shofar* verses). Because of the long and involved nature of this *Amidah,* few individuals were familiar with it, and the Talmud stipulates that even the learned depended on the rendition of this *Amidah* by the reader (R.H. 34b). In some rites the *shofar* is sounded during the silent *Amidah* as well as during the reader's repetition of it after the *Kedushat Hayom* (which also concludes the *Malkhuyot* section), as well as after the *Zikhronot* and the *Shofarot.* The order of the *Amidah* is then as follows:

I. *Avot:* concluding with *Magen Abraham.*
II. *Gevurot:* concluding with *Mehayyeh Hametim.*
III. *Kedushat Hashem:* concluding with *Hamelekh Hakadosh.* This section includes also the three *Uvekhen* prayers (see pp. 100-103).
IV. *Kedushat Hayom:* concluding with "evermore wilt Thou reign in glory." This section contains: *Attah Behartanu, Umipne Hataenu,* and the verses specifying the sacrifices offered in

ancient times on that day; and *Alenu*, which
introduces the ten "Kingship" verses. The inclusion of the *Malkhuyot* in this section is in
accordance with Rabbi Akiba's opinion (Mishnah R.H. 4:5).

V. *Zikhronot:* beginning with *Attah Zokher* as the
introduction to the ten "Remembrance" verses
and concluding with, "Our God, and God of
our Fathers, be mindful of us for good and
remember us . . . unto salvation and mercy."

VI. *Shofarot:* beginning with *Attah Nigleta* as the
introduction to the ten *shofar* verses and concluding with "Sound the great *shofar* for our
liberation."

VII. *Avodah:* beginning with *Retzeh* and concluding
with "Who restores His Presence to Zion."

VIII. *Hodaah:* beginning with *Modim* and concluding
with "Thou whose Name is good and to whom
it is good to render thanks."

IX. *Berakhah:* beginning with *Sim Shalom* and concluding with "Blessed art Thou, O Lord, who
makest peace."

הִנְנִי הֶעָנִי מִמַּעַשׂ

I am poor in deeds

Deficient in good deeds I am overwhelmed and awed as I stand
here as the emissary of Thy people. Though I am a sinner and
though I am lacking in character and piety, I implore Thy
mercy and pray that my prayer may find acceptance before Thy
throne. . . . Praised art Thou who hearest prayer.

Of uncertain date and unknown authorship, *Hinneni*
is a deeply stirring personal prayer, in which an east
European cantor expressed the feelings that overwhelmed
him as he approached the lectern to intone the *Musaf
Amidah*. The author is supremely aware of the gravity of
his responsibility. He knows that according to rabbinic
teaching, on Rosh Hashanah and Yom Kippur, even the
most learned among the congregants fulfill their obligations by listening to the reader's rendition of the *Amidah*,
while on other occasions, only the unlearned are so absolved. The *Musaf* of Rosh Hashanah is in this respect

162   Justice and Mercy

especially singled out in the Talmud (R.H. 34b), since few congregants were familiar with its nine blessings and accompanying biblical verses of the *Malkhuyot, Zikhronot,* and *Shofarot* (pp. 179-80). To these considerations must be added the author's acute awareness of his personal inadequacy. He thinks of the high qualities of piety and practice enumerated in the Talmud for eligibility to serve as a *sheliah tzibbur* (pp. 82-83), and prays that his rendering of the prayers may be accepted as if he too were a person whose behavior during his youth was unblemished, who enjoys the love of his fellowmen, whose voice is pleasing, and whose recitation of the liturgy is fluent.

Because *Hinneni* is a personal prayer and not part of the prescribed liturgy, it ends with a *barukh* blessing in which the Tetragrammeton *(Adonai)* is omitted. *Hinneni* is recited before *Musaf* on Rosh Hashanah and on Yom Kippur. It is not recited before the *Shaharit Amidah* because of the liturgical rule that there must be no interruption between the *Geulah* and the *Tefillah* (pp. 80-81).

After completing this prayer, the reader repeats the *Musaf Amidah,* see pages 160-61.

READER'S REPETITION OF THE
MUSAF AMIDAH: ROSH HASHANAH *

אָפַּד מֵאָז

This day hath been ordained of old as a day of reckoning

Rosh Hashanah celebrates the birthday of mankind. Creation began, according to rabbinic tradition, on the twenty-fifth day of Elul, and man was created on the first day of Tishri.

As the record books of our life are opened, our deeds proclaim themselves before the Throne of Judgment. Our plea is that when we sound the *shofar* in reaffirmation of God's Kingship, He will remember for us the covenant made with our patriarchs, extend us His pardon,

---

* For our discussion of the opening sections of the *Amidah,* see pp. 85 ff.
** *Uppad Meaz* is recited only on the first day.

and be for us as He was for Abraham, a stay and a shield.

The opportunity of repentance is therefore the Creator's gift to a creature whose actions are free. It is man's ability to "return" to God which signalizes his freedom. This is the message, the task, and the teaching transmitted by the patriarchs to their children, and through their posterity, to all mankind.

Rabbinic sources

This alphabetical acrostic by Kalir is the first part of a *kerovah* for Rosh Hashanah. Among the midrashic allusions that it contains, are the following:

Uppad Meaz ("ordained of old")

Adam was created on the first day of Tishri, and in a period of twelve hours went through an entire spiritual odyssey. Created on the first hour of the first Rosh Hashanah day, he sinned on the tenth hour of the same day, was judged on the eleventh hour, and pardoned on the twelfth. God then assured him that in the future, when his descendants stand in judgment before Him on Rosh Hashanah, they, like him, would obtain a free pardon (*Leviticus Rabbah*, 29:1).

Zeh melitz kehirhiv batzar ("God Himself made the plea for man's relief from distress")

By opening for Adam the gates of repentance, God acted as man's protector in the grievous situation brought about by his sinful behavior (*Genesis Rabbah*, 21:6).

Tiat hotzev gevaot vetzurim . . . ("The choice plants of the Creator of hills and rocks were then born")

On Rosh Hashanah the patriarchs were born (*Rosh Hashanah 10a*).

Keyosheve netaim hemmah hayotzrim lelammed botzedek laatzurim ("They are the builders who dwelt in the garden and who plead for those assembled in the Synagogue")

The phrase: *keyosheve netaim hemmah hayotzrim* comes from I Chronicles 4:23 and is midrashically interpreted to refer to the souls of the righteous (i.e., the patriarchs) who dwelt in the garden of Eden (*yosheve netaim*). God took counsel with them before He created man (*Genesis*

Rabbah, 8:7), and on Rosh Hashanah they plead for those assembled in prayer.

תְּפֶן בְּמָכוֹן

**When seated on Thy judgment throne, hearken
to the sound of the *shofar****

This plea, that God may listen to the *shofar* sounds and spare the world, is in effect a beseeching that the Judge of all men may temper justice with mercy. We invoke the merit of the patriarchs and the covenant made with them. The binding of Isaac is recalled as an example of true dedication to God and as a reminder of the special merit accruing therefrom to his descendants.

Comments on the text

This alphabetical acrostic in the inverted order is the second part of Kalir's *kerovah.*

The appeal to God that He move from the throne of judgment to that of mercy, is inspired by the rabbinic teaching that when God assesses the world from the throne of judgment, he is inclined to emphasize *Middat Hadin* (His attribute of justice). But when Israel sounds the *shofar,* He moves to the throne of mercy in order to judge it mercifully with *Middat Harahamim* (His attribute of mercy) (*Leviticus Rabbah,* 29:3).

The polarity of the divine attributes of justice and love is exemplified in the following passage:

Rabbi Johanan said in the name of Rabbi Jose: "Whence do we learn that the Holy One, blessed is He, prays? From the verse: 'Even them will I bring to My holy mountain, and make them joyful in My house of prayer' " (Isa. 56:7). Scripture does not say *their* house of prayer, but *My* house of prayer. Thus we deduce that God prays. What does God say in His prayer? Said Rabbi Zutra ben Tobia, in the name of Rab, "He prays as follows: 'May it be My will that My mercy may subdue My wrath, that My love may have supremacy over all My other qualities, so that I may deal with My children in accordance with the attribute of mercy, overlooking the rigorous demands of stern justice' " (Ber. 7a).

* *Tefen Bemakhon* is recited only on the first day.

Dibrot eleh divre haberit ("Remove the harsh terms of these words of the covenant in consideration of Thy thrice given compact")

The "harsh terms" (*eleh divre haberit*) refer to the expression in Deuteronomy 28:69: "These are the words of the covenant," which concludes the chapter describing the severe chastisements to which Israel would be subjected because of its disobedience. The "triple covenant" alludes to the statement of Rabbi Akiba that on Mt. Sinai there were revealed for the first time the principles and details of the Torah, that they were taught a second time in the Tabernacle, and a third time at the plains of Moab (Sotah 37b).

מֶלֶךְ עֶלְיוֹן

The King Most High, eternal is His power, everlasting His glory, and forever His acclaim

God, the King Most High, reigns forever. He knows all and is all-powerful. He fathoms our innermost secrets and outlives all that lives. Infinite in the sway of His power, He is near to those who seek His help. Not so dependable are those lesser beings—the princes and powers of the world—to whom men are wont to offer their allegiance. The human "pauper king," on whom men depend, is powerless. He is destined for the grave. The sleep of death is his end, and into the void he vanishes. But God, the King Most High, His power is everlasting, His glory is eternal, His praise endures forever.

The author of this *piyyut* is unknown, but its structure is similar to that of a *piyyut* in the *Shaharit* of the second day of Rosh Hashanah, composed by Rabbi Simon ben Isaac ben Abun of Mayence (see page 56). It is not known which one antedated the other.

וּנְתַנֶּה תֹּקֶף

Let us declare the utter sanctity of this day.
Thou openest the book of records from which
man's destiny is read, the seal of each man's
hand being in that book. A still small voice
is heard.

Repentance, prayer and good deeds

Because this prayer expresses so dramatically an awareness of the unpredictability and uncertainty of human
life, it has occupied a pre-eminent place among the liturgical preferences of the Jews. With vivid imagery, the
author depicts the heavenly scene on the Day of Judgment. The *shofar* is sounded, there is heard but a still
small voice to herald the appearance of the Divine Judge.
The angels are in terror, for judgment is to be decreed
against the habitants of heaven, as well as against those
of earth. In the eyes of God, no being, however angelic,
has perfect purity. One by one, as sheep are counted by
the shepherd, each life passes in review before Him, and
its fate is inscribed in a book of records which contains
the seal of every person's hand. The sense of doom, of
almost unrelieved despair, is heightened in us as we are
told that on Rosh Hashanah the decree is written and
that on Yom Kippur it is sealed.

It is not the poet's intention, however, to induce a
fatalistic resignation; but rather the opposite, to deny
that man's life is subject to an irremediable fate. The
prayer, in fact, reaches its climax when it assures us that
it is within man's power to annul an evil decree, to reopen
the future, and to reclaim the initiative it gives. The quan-
tity of man's life is in the hands of God, the quality of
his life is in man's hands only. "Everything is in the
hands of God except the fear of God" (Ber. 33b). Everything is foreseen, yet freedom of choice is granted (Ab.
3:15). In its climactic declaration, the prayer affirms that
man can change the future by changing himself. It suggests a threefold means of annulling "the evil of the
decree":

1. Repentance: A courageous break with evil and a
   "return" to God.

2. Prayer: A re-establishment of our relationship with God.
3. *Tzedakah* (deeds of kindness): Tangible acts of love and concern for our fellow men.

Guilt is always more painful than actual punishment. To feel responsible for one's virtues and one's defects is the foundation of moral conduct. Judaism teaches that acts in defiance of the moral law are requited with just retribution. Conceived in terms of external fortune, this is not always confirmed by experience. The prosperity of the wicked and the suffering of the righteous have always puzzled religious thinkers. "But the doctrine of retribution is fully confirmed by experience when it is understood as the fact of disintegration of personality which inevitably results from yielding to some dominant impulse or desire" (M. M. Kaplan). Every sin is a violence against one's nature. The rabbinic conviction that sin is its own punishment, and that wrongdoing dulls the conscience and the heart of man, is validated and confirmed by many who, after a lifetime of selfishness, leave behind them a legacy of frustration and futility.

Comments on the text

The authorship of *Unetanneh Tokef* is still disputed. It is said by some to have been introduced into the liturgy by Kalonymos ben Meshullam of Mayence (*ca.* 1100). Associated with this exalting *piyyut* is a popular tale ascribing its composition to Rabbi Amnon, an affluent scholar of distinguished lineage, who, in a moment of weakness, postponed for three days his answer to a request that he become an apostate from Judaism. Tormented with remorse, he spent the three days in regret at his failure to reaffirm immediately the constancy of his belief in the faith of his fathers. On the third day, because he then failed to give an affirmative reply, he was arrested and tortured. As Rosh Hashanah was then being observed, he asked that he be brought to the synagogue. When the *Kedushah* was about to be recited, Rabbi Amnon asked for a brief pause, recited the *Unetanneh Tokef* prayer and then expired. Its inclusion in the liturgy is said to have been in answer to the request made of Rabbi Kalonymos by Rabbi Amnon when the latter appeared to him in a dream.

In an erudite and comprehensive study of comparative liturgy, Eric Werner, of the Hebrew Union College-Jewish Institute of Religion, offers a fascinating summary of more recent research on the origins of the *Unetanneh Tokef*. He tells us that M. Zulay of the Hebrew University of Jerusalem, the author of a volume on the *piyyutim* of Yannai, had confirmed the theory that the *Unetanneh Tokef* originated as early as the Byzantine rule (*ca.* 800). Dr. Werner shows that there is a remarkable similarity in style and form between *Unetanneh Tokef* and its Byzantine and Middle-Latin parallels. Yet the Jewish differential can be clearly discerned by a comparison with this part of the Middle-Latin *Dies Irae:*

> What a tremble will be there!
> The book will be opened
> All hidden things will appear
> The awesome trumpet will sound
> Over all the graves.
> Whom shall I ask for protection even
> When the just ones are not safe?
> Counting the sheep, grant me space
> Among the lambs, segregate me from the goats
> My prayers are not worthy, but Thou,
> Good one, be gracious unto me.
>
> (Werner, *Sacred Bridge,* p. 254)

Here, as in the *Unetanneh Tokef,* judgment takes place in heaven, but emphasis is placed upon the "Last Judgment," after the dead are revived and the redeemed are segregated from those condemned. In the Jewish version, however, the Judgment Day occurs on Rosh Hashanah, and the sealing of the Judgment is on Yom Kippur. The decision relates to this life, and the decree can be remedied and even repealed by the decision of repentance. Indeed, so pronounced is Judaism's predisposition to direct attention to the quality of man's life on earth, that, in a foreshadowing of the procedure at the "last judgment" Raba (4th century C.E.) suggests that among the questions to be asked of man are the following:

Did you conduct your business with integrity? Did you set aside fixed times for study of Torah? Did you concern yourself with the duty of raising a family? Did you retain a confident faith in the fulfillment of the prophetic ideals of Israel's redemption and the coming of an era of universal peace? (Shab. 31a).

"the seal of every man's hand is set thereto"

This idea is based on a homily suggested by the verse: "He sealeth up the hand of every man, that all men whom He hath made may know it" (Job 37:7). In commenting on this verse, the Midrash states that when Adam sinned, God caused all generations of the future, righteous and wicked alike, down to the Resurrection, to pass before Adam, and said to him: "See how you have brought death upon the righteous." When Adam heard this, he was distressed that by his action death would come even upon the righteous. He pleaded with God not to record it against him that he brought death upon them. Adam was then assured that every man would be asked to record the deeds he has done and to set the seal of his own hand to his own record. The Midrash then continues to say that when God sits in judgment over His creatures, He brings their record books and exhibits to them their own deeds (*Tanhuma,* ed. Buber, *Bereshit,* 29).

This Midrash serves to remind us of the teaching that a person must hold himself fully responsible for the quality of his life. He must not succumb to the temptation to blame his conduct on forces beyond his control. The moral quality of our life is determined by the extent to which we believe that the seal of our own hand is set to the record of our deeds.

"a still small voice"

This phrase is first found in this biblical context:

And He said "Go forth, and stand upon the mount before the Lord." And, behold, the Lord passed by, and a great and strong wind rent the mountains, and broke in pieces the rocks before the Lord; but the Lord was not in the wind; and after the wind an earthquake; but the Lord was not in the earthquake; and after the earthquake a fire; but the Lord was not in the fire; and after the fire a still small voice (I Kings 19:11-12).

That even among men, regal majesty is accompanied by "a still small voice" is the teaching of this charming tale:

Rabbi Sheshet was totally blind. Once, when the entire population of the town went to welcome the king on his visit to the city, Rabbi Sheshet went along with the people. A scoffing unbeliever said to him: "Whole pitchers go to the well, but why do broken pitchers go there?" Said Rabbi Sheshet, "Come along and you will see that my sight is keener than yours." The first regiment passed by. As a tumultuous noise was heard, the scoffer shouted; "The king is here!" Said Rabbi Sheshet, "The king is not yet here!" A second regiment passed by, and again there was a loud noise. Again the scoffer exclaimed, "The king is here!" But Rabbi Sheshet said, "The king has not yet arrived." A third regiment appeared, and it marched amidst a deep silence. This time Rabbi Sheshet exclaimed "I am sure that the king is about to appear." And the king did appear. "How did you know?" asked the scoffer. Rabbi Sheshet then explained to him that earthly majesty, like heavenly majesty, makes its appearance with the dignity of a still small voice (Ber. 58a).

The true builders of civilization and the real benefactors of humanity are not necessarily those who attain public fame and achieve wide acclaim. There are heroes of the common life who, as they do their work quietly and anonymously, impress their presence upon the lives of others. Theirs is a still small voice which speaks with a dignity and majesty that is a reflection of the divine in man.

One calls to mind Akiba's wife, who encouraged him to spend many years in the study of Torah, while she remained at home suffering privation. Upon his triumphant return, when he was acknowledged as the most eminent scholar of his time, his wife, who had not seen him for these many years, tried to make her way through the masses of his admiring disciples. Akiba, noticing that his pupils were trying to shield him from a woman dressed in tattered clothes, recognized his wife and said to his pupils: "Make way for her. All that I am and all that you are we owe to her" (Ket. 63a).

"All who enter the world dost Thou cause to pass before Thee, one by one, as a flock of sheep (*kivene maron*)"

The term *kivene maron* occurs in the Mishnah (R.H. 1:2), and is interpreted in the Talmud as "sheep" (R.H. 18a). However, older texts of the Mishnah and texts of the *Tosefta* and the Jerusalem Talmud point to the reading *kivenumeron* which is from the Greek word *nomeron,* meaning a regiment of soldiers. Saul Lieberman suggests that there is visualized here a troop of soldiers climbing up, one by one, on a narrow incline (*Tosefta Ki-fshutah, Moed,* pp. 1022-23). This original meaning offers us an even more vivid picture of each person being judged as an individual by the moral quality of his life.

"Man's origin is dust and he returneth to the dust"

The uncertainty, unpredictability, and evanescent nature of human life is depicted here in graphic metaphors equating man with a fragile potsherd, withering grass, a fading flower, a passing shadow, floating dust, and a vanishing dream. This devaluation of human life purports to fortify the belief that God takes cognizance of the inner drives that account for man's lack of moral constancy and that often disfigure his humanity. No life, however, is irremediably doomed to meaninglessness. The sinner can redeem himself by taking the initial step of repentance towards the reclamation of his worth and dignity as a moral being. Then his life assumes great significance in the eyes of God, for God needs man to sanctify His name on earth, even as do the inhabitants of the heavens above. Once finite man adopts as his vocation the glorification and hallowing of God's name, his life assumes infinite worth. Israel, the people which in its very name bears the Name of God, is to act and serve as the divinely commissioned vanguard of the terrestrial hosts, expressing the praise of God in thought, word, and deed.

THE *KEDUSHAH*

עֲשֵׂה לְמַעַן שְׁמֶךָ

וְקַדֵּשׁ אֶת שִׁמְךָ עַל מַקְדִּישֵׁי שְׁמֶךָ

Act for the sake of Thy name
Make Thy holiness manifest
over those who hallow Thy name

As in the *Shaharit* service, the *Kedushah* is introduced by a number of *piyyutim** which enlarge on its mystical

* In a recent study of the mystical element in Jewish liturgy, Gershon Scholem has shown that there was a plethora of *Kedushah*

theme of the chorus of heavenly beings who are joined by the worshiping congregation of Israel in announcing the majesty of God.

The *Kedushah* of the *Musaf* is unique in that it includes the responses of "Hear O Israel, the Lord our God, the Lord is One" (Deut. 6:4), "to be your God" (Num. 15:4), and "I am the Lord your God" (*ibid.*)—these being the opening and closing verses of the *Shema*. The reason that has been given is that between 438-528 C.E. the Persians forbade the Jews of Babylonia to say the *Shema*, since its monotheism contradicted Zoroastrian dualism. The Persian government officials would station themselves in the synagogues during those hours of the morning which were the prescribed hours for the reading of the *Shema* (until about 10 A.M.). Assured that the *Shema* had been omitted, they would leave. Once they had left, the *Shema* was recited in the *Kedushah* of the *Musaf*, and the practice was retained even after the persecutions ceased.*

Comments on the text

The usual introduction to the *Kedushah* is: *Nekaddesh et shimkha baolam* ("We sanctify Thy name on earth") in the *Shaharit*, and *Naaritzekha venakdishekha* ("We revere Thee and declare Thy sanctity") in the *Musaf*. Here, however, a different introduction, *Aseh lemaan shemekha* ("Act for the sake of Thy name"), leads the congregation into the response: *Kadosh, Kadosh, Kadosh* ("Holy, Holy, Holy is the Lord of hosts").

There are differences in the opening words of the *Kedushah* of the *Amidah* which date back to the varying liturgical practices of Palestine and Babylonia. The two main variations are these: The Sephardic rite for the *Musaf*

hymns (belonging to the mystic *Hekhalot* [Temple] literature) addressed to God as He is seated on His heavenly throne, while the *Hayyot Hakodesh* (the celestial creatures), who are the bearers of the throne (Ezek. 1:5 ff.), sing songs of praise. Scholem now dates these mystic hymns much earlier than the fifth century C.E.— even as early as the second century C.E. Gershom Scholem, *Jewish Gnosticism, Merkabah Mysticism, and Talmudic Tradition* (New York: The Jewish Theological Seminary of America, 1960), p. 20 ff.
* Louis Ginzberg, *Ginze Schechter* (New York, 1929), pp. 524 ff.

Kedushah begins, "A crown (*keter*) . . . the angels on high offer to Thee . . . and so do Thy people who are gathered below; all of them sound the 'Thrice Holy to Thee,'" etc. The Ashkenazic rite opens as follows: "We will revere and sanctify Thee as is done in the assembled worship of the holy seraphim who sanctify Thy Name . . . as it is written in the words of the prophet: 'Holy, Holy, Holy,'" etc.

Despite the esoteric references to the mystery that surrounds God's majesty and the feelings of sublimity which the words of the *Kedushah* convey, the prayers and hymns which precede and follow it, far from accentuating the transcendence and awesome Presence of God, imply that His holiness manifests itself in His goodness towards His creatures (*Hamol Al Maasekha*) and in His merciful acceptance of the repentant sinner (*Vekhol Maaminim*).

The meaning of God's holiness is expressed in these concluding lines leading up to the blessing: *Hamelekh Hakadosh* (the holy King):

Thou art holy and awesome is Thy name and there is no God but Thee, as it is written: "The Lord of hosts is exalted through justice, and God the Holy One is sanctified through righteousness" (Isa. 5:16).

The word for righteousness here is *tzedakah*. In rabbinic terminology, *tzedakah* means love. Our verse, in its liturgical usage, declares that God's power manifests itself by His judgment of men, while His holiness is made manifest to them by His love and forgiveness. God is *kadosh* (i.e., kind) and also *nora* (awesome). There is no other God (i.e., judge) besides Him (cf. *Midrash Tehillim*, 101:1).

וְכֹל מַאֲמִינִים

And all believe that He is the faithful God

This ninth-century, twofold alphabetical acrostic has been ascribed to Yohanan ha-Cohen, but M. Zulay says that Yannai (*ca.*550 C.E.) may have been its author. Declaring that God holds in His hand the scales of justice, the *piyyut* affirms that He is merciful even as He fathoms our secret devisings. God extends His love to those who are righteous and also to those who go astray. Powerful above all who wield power, He is great and gracious in forgiveness. Equally accessible to all, His hand is extended to those who knock at the gates of repentance.

The essential message of this *piyyut* is that God is not only a king, but also a merciful father. To feel the friendship of the Creator of the universe while accepting personal responsibility for the quality of our life is the dual meaning of the concept that God is both Father and King.

By uniting our being with Him, by linking our name with His, and by sanctifying His name in word and deed, we introduce meaning into our life and purpose into our existence.

For our discussion of the three Uvekhen *prayers which are recited here, see pp. 100-03.*

וְיֶאֱתָיוּ

All the world shall come to serve Thee

How one would like to catch a glimpse of that early hymnologist to whom we owe the well-known *piyyut, Veyetayu.* In its iconoclastic victory of monotheism over all kinds of idolatries, ancient as well as modern, it might best be described as the *Marseillaise* of the people of the Lord of Hosts—a *Marseillaise* which is not followed by a reign of terror, but by the Kingdom of God on earth, when the upright shall exult and the saints triumphantly rejoice (Solomon Schechter).

This hymn, of unknown origin, is inserted after the *Uvekhen* prayers to complete the portrayal of the perfected world and the united humanity which would ensue after the universal recognition of the sovereignty of God. The self-imposed constraints of the alphabetical acrostic seem to have liberated rather than impeded the free flow of the poetry and the ascending sense of exaltation which leads us on to this triumphant climax:

And the islands laugh exultant/That they belong to God./And all their congregations/So loud Thy praise shall sing,/That the uttermost peoples, hearing,/Shall hail Thee crowned King.

Comments on the text

The extant Hebrew text contains glosses and interpolations which confuse the alphabetical order and disturb
the rhythm of the hymn. The correct text as given by
H. Brody is:

וְיִזְבְּחוּ לְךָ אֶת זִבְחֵיהֶם

וְיַחְפְּרוּ אֶת עֲצַבֵּיהֶם

וְיִטּוּ שְׁכֶם אֶחָד לְעָבְדְּךָ

They shall bring to Thee their offerings
and repudiate their idols
and serve Thee in one accord.

אַתָּה בְחַרְתָּנוּ

Thou hast chosen us from all people

We now begin the section leading to the *Kedushat
Hayom* ("The Sanctification of the Day"), the fourth
blessing of the *Musaf Amidah.* As we refer to the privilege which is ours, to observe this Day of Remembrance,
our thoughts are directed to the biblically ordained sacrificial service which was, in ancient times, performed on
this day in the Temple at Jerusalem. Reflecting upon the
fact that we are denied the opportunity of celebrating the
day in like manner, we enter upon a self-critical prayer:
Umipene Hataenu ("Because of our sins").

וּמִפְּנֵי חֲטָאֵינוּ

Because of our sins, we were exiled from our land

"When in the mood of blaming, blame yourself"

Why was the first Temple destroyed? Because there then prevailed among the people these three heinous sins: idolatry, unchastity, and bloodshed.

Why then was the second Temple destroyed? Were not
people then meticulous in their devotion to the Torah, to the

Mitzvot, and to deeds of kindness? True; nevertheless the second Temple was destroyed because people harbored baseless hatreds toward one another. From this we learn that baseless hatred is accounted as heinous as the three sins: idolatry, unchastity, and bloodshed together (Yoma, 9b).

When God was about to give the Torah, no other people but Israel would accept it. Hence Israel is more responsible than others for failing to live by the Torah. This is to be understood in the light of this parable: A king had a field which he wished to put in charge of a laborer. He asked each of five men the same question: "Will you take over this field?" The first four men each in turn refused to undertake the work saying: "I have no strength, this work is too hard for me." When the fifth man was asked: "Will you take over the field?" He replied: "Yes, on condition that you till it." The reply was again: "Yes." But as soon as the man took possession of it, he let it lie fallow. With whom was the king angry? Surely not with those who had said that they could not perform the work. He was angry only with the one who had undertaken the responsibility and then failed to carry it out. So God took Israel severely to task, for of all the nations, Israel alone undertook to live in accordance with the Torah (*Exodus Rabbah,* 27:9).

The morally sensitive are not satisfied with a disinterested study and interpretation of history. Seeking the spiritual significance of events, one plots the map of history with the moral co-ordinates that may account for the fortunes and misfortunes of individuals and peoples. This prayer reflects such an attitude. The objective fact was that the superior forces of the Roman armies foredoomed the destruction of the Temple in 70 C.E. and made inevitable the exile which followed. But, as evidenced by the passages cited above, and by the noble, self-accusing prayer of *Umipene Hataenu,* such "cause and effect" thinking was not the style of our ancestors. To them, the measure of all things was not nature, but man: "Because of our sins we were exiled from our land and removed far away from our country." The thesis that when a people defies moral scruples, its resistance weakens and its downfall results, has as much evidence in its favor as the theories which account for all the vicissitudes of history solely on economic, military, or political grounds. To deny the decisive role of free action in human life is to enthrone "iron necessity." Man is made by events when he regards himself solely as a product rather than as a cause of what happens. He "makes history" by mobilizing his powers of reason, imagination, and moral insight, thereby transcending the limitations of his nature and his environment. The self-accusing mood of this prayer is in the spirit of the admonition of Bahya ibn Pakuda (Spain, 11th century) who said: "When you are in the mood of praising, praise God, when in the mood of blaming, blame yourself."

"Lead us with joyous song unto Zion, Thy city"

The Prayer Book reverberates with yearning for the return of the Jewish people to the Holy Land, for the re-establishment of the sanctuary at Jerusalem, and the restoration of the sacrificial system of worship. In recalling the ancestral longing for *Eretz Yisrael,* we affirm that Judaism is more than an abstract philosophy of the good life, that Jews are more than a community of "co-religionists." Judaism is the spiritual self-awareness of a living people, and Jews are an identifiable people with a sense of common history, common cause, and common destiny. That destiny is to serve mankind as exemplars of the highest spiritual values which it has developed from the dawn of its history. A restored Jewish life in *Eretz Yisrael* means more than the establishment of another autonomous nation. It implies that Judaism can flourish at its best and at its highest in its natal environment. This is what the many references to *Eretz Yisrael* as the site of God's sanctuary can mean to us in this day, when Judaism can thrive only through a reciprocal spiritual relationship between *Eretz Yisrael* and the Diaspora.

Prayers for the restoration of sacrifices

Our ancestors prayed for the restoration of Jerusalem as a holy city, and of the Temple as "a house of prayer for all peoples." In their view of the restoration, they experienced no difficulty when they hoped for the reinstatement of the biblically instituted sacrificial system—a system meticulously defined in *Kodashim,* the fifth order of the Mishnah. The prophets did, indeed, denounce the offering of sacrifices without sincerity, and the performance of ritual without righteousness. Perhaps the boldest denunciation was that of Isaiah: "To what purpose is the multitude of your sacrifices unto Me? I am full of the burnt-offerings of rams, and the fat of fed beasts; and I delight not in the blood of bullocks or of lambs or of he-goats" (Isa. 1:11). But they did not envision the actual abolition of the sacrificial system. They saw nothing incongruous in the idea that Jerusalem would again become the site of a sanctuary where the offering of daily and special sacrifices would testify to an entire people's obedience to God. Thus, when Isaiah depicts restoration in most universalistic terms, he refers to the sacrifices in these incandescent words:

Also the aliens that join themselves to the Lord, to minister unto Him, and to love the name of the Lord, to be His servants, every one that keepeth the sabbath from profaning it, and holdeth fast by My Covenant; even them will I bring to My holy mountain, and make them joyful in My house of prayer; their burnt-offerings and their sacrifices shall be acceptable upon mine altar; for My house shall be called a house of prayer for all peoples (Isa. 56:6-7).

To this age the idea of animal sacrifices is uncongenial. But its underlying rationale is for us still a valid and potent idea: that man comes to experience the *nearness* of God (*korban*—"sacrifice"—means to "come near" to God) by offerings of his self and his substance. When today, we recite prayers for the restoration of the sacrifices at a rebuilt Temple in a renewed Jerusalem, we acknowledge our oneness with our fathers in their hope that Jerusalem may become a holy community and a light to the nations. The ancient sacrifices are to us symbolic of the duty to dedicate all that we have and all that we are to the service of God.

Supplementary comment

On Rosh Hashanah, the words that introduce the biblical text describing the prescribed offerings are: *veet musefe yom hazikkaron hazeh* ("and the additional offerings of this Day of Remembrance"). The plural form, *additional offerings,* is accounted for by the fact that as Rosh Hashanah is also the new moon of Tishri, two additional offerings were brought, one for the *Rosh Hodesh* (new moon) and one for Rosh Hashanah. There are indications in the Talmud that in earlier times the Rosh Hashanah liturgy called for even more specific references to *Rosh Hodesh* (Mishnah Erub. 3:9; cf. Soferim 19:5).

The New Year (Rosh Hashanah)   179

הֱיֵה עִם פִּפִיּוֹת

Inspire the lips of the messengers of Thy people

The *Amidah* is about to enter upon its most solemn
phase: the three *Musaf* soundings of the *shofar,* and the
recitation of the *Malkhuyot, Zikhronot,* and *Shofarot*
verses.

Much depends on the *sheliah tzibbur*'s faithful, fluent,
and melodious rendition of these parts of the services—
parts with which even the learned in the congregation
are not fully conversant, because of the many biblical
passages and the two additional *Amidah* blessings included in them (R. H. 35a). Before the reader commences
this climactic part of the *Musaf Amidah,* this prayer,
found in all versions of the liturgy, is recited in his behalf. It implores God to "teach them (the emissaries of
the congregation) what they shall say, instruct them what
they shall speak, grant unto them what they ask and
make known to them how they may glorify Thee."

אוֹחִילָה לָאֵל

I beseech God

This brief *reshut* (permission) is recited by the *sheliah
tzibbur.* Cognizant of the many who depend on him for
the fluent and fervent rendition of the prayers, he be-
seeches divine help. For though man's sincerity flows
from his own heart, the gift of expression comes from
God. He therefore prays with the psalmist: "O Lord,
open Thou my lips; and my mouth shall declare Thy
praise" (Ps. 51:17).

Malkhuyot, Zikhronot and *Shofarot*

At this point, the *Amidah* is subdivided into these three
distinct sections:

I. *Malkhuyot*

Ten biblical verses introduced by a prelude (*Alenu*) and
concluded by a prayer and a blessing. The theme of the
Malkhuyot is the Kingship of God, which Israel is privileged to acknowledge, and which, it prays, will be acknowledged by all mankind.

II. *Zikhronot*

Ten biblical verses, each containing a reference to God's "remembrance" of those who do not forget Him. These verses also have a prelude "Thou rememberest" (*Attah Zokher*), and are concluded by a prayer and a blessing. The theme of the *Zikhronot* is that as Judge, God "remembers" the deeds of men and nations, and is merciful in judgment. We therefore implore Him to "remember" His everlasting covenant with Israel.

III. *Shofarot*

Ten biblical verses which variously refer to the *shofar* blasts of the revelation at Mt. Sinai, to the *shofar* sounds that accompanied the Temple service, and to the *shofar* of messianic redemption and liberation. The *Shofarot* verses likewise are introduced by a prelude "Thou didst reveal" (*Attah Nigleta*) and are concluded by a prayer and blessing imploring God to speed the fulfillment of Israel's messianic hopes.

The Mishnah stipulates that the *shofar* be sounded at the end of each section, and that in each, the Bible verses be cited in this order: Three from the Torah, three from the *Ketuvim* (Writings), three from *Neviim* (Prophets), and a tenth verse from the Torah (Mishnah R.H. 4:6). Though the *Ketuvim* are the third division of the Bible, the verses from this division come immediately after the Torah verses. The reason given by all authorities is that since they are all cited from the Psalms of David, they antedate the verses from the Prophets. The prologues are ascribed to Rab, the third-century Babylonian Amora, and are mentioned in the Talmud as *Tekiatah de-Rab* (the *shofar* prayers of Rab).

עָלֵינוּ לְשַׁבֵּחַ

Let us praise the Lord of all. We bend the knee and bow the head before the King of Kings, the Holy One, blessed be He

This prayer, attributed to Rab, the Babylonian Amora just mentioned opens the *Malkhuyot* section. It is read throughout the year at the conclusion of each of the three daily services, because it expresses Israel's sense of privilege at having been the first among the earth's peoples to purge itself of idolatry. It voices the hope for the time when all mankind will abandon its idolatries, and when the world will be perfected by the universal recognition of the Kingship of God.

The intent of the particularistic note in *Alenu,* where we express our gratitude to God that "He has not made us like nations of the world," becomes clearer when we restore that portion of the *Alenu* which was excised by medieval censors:

It is our duty to thank God . . . that He did not make us like other peoples on earth . . . *inasmuch as they worship idols of vanity and emptiness and pray to gods that cannot help* whereas we kneel in worship and acknowledge only the Supreme King of Kings, the Holy One blessed is He.

עַל כֵּן נְקַוֶּה

We therefore hope to behold the glory of Thy might, when the world will be perfected under the Kingdom of the Almighty

Having expressed gratitude for being raised up by God to abjure idolatry and acknowledge His sovereignty, Rab's prayer continues with this utterly universalistic petition that paganism may vanish, idolatry be abandoned, and that as God's sovereignty over all mankind is recognized, "all may accept the yoke of Thy Kingship." Man's bondage to evil will end when divisive and corrupting idolatries will pass, when he assumes in their stead a voluntary obedience to the will and the law of God.

In the Middle Ages, many who died for the "Sanctification of the Name" uttered with their last breath the words of this prayer. Joseph ha-Cohen, a medieval chronicler, in his "Vale of Tears" relates the following:

During the persecution of the Jews of Blois, France, in 1171, where many masters of the law died as martyrs at the stake, an eyewitness wrote to Rabbi Jacob of Orleans that the death of the saints was accompanied by a weird song resounding through the stillness of the night, causing the churchmen who heard it from afar to wonder at the melodious strains, the like of which they had never heard before. It was ascertained afterwards that the martyred saints made use of the *Alenu* as their dying song.

Kneeling and prostration in Jewish worship

As the reader recites "We bend the knee and prostrate ourselves before the King of Kings," he kneels and bows his head to the ground. In many synagogues all the worshipers join him in this gesture of obeisance and adoration. This is also the practice on Yom Kippur, when *Alenu* is recited during the Musaf *Amidah*. In addition there are on Yom Kippur three complete prostrations, with the face actually touching the ground, during each of the three confessions in the *Amidah* (Mishnah Yoma 6:2). On other occasions, kneeling and prostration were abolished and even prohibited in Jewish worship, because Christianity had adopted these gestures of adoration. The very fact that the name of the main prayer in the liturgy is called *Amidah* (standing), and that even bending the knee and bowing the head were restricted to two blessings of the *Amidah* (see p. 12), indicates a deliberate departure from kneeling and prostration. In Babylonia, where there were few Christians, a form of prostration was practiced (Meg. 22b). In Geonic days even this was modified to a bowing of the head forward on the arm, as is still the practice in the synagogue during the weekday *Tahanun* prayers.

The reader is assisted as he rises from his kneeling position, so that his feet may be kept together for the continuation of the recitation of the *Amidah* (see p. 13).

The ten *Malkhuyot* verses

Al Ken Nekaveh leads to the first of the ten "kingship" verses, culled from the three divisions of the Bible. The ninth verse is: "And the Lord shall be King over all the earth; in that day the Lord shall be One and His Name One." When the *Alenu* was adopted into the daily service, only the first verse, "The Lord shall reign for ever and ever," and the ninth verse, "The Lord shall reign over all the earth; in that day the Lord shall be One and His Name One," were retained.

Each of the first nine verses alludes to God's sovereignty, as each contains a word formed from the root *malokh* (to reign). The tenth *Malkhuyot* verse is, "Hear

O Israel: the Lord our God, the Lord is One." Though it contains no word with the root *malokh,* it is considered as a "kingship" verse, since it contains the word *Elohim* which, according to Rabbi Jose, has a "kingship" connotation (R.H. 32b). Moreover, *Shema Yisrael* is "a declaration of the acceptance of the kingship of God" (Mishnah Ber. 2:2).

On the prayer, Melokh Al Kol Haolam *which follows, see our previous discussion, pp. 109-11.*

הַיּוֹם הֲרַת עוֹלָם

This day the world was called into being; this day all the creatures of the universe stand in judgment before Thee

Rights and duties

The idea that we stand in judgment before God "as children or as servants" expresses the polarity of Judaism's conception of God as a merciful Father and as a demanding Ruler. This dual conception highlights two related aspects of the human situation. As a child of God, man is endowed with certain rights. Such rights have been defined and redefined throughout western history—whether partially, in such documents as the Magna Carta, or more fully, in the Bill of Rights of the Constitution of the United States, and in the Declaration of Human Rights formulated by the United Nations. So long as we respect the rights of others, these rights are inalienably ours, since they emanate not from a "social contract" or as a beneficence of "we the people," but from God who is the Father of all.

But it is not enough to talk of human rights without emphasizing human duties. We dare not magnify human rights and minimize human obligation, for though man is a child of God, he must also hold himself accountable as a servant of God. Rights without duties lead to lawlessness, even as duties without rights can lead to slavery and to the abasement of individuality. If such objectives as self-realization or self-expression are not to lead to an arrant egotism, we must be no less ardent in exercising self-examination and self-control.

184   **Justice and Mercy**

On the concept that Rosh Hashanah is "the birthday of the world," see pp. 162-63.

אֲרֶשֶׁת שְׂפָתֵינוּ

May the entreaty of our lips find favor before Thee

This epilogue, found in the German and Roman liturgical rites, concludes each of the three series of the *shofar* blasts of the *Musaf* service.

אַתָּה זוֹכֵר

Thou rememberest the deeds of men and nations

"To the end of all generations"

The prelude to the *Zikhronot* asserts that there appears before God "the record of every man's deeds, his works and his ways, his thoughts and his schemes, his plans, and the motives of his acts." It further affirms, "Happy is the man who forgets Thee not and the son of man who finds strength in Thee." This unquestioning faith enabled the Jew to face the future with courage, in the most trying circumstances. His endurance and strength were derived from the belief that God "surveys and sees all that happens to the end of all generations." Rather than presume to sit in judgment over God's government of the world, he chose to subject his own life to God's scrutiny. To know that God did not abdicate His rule once He created the world, nor that God abandoned man to blind fate and random chance, was to him sufficient reason so to live as to merit God's merciful "remembrance." The faith expressed in the prelude to the *Zikhronot* can be for us, as well, a faith for confident and courageous living. Our inability to plot the curve of retribution and reward in the unfolding of history should not dampen our belief in God's providence. Regardless of the individual's personal fortunes, God's "remembrance" of our deeds of virtue and valor redeems our life from meaninglessness by validating our struggles for the enthronement of the moral law in the life of all men.

זָכְרֵנוּ בְּזִכָּרוֹן טוֹב לְפָנֶיךָ

Remember us with a hopeful remembrance

The last of the *Zikhronot* verses, "I will for their sakes remember the convenant of their ancestors, whom I brought forth out of the land of Egypt in the sight of the nations, that I might be their God: I am the Lord" (Lev. 26:45), is integrated into the blessing of this section. Envisioning Israel's future redemption, the *Zikhronot* section reaches a climactic conclusion as it refers to the *Akedah*, the prototype and the symbol of merit and moral example accumulated for the Jew by the martyred heroes of the past.

אַתָּה נִגְלֵיתָ

Thou didst reveal Thyself in a cloud unto Thy holy people

Revelation as a cumulative experience

In the Torah, the first mention of the *shofar* is in the account of the revelation at Sinai: "And it came to pass, on the third day, when it was morning, that there were thunders and lightnings and a thick cloud upon the mount, and the voice of a horn (*shofar*) exceeding loud; and all the people that were in the camp trembled" (Exod. 19:16). Since this is the first of the *Shofarot* verses, the prelude to the *Shofarot* consists of a stirring retelling of that which transpired at Sinai. The prelude focuses our attention on the extraordinary nature of that revelation. God revealed Himself not to the chosen few, but to an entire people—"to teach Thy people *Torah* and *Mitzvot*." Yehezkel Kaufmann, in his monumental study of the religion of the Bible, points to the stunning originality of the idea that an entire people was the recipient and vehicle of God's revelation. The concept implies that the moral law is to be regarded not as the doctrine of sages or the dictate of earthly rulers, but as the will of God made known to an entire people consecrated to be "a kingdom of priests, and a holy nation" (Exod. 19:6). Israel is a people not thrown together by accidental circumstances, but drawn together by an indissoluble covenant with God—a covenant that might be defied, but not denied; broken, but not annulled. Throughout history this people was haunted by the memory of its corporate commitment, and inwardly plagued by its all too frequent backsliding from provisions of the covenant.

One would expect such a fixation on one event in the past to produce a static and monolithic conception of the character and content of the revelation. But the very notion that the whole people was the vehicle of divine revelation saved Judaism from an arid, literal biblicism. It gave rise to the belief that the "oral law" is the authentic and living interpretation of the "written law," so that Revelation came to be regarded as a continuing process. The Rabbis seem to have grasped intuitively an idea akin to the modern concept of historical evolution, when they asserted that at Sinai both the oral and the written laws were revealed. Rabbi Haggai even went so far as to say that the oral teachings took precedence over those that were written (TP Peah 17a), and that all the teachings of future scholars were revealed to Moses on Mt. Sinai (*ibid.*). Judaism's hospitality to the idea that Revelation is a cumulative process is reflected in this interesting passage:

"They [the sayings of the wise] are given from one shepherd" (Eccl. 12:14). The Holy One, blessed is He, said: "If a person of modest scholarly attainments tells you something and you derive spiritual delight from his insight, do not regard it as something you heard from an inferior scholar. Moreover, you must even regard it as having been told you by a great sage. And even more than that! You must regard it as having been heard from the mouth of a prophet, and even beyond that, you must regard it as if you had heard it from Moses himself . . . and even much more than that! You must regard it as if you have heard it from God himself" (TP Sanh. 28a).

An even bolder extension of the idea of Revelation is implied in the statement that where scholars offer two mutually contradictory opinions on a legal problem or on the interpretation of a biblical verse, both opinions are considered to be "the words of the living God," since both are equally the result of a reverent search for an understanding of the Torah (Erub. 13b).

What was implicit in the rabbinic expansion of the

concept of revelation must become an explicit principle in our day, when Jewish tradition faces the challenge of new ideas and of discoveries of major proportions. As a viable religion, Judaism must continue to be a vehicle of God's continuous Revelation to His people, for the voice that Israel heard at Sinai "did not cease" (Onkelos on Deut., 5:19).

The *Shofarot* verses continue with three passages from the Psalms in which the *shofar* is mentioned as a musical instrument used in the Temple services. In the three verses from the prophetic books, the *shofar* sounds are identified with the messianic restoration of the Holy Land. Amidst throngs worshiping in a rebuilt sanctuary at Jerusalem, a redeemed people will again sound the *shofar* on their days of joy, their festivals, and new moons, and win the favor of God "who hears the sounds of the *shofar* and gives heed to its blasts." The tenth verse of the *Shofarot,* like the tenth verse of the two other series, comes from the Torah (Num. 10:10) and is fittingly integrated into the blessing which concludes this section.

For a discussion of the concluding sections of the Musaf Amidah *which follow here, see pp. 112-21.*

הַיּוֹם תְּאַמְּצֵנוּ

This day mayest Thou strengthen us

The peaks of time

It is quite evident that we have here the four opening lines and the four concluding lines of a complete alphabetical acrostic. Abudraham mentions some of the missing lines:

This day do Thou give us glory	הַיּוֹם תְּהַדְּרֵנוּ
This day do Thou gather us	הַיּוֹם תּוֹעֲדֵנוּ
This day do Thou remember us	הַיּוֹם תִּזְכְּרֵנוּ
This day do Thou be gracious to us	הַיּוֹם תְּחָנֵּנוּ
This day do Thou purify us	הַיּוֹם תְּטַהֲרֵנוּ
This day do Thou rectify us	הַיּוֹם תְּיַשְּׁרֵנוּ

Quantitatively, every day has the same twenty-four hours. But qualitatively, not all days are the same. Chaim

Nachman Bialik, the great modern Hebrew poet, said that time, like space, has its peaks, its valleys, and its plains. The peaks of time are those days on which are signaled the exaltation of the spiritual life—the days of transcendent joy, self-discovery, illumination, and renewal. When our life is ordered in accordance with a calendar of significant days, the freshness and novelty of life is apprehended anew, as we forsake the boredom and the ennui expressed by Kohelet in these lines:

All things toil to weariness;
Man cannot utter it,
The eye is not satisfied with seeing,
Nor the ear filled with hearing.
That which hath been is that which shall be,
And that which hath been done is that which shall be done
And there is nothing new under the sun.

Ecclesiastes 1:8-9

The degree to which we make *hayom* (the day) a sublime moment in our spiritual odyssey affects the quality of our life and enables us to say, *Zeh hayom asah Adonai,* "This is the day which the Lord hath made; we will rejoice and be glad in it" (Ps. 118:24).

ORDER OF THE *MINHAH* SERVICE: ROSH HASHANAH

The *Minhah* service consists of four parts:

   I. *Ashre* and *Uva Letziyyon.*
  II. The *Amidah,* which is the same as that of the *Maariv* (see p. 119).
 III. *Avinu Malkenu* (see p. 119), which is omitted on Sabbaths.
  IV. *Alenu* (see pp. 36; 180-81).

When Rosh Hashanah falls on a Sabbath, the Torah is read as on every Sabbath afternoon. The portion read is Deuteronomy 32:1-12, which comprises the opening verses of the *Sidrah Haazinu,* the Torah Reading for *Shabbat Shuvah*—"The Sabbath of Repentance."

THE DAY OF ATONEMENT (YOM KIPPUR)

THE FUNDAMENTAL CONCEPTS
IN THE YOM KIPPUR LITURGY:
AN INTRODUCTION

The Torah establishes no explicit association between Rosh Hashanah and Yom Kippur. The former is briefly described as "a day of blowing the horn" (Num. 29:1), while Yom Kippur is more elaborately defined as "a day of atonement, to make atonement for you before the Lord . . . and ye shall afflict your souls" (Lev. 23:28; 32). The Rabbis, however, invested both Holy Days with a unity and continuity of mood and meaning which is symbolized in the designation *Aseret Yeme Teshuvah* (Ten Days of Repentance), embracing the two Holy Days as well as the days that intervene between them.

Sin as rebellion

The Yom Kippur prayers mirror the religious attitudes and beliefs expressed in the Rosh Hashanah liturgy. In the latter, we reaffirm God's sovereignty over the life and destiny of men and nations, and acclaim Him as the Judge on whose mercy we must rely, lest we be condemned by our own misdeeds to a life of futility. The "evil decree," which we may have earned by our acts of omission and commission, can be reversed by devoting the "Days of Awe" to a *heshbon hanefesh,* a rigorous moral self-examination—a redirection of our life—so that it might be lived "under the yoke of the Kingship of God," in obedience to the divine will: "If you have accepted My Kingship, you must also obey My decrees" (*Sifra,* "Ahare Mot," 13). A sin is therefore more than an immoral act. It is disobedience to God's will, a defiance of His kingship, and an act of rebellion against Him. In the three words, *het, avon, pesha,* used in the High Priest's confession on the Day of Atonement, there can be discerned three gradations of sin, the stages by which man "throws off the yoke of God's rule and subjects himself to the yoke of man's rule" (Sotah 47b). *Het* connotes an unwitting offense; *avon,* a deed of insolence; and *pesha,* an outright act of rebellion against God (Yoma 36b). The inner corrosion that sets in even when one commits an unwitting offense gives sin a growing power over the sinner. Trivial sins lead to more serious ones, for the evil impulse constantly prods a man to more flagrant acts of rebellion. At first, sin appears as innocent as the thin thread of the spider's web, but soon it takes on the thickness of a rope from which one cannot easily extricate himself (*Gen. Rabbah,* 22:6). First, sin wins his way into a person's life by posing as a humble wayfarer, then it becomes a welcome guest, and finally it exacts obedience as the master of the house (Suk. 52a).

The three cardinal sins for which a person must be ready to undergo martyrdom rather than to submit to their coerced commission are: idolatry, adultery, and murder (Sanh. 74a). In his *Some Aspects of Rabbinic Theology,** Schechter shows how the Rabbis identified certain immoral acts as aspects of one or another of the cardinal sins: Pride and slander are forms of idolatry, for they cause God's presence to depart from the earth, in that God cannot dwell in the same place with a person guilty of such vices (Ar. 15b); capricious hatred of another person is tantamount to the commission of the three cardinal sins combined (Yoma 9b); humiliating one's fellow man in public is like shedding his blood (B. M. 58b), as is the failure to visit a sick friend (Ned. 40a), or the refusal to grant a loan to a needy person (Sotah 40b).

Sin and suffering

Neither prophet, nor psalmist, nor sage ever arrived at a concise formulation of the causal or consequential connection between sin and suffering. Job's eloquent protest against the notion that suffering is an inexorable retribution for sin serves to point up the difficulty of "justifying the ways of God to man." Rabbi Yannai was so baffled by this problem that he declared that it is not within man's power to understand the reason for the prosperity of the wicked and the afflictions of the righteous (Ab. 4:15). Yet the Rabbis asserted that suffering should at least prompt a person to seek to determine whether by his own behavior he may have deserved chastisement. "When a person sees that affliction has come upon him," said

* Solomon Schechter, *Aspects of Rabbinic Theology* (New York: Schocken Books, Inc., 1961), pp. 219-241.

Rabba, "he should first examine closely his own conduct. Should he fail to find a moral defect which might account for his suffering, he might attribute it to his neglect of the study of Torah. Should this also not prove to be the cause, he might then regard his suffering as 'a chastisement of love,' aiming to test and refine his character" (Ber. 5a).

The Yom Kippur liturgy is suffused with the belief that sin alienates man from God, who is "the Righteous One of the world" (Yoma 37a), and that the sinner is in desperate need of reconciliation and atonement. This idea is tersely expressed in the Book of Isaiah: "Your iniquities have separated between you and your God" (Isa. 59:2).

All in need of atonement

Atonement is every man's need, for "there is not a righteous man upon earth, that doeth good and sinneth not" (Eccl. 7:20). Even those whose conduct may be deemed blameless are guilty. The Talmud lays down the principle that a person is held accountable for the sins of his family, or of his community, or even "of all mankind" when he fails to employ the influence he commands for the correction of abuses (Shab. 53b). A forceful statement in the *Tosefta* demands of every individual a deep sense of personal accountability, since his conduct may affect the destiny of the whole world: "He who commits a good deed may incline the balance with regard to himself and all mankind toward the side of good;-and he who commits a sin may incline the balance with regard to himself and all mankind toward the side of guilt" (*Tosefta Kid.*, 1:13). A striking example of the responsibility expected of leaders is a midrash which condemns timid persons whose regret at evil stops at the threshold of action. The prophet Ezekiel relates that in a vision he heard a heavenly voice ordering six men to bring destruction on the inhabitants of Jerusalem because of the abominations they practiced. One of the men was instructed to put a saving mark on the foreheads of the men "that sigh and that cry" over the abominations committed in the city (Ezek. 9:4). The Midrash embellishes this story and informs us that "that very moment a denunciation sprung up before God" and protested against the exemption of those who groan and sigh. "Has any of them ever had his head smashed because of Thee or offered his life for the sanctification of Thy name?" (*Yalkut Ezekiel*, 349; cf. Shab. 54a)

Repentance: the cure for sin

Built into the structure of the world even before it was created, repentance is the antidote to sin (Pes. 54a). *Teshuvah* (repentance) is not a form of self-castigation, nor is it a traumatic experience of sudden conversion. It demands of the sinner that he forsake each particular sin, expunge it from his life, and firmly resolve never to repeat it (Maimonides, *Hilkhot Teshuvah*, 2:2). The sinner's repentance must be of such a transforming nature that when an occasion again presents itself to commit the same offense, he will resist the temptation because of a firmer commitment to righteous conduct (*ibid.*, 2:1). Repentance is therefore by no means a superficial gesture of atonement. "If any one says to himself, 'I will sin and repent (and then) I will sin and repent (again),' no opportunity is granted him to repent" (Mishnah Yoma 8:9).

"The spirit of man is the lamp of God, searching all the inward parts" (Prov. 20:27). The "lamp of God" is the human conscience, which sharply distinguishes man from other creatures. Periodically our conscience makes us painfully aware of the distance between our conduct and our ideal self, that self which enables us to believe that man is made in the divine image. We are born into the world with the freedom to choose between servitude to the material world or service to God. When we betray our nobler self, we cause unhappiness to others and thus sin against God and man. Originating in a sense of unworthiness, because of our being ashamed of our conduct, repentance strengthens our determination to seek release from the grip of our sins. The unrepentant sinner readily and easily forgives himself; the repentant person prays fervently with the psalmist: "Create me a clean heart and renew a steadfast spirit within me" (Ps. 51:12). If he fortifies this prayer with a resolute will, he will succeed in building a nobler life upon the ruins of the old.

God, "Who forgives and pardons our sins"

The Yom Kippur liturgy addresses God as "He who forgives and pardons our iniquities, and the iniquities of

His people, the house of Israel and who cancels out our wrongdoing year by year." As divine forgiveness is the fruit of true repentance, so is repentance the product of man's free initiative. The sinner is encouraged by the assurance that once he initiates the process of his moral rehabilitation, he will be aided, for "He who comes with the resolve to purify himself, will receive divine help" (Yoma 38b). Even if the sinner opens the door of repentance only slightly, "be it even of the width of a needle," God will open it so wide "that whole wagons and chariots could pass through it" (*Song of Songs Rabbah,* 5:2). No matter how repellent one's conduct and how perverse one's character, no man should consider himself to be irredeemable, for repentance can effect a cure for his moral ailment. To prove the therapeutic effect of repentance, the Rabbis cite the example of Manasseh. The Bible depicts the reign of this king as one of unconfined evil. Child sacrifice, idolatry, and necromancy were openly practiced as Manasseh caused his people to revert to the abominations of the ancient Canaanites (II Kings 21:1-15). Rabbinic lore however, takes full advantage of a brief statement in the Second Book of Chronicles that says that the Assyrians carried Manasseh off to Babylon in chains, and that in his extremity he prayed for forgiveness and was then restored to his throne (II Chronicles 33:12-13). The Rabbis inform us that when the angels stopped up the windows of heaven so that the prayer of Manasseh might not ascend to God, God bore a hole beneath His throne and received the prayer of Manasseh, while rebuking the angels: "If I did not accept this man's repentance, I would be shutting the door in the face of all repentant sinners" (Sanh. 103a).

Repentance is available at all times, even at the moment of one's death (Ab. 2:10). It is as wide as the sea, and like the sea, it is always accessible for man's purification (*Pesikta de Rav Kahana,* 157a). The days between Rosh Hashanah and Yom Kippur are especially propitious—the days of which the prophet (Isa. 55:6) speaks: "Seek ye the Lord while He may be found" (R.H. 18a).

Restitution

The prerequisites of repentance are restitution and the confession of one's sins before God. "When a man or a woman shall commit any sin that men commit, to commit a trespass against the Lord . . . then they shall confess their sin which they have done; . . . and shall make restitution . . . unto him in respect of whom he hath been guilty" (Num. 5:6). Where complete reparation and restitution are not possible, full repentance is deemed to be unavailable. Maimonides cites from an unknown source twenty-four hindrances to repentance, among which the following are listed:

1. A person directs abusive language at a group of people; he cannot repent since he does not know the person or persons whose feelings he has outraged with his insulting words. He cannot take steps towards reconciliation, and without effecting reconciliation with the person whom one has hurt, one's repentance is not acceptable.

2. A person receives stolen goods from a professional thief, and as the original owner of the goods cannot be identified, restitution is therefore impossible. Repentance without restitution is of no avail.

3. A person fails to announce his finding of a lost article and is therefore not able to return it to its rightful owner. For him repentance is not available since restitution is not possible.

4. A person who appropriates to himself what belongs to the poor and the underprivileged. Since such people are usually homeless, they cannot be located and restitution cannot be made.

5. A judge who accepts a bribe. He can never precisely determine the degree to which his acceptance of the bribe perverted his judgment and deprived a litigant of his rights.

(Hilkhot Teshuvah, 4:3)

The Mishnah makes mention of a special enactment which was made to encourage repentant sinners to make restitution. A person who stole a beam and built it into his own house, should, according to the strict rule of restitution, be required to tear down the structure and return the beam to its rightful owner. But in an "enactment in behalf of the repentant" *(takkanat hashavim)* it was ruled that the thief need only repay the owner the cost of the beam (Mishnah Git., 5:5).

To seek repentance without abandoning a sinful habit was deemed to be as foolish and as futile as the action of a ritually unclean person who immerses himself in a bath, while holding in his hand the dead reptile that caused his impurity (*Tosefta Taan.*, 1:8). The Rabbis spared no effort to counter and contradict the belief that the rites and prayers of Yom Kippur were magical and mechanical means of absolution.

Confession

An offense against man is a sin against God. Hence, after restitution has been made, it is deemed necessary to utter words of confession to God. The formula of confession suggested by Maimonides is: "O God I have sinned, I have committed iniquity, I have rebelled against Thee. I have done thus and thus. I regret these deeds and am ashamed of them and will never repeat them" (Maimonides, *Hilkhot Teshuvah*, 1:1).*

"You shall afflict your souls" (Leviticus 23:37)

The rules for self-denial on Yom Kippur are thus outlined in the Mishnah: "On the Day of Atonement, eating, drinking, washing, anointing, putting on sandals, and marital intercourse are forbidden" (Yoma 8:1).

The Mishnah and the Gemara, both in the Palestinian and Babylonian Talmud, proceed to discuss meticulously the measure of food and drink that would make a person culpable. Abstention from food and drink are considered to be biblically mandatory. The other forms of self-denial are derivative (Yoma 74a). A sick person is absolved from fasting and even forbidden to fast, if a doctor, regardless of his faith, states that fasting might endanger the patient's health (*Orah Hayyim*, 618:1). Even if a hundred physicians state that the fast will not imperil the patient's health, and the patient agrees with them, but two physicians disagree with the opinion, or even if one physician and the patient insist that he must not fast, the fast must be broken (*ibid.*, 518:2). Interesting is the psychological insight revealed by this passage:

Rabbi Mana visited Rabbi Haggai (on a fast day). The latter complained that he was very thirsty. Rabbi Mana advised him to take a drink. He left the house and returned an hour later; he asked Rabbi Haggai, "How did you fare with your thirst?" Rabbi Haggai answered, "The very moment you permitted me to take a drink, my thirst left me" (TP Yoma 43d).

* For the discussion of the *Al Het* confession, see pp. 216-21.

Even in biblical times, leather shoes were considered an apparel of luxury: "How beautiful are thy steps in sandals, O princes' daughter" (Song of Songs 7:2). When David fled from Absalom, "he had his head covered, and went barefoot" (II Sam. 15:30). As a sign of mourning, Isaiah took off his shoes (Isa. 20:2). For this very reason a mourner does not wear leather shoes. Abstaining from leather shoes was therefore considered a suitable form of self-deprivation on Yom Kippur.

An additional value can be attributed to the practice of not wearing leather shoes on Yom Kippur. The entire day serves as a vivid reliving of the Temple days. Leather shoes were forbidden, too, in a holy place. When Moses was about to approach the burning bush he was commanded, "Put off thy shoes from off thy feet for the place whereon thou standest is holy ground" (Exod. 3:5). *Kohanim* must remove their shoes when they go up to pronounce the Priestly Benediction (R.H. 31b). It was forbidden for any person to enter the Temple Mount with his staff, with his sandals, or his wallet (Mishnah Ber. 9:5).

The concept that Jews, as members of "A kingdom of priests and a holy nation," experience a heightened degree of holiness on the *Yom Hakadosh* (The Holy Day) can be therefore appropriately associated with this ancient form of self-deprivation.

THE ORDER OF THE
KOL NIDRE (MAARIV) SERVICE

Though *Kol Nidre* is not an integral part of the standard evening liturgy, its popularity caused its name to be bestowed on the entire service which is often referred to as "the *Kol Nidre* service." On other holidays, the *Sheheheyanu* blessing, in which gratitude is expressed for our having been kept in life to celebrate the particular festival, is recited at the conclusion of the *Kiddush*. Since no *Kiddush* is recited on Yom Kippur, the *Sheheheyanu* blessing is uttered immediately after the *Kol Nidre* has been rendered. When Yom Kippur falls on a Sabbath, Psalm 92, "A Psalm, a Song, for the sabbath day," and

Psalm 93, "The Lord reigneth. He is clothed in majesty," are recited here to mark the beginning of the Sabbath at dusk. The recital of the *Maariv* with the evening *Shema* does not precede the Sabbath Psalm, since the *Shema* can be read at any time after sunset (Mishnah Ber. 1:1).

The first part of the *Maariv* service is the standard evening liturgy with the blessings that accompany the *Shema* (see pp. 27-29).

The theme-verse of Yom Kippur, recited before the *Hatzi Kaddish,* is: "For on this day shall atonement be made for you, to cleanse you; from all your sins shall you be clean before the Lord" (Lev. 16:30). Liturgically the verse is punctuated in accordance with this passage from the Mishnah:

R. Elazar ben Azariah expounded this: "From all your sins shall you be clean *before the Lord"*—for transgressions between a man and God, Yom Kippur effects atonement, but for transgressions between a man and his fellow man, Yom Kippur effects atonement only if he has become reconciled with his fellow man (Mishnah Yoma 8:9).

As on Sabbaths and all holidays, the standard *Amidah* for Yom Kippur consists of seven blessings. They are: 1) *Avot;* 2) *Gevurot;* 3) *Kedushat Hashem;* 4) *Kedushat Hayom,* which ends with the blessing: Blessed art Thou . . . who pardonest and forgivest our iniquities . . . who makest our trespasses to pass away year by year, Thou King over all the earth, who sanctifiest (the Sabbath and Israel and the Day of Atonement; 5) *Avodah;* 6) *Modim;* 7) *Berakhah* (cf. pp. 32-33).

When Yom Kippur falls on Sabbath, the *Amidah* is immediately followed by *Vayekhullu* ("And heaven and earth were finished") and its accompanying prayers (see p. 34). At the end of the *Amidah,* before Elohai Netzor ("Guard my tongue from evil") the *Viddui* (confession), is recited. (For the discussion of the *Viddui* see pp. 216-21.)

The *Maariv Amidah* is not repeated by the reader, because its recitation during the evening is, according to some opinions, not obligatory but voluntary (cf. p. 34). The *Amidah* is followed by *Selihot* (see pp 205 ff.) and

by the repetition of the *Viddui*. On Sabbaths, the concluding sections of the *Selihot,* as well as *Avinu Malkenu,*
are omitted because the original association of these
prayers with fast days makes them incongruous with the
serenity of the Sabbath (see p. 119).

THE *KOL NIDRE* SERVICE

בִּישִׁיבָה שֶׁל מַעֲלָה

**By the authority of the Heavenly Tribunal and
of the court below . . . we declare it is lawful
to pray together with those who have trans-
gressed**

According to Rabbi Mordecai ben Hillel (d. Germany,
1298), this formula was instituted in the thirteenth century by Rabbi Meir ben Barukh of Rothenburg (d. 1293)
to permit transgressors who had been excommunicated
because of their defiance of communal regulations to
worship with the congregation. An interesting talmudic
passage affords the midrashic foundation of this "permission." The Talmud notes that among the ingredients of
the spices for the incense offering prescribed in the Torah
is galbanum, which has an unpleasant odor (Exod.
30:34). In this, Rabbi Simon the Pious finds a symbolic
validation of the rule that a public fast in which sinners
do not participate is no fast (Ker. 6b).

It is also plausible to assume that the reference to the
"tribunal" is related to the absolution of vows with which
the *Kol Nidre* formula was originally associated and
which process required a "court" of three (See page
203).

Comments on the text

R. Meir ben Barukh of Rothenburg, who introduced this
formula into the *Kol Nidre* service, was a scholar, a litur-
gist, and a noted authority in talmudic law. Born about
1220 in Worms, Germany, he died in a prison at Ensisheim, Alsace, in 1293. In his youth he was a pupil of
noted talmudists, among whom was Rabbi Yehiel of
Paris, who defended the Talmud against its maligners. In

1244 Rabbi Meir witnessed the public burning of twenty-four cartloads of talmudic manuscripts in Paris, and wrote a touching elegy lamenting that desecration. Returning to Germany in 1245, Rabbi Meir established a talmudical Academy at Rothenburg, and soon his authority as a scholar and as a legal authority was widely recognized. In 1286 Rabbi Meir was recognized by an apostate Jew, and he was arrested while passing through Lombardy on his way to Palestine, where he was going to settle with his family. He was brought back to Germany at the instance of the Archbishop of Mayence, and Emperor Rudolph had him confined to the fortress of Ensisheim. A huge sum was raised for his ransom, but Rabbi Meir refused to accept his release on this basis, for fear that it might create a precedent for subsequent acts of extortion from Jews through the imprisonment of their rabbis. During the seven years of his confinement, he was permitted to meet with his disciples, and composed several of his works within the walls of the prison. He died in prison, and fourteen years elapsed before his body could be ransomed at a heavy cost and buried in the city of Worms.

כָּל נִדְרֵי

All vows from this Day of Atonement unto the next Day of Atonement shall not be vows

Our high resolves and our low achievements

The archaic and technical language of the text of the *Kol Nidre* is in itself a subject of intriguing complexity (and we will treat this in a supplementary comment). For us today, *Kol Nidre* can symbolize the need to deepen our sensitivity toward the resolutions which we make in our finest moments of spiritual decision. A feeling of discontent may, in a solemn moment of self-examination, prompt a person to resolve to change his ways. But too often he lacks the tenacity needed for effecting a radical break with strongly entrenched habits. *Kol Nidre* can serve us as a reminder that only by resolute will and by severe self-discipline can we hope to lessen the distance between what we are and what we ought to be. The chant of the *Kol Nidre,* the speaking of the archaic formula of absolution, should move us to a meditation of this nature:

In this moment of solemnity we enter an atmosphere charged with the highest sanctity. Happy are we that the cleansing of our souls comes from God. Before Him we lay bare our secret selves and reflect on how our life is beset by the dilemma of high promise and great expectations shattered on the reef of waywardness. *Kol Nidre!* All our vows spoken with good faith, forgotten. *Kol Nidre!* All our resolves fashioned with eager determination, forgotten! *Kol Nidre!* All our goals conceived with honorable intent, forgotten! Because of our inconstancy of will, our achievement is so often too small. Forgive us, then, for having failed Thee and fortify our desire to serve Thee with deeper conviction and greater consistency. Forgive the entire congregation of Israel and the stranger who dwells in its midst, for our sin is not one of design but of human weakness. Answer us as Thou hast promised Moses, "I extend My pardon in accordance with your plea."

"Our vows shall not be vows; our bonds shall not be bonds; and our oaths shall not be oaths"

Rabbi Moshe Mordecai Epstein (1863-1933), head of the Yeshivah of Slabodka, offered an interesting reinterpretation of the concluding words of the *Kol Nidre.* He suggested that we should regard them as a confession of our lack of moral constancy. The self-righteousness and smugness which stand in the way of our spiritual growth need to be dispelled by a confession, in utter humility, that so often the vows we make are no vows, our resolves no resolves, and our oaths no oaths. When accompanied by such a meditation, the recital of *Kol Nidre* prepares us for the soul-cleansing experience of the Yom Kippur day.

The reader and the two men who hold the scrolls during the chanting of *Kol Nidre* may be said to be reminiscent of the "court" constituted by the three laymen before whom one appeared for the annulment of vows. *Kol Nidre* is recited three times because it was a practice for legal formulae to be so recited (Mishnah Men. 10:3). Because the recitation of *Kol Nidre* partakes of the nature of a court procedure, which could not be conducted on a holiday, it is recited before sunset, and since it is chanted before dark, it is the practice to put on the *tallit* then, and to wear it during the entire evening service, thereby underscoring the uniqueness and solemnity of Yom Kippur.

The origin of *Kol Nidre*

The archaic text of *Kol Nidre* must be viewed in the light of the provisions made in the Talmud for the absolution of certain types of vows. Because the Torah values the sacredness of the spoken word so highly, an entire tractate of the Talmud is devoted to a delineation of the conditions involved in the fulfillment of vows, and of the procedure under which certain vows could be annulled. Vows involving communal obligations or affecting the welfare of other persons could never be annulled. Such vows came under a ruling stipulating that one who fails to honor a pledge is guilty of desecrating his word (Rashi on Num. 30:3). But there was another type of vow which involved only the person of the votary; as, for example, when a person resolved to undergo some self-discipline. But even such vows affected the principle of the sacredness of a man's explicit word. Hence their annulment called for a special procedure. They could be annulled only by the appearance of the votary before a recognized scholar (*hakham*)—or before a "court" of three ordinary laymen—who interrogates the votary and endeavors to find extenuating reasons that might warrant the absolution of the particular vow.

The problem of the absolution of vows was further complicated by the fact that many people were in the habit of making, in their business and social relations, statements in the form of impulsive vows. The Mishnah does not consider such vows to be binding. It assumes them to be rhetorical exaggerations which are not to be taken seriously. Among the vows which have no binding effect, the Mishnah (Ned. 3:1) lists the following:

1. Vows of inducement: As when an eager seller says to a prospective buyer: "May such and such be forbidden me if I reduce the price of this article below a *sela* (four dinars)," and the buyer retorts: "May such and such be forbidden me if I pay you more than one shekel (two dinars)." When they compromise on three dinars it is to be assumed that each had merely uttered a "vow of inducement."

2. Vows of exaggeration: As when a person says, "May such and such be forbidden me if I did not see a serpent as big as the beam of an olive press."

3. Vows made in error.

4. Vows made under coercion.

An obscure passage in the Mishnah accounts for the opening words of the *Kol Nidre*. The Mishnah states that a person may say: "Let no vow that I vow hereafter be binding"—provided that he is mindful of this in the moment of his vow (Mishnah Ned. 3:1). In the course of its discussion and clarification of this passage, the Talmud states that this formula is to be said "at the beginning of the year" (Ned. 23b). This form of absolution in advance, though intended to be valid only for impulsive vows, was deemed objectionable by Raba, who forbade a young colleague to give a public discourse on this matter "lest people tend to deal lightly with vows" (*ibid.*).

There are two versions of the *Kol Nidre* text. The earliest, still used in the Sephardic rite, asks absolution for vows made "from last Yom Kippur to this Yom Kippur." The Ashkenazic version, which was introduced by Rabbenu Tam (France, 12th century), asks absolution for future vows to be made "from this Yom Kippur unto the next Yom Kippur." Both were subjected to a barrage of objections from some of the most noted Geonic authorities, among them Saadyah Gaon, Amram Gaon, and Natronai Gaon. They could find no valid legal authorization for such forms of absolution, and Rabbi Amram deemed the *Kol Nidre* to be "a foolish custom." Some claimed that *Kol Nidre* was intended only for impulsive vows which the Mishnah deems to be not binding, so that people might learn that even in such matters our yea must be yea and our nay, nay (*Shibbale Haleket*, 317).

How *Kol Nidre* came to occupy so prominent a role in the Yom Kippur eve service in the face of so many objections, is a moot question. In a comprehensive analysis of the various theories which have been propounded, Israel Davidson asserts that no one theory satisfactorily accounts for all the questions that have been raised. Towards the end of the nineteenth century, Joseph Bloch had proposed the theory that *Kol Nidre* arose in the seventh century when secret Jews, who had been converted to Christianity after persecution by the Visigoths (590-711 C.E.), would come to the synagogue on Yom Kippur eve. According to him, *Kol Nidre* was their expression of overwhelming grief at their apostasy, and was their means of seeking absolution for vows they had been forced to make to an alien faith. Bloch claimed that in subsequent centuries, during the persecutions by the later Byzantine rulers (700-850 C.E.), and still later under the Spanish Inquisition (1391-1492), the *Kol Nidre* served a similar purpose. Davidson finds this explanation to be wholly inadequate as an account of the actual origin of *Kol Nidre,* though he does not deny the possibility that "secret Jews" may have adopted it as a means of absolution for failure to redeem the vows they had made to return to the faith of their fathers.

The *Kol Nidre* formula often exposed the Jews to the charge that the oath of a Jew was not to be believed. Explanations given by Rabbi Yehiel of Paris (1240 C.E.) that *Kol Nidre* was never intended to apply to vows "between man and man," did not avail to silence the enemies, and the charges were renewed from time to time. In America, Reform Judaism eliminated the *Kol Nidre* from its liturgy for several decades. But *Kol Nidre* survived all these vicissitudes. In the last edition of the Reform *Union Prayer Book* it has been restored with its full Aramaic text. After the eleventh century, the practice arose of chanting *Kol Nidre* first in a low and soft voice and then gradually in increasing volume at each repetition. Some prolonged the singing until nightfall to enable latecomers to hear at least one rendition. A set traditional melody for *Kol Nidre* is first mentioned by Rabbi M. Jaffa of Prague (16th century).*

SELIHOT

Each of the five services in the Yom Kippur liturgy contains a section of *Selihot* (Forgiveness Prayers), of which the confession of sins is an integral part. The *Selihot* for

* A. Z. Idelsohn, *Jewish Music in its Historical Development* (New York: Holt, Rinehart, and Winston, Inc., 1929), pp. 159-60.

Kol Nidre eve begin with *Yaaleh* ("Let our prayer ascend").

The prayers and *piyyutim* of the *Selihot* are inspired by the belief that God is "a God ready to pardon" (Neh. 9:17), and that He is "good and ready to pardon" (Ps. 86:5). Throughout the Bible this theme recurs. David prayed: "Pardon my iniquity for it is great" (Ps. 25:11). Solomon, in his prayer at the dedication of the Temple, prayed: "Hear Thou in heaven, and forgive the sin of Thy servants, and of Thy people Israel" (I Kings 8:36), and Daniel appealed to God's "compassions and forgivenesses" (Dan. 9:9).

In the *Selihot* we express our feeling of moral deficiency and our deep contrition and remorse. Such a feeling comes from a searching self-scrutiny which exposes the egocentric motives of our behavior. So often our conduct heaps hurt and sorrow on others. Even when our actual behavior seems to be blameless, we stand guilty of acts of omission, as we fail to bring succor to the suffering and rescue to the victims of injustice. Iron is weighed by the ton, but gold is weighed by the gram. The more developed a person's moral sensitivity is, the keener is his awareness of his moral insufficiency. In the Jew the feelings of contrition and remorse were further deepened by the belief that he had a share in the corporate guilt of Israel—a guilt which brought about the exile and delayed the promised redemption, for "Every generation during which the Temple is not rebuilt is to be considered as blameworthy as if it had caused its destruction" (TP Yoma 38c).

Daniel expressed for future generations the assurance of divine forgiveness which is the climactic note of the *Selihot* prayers. Daniel prayed: "We do not present supplications before Thee because of our righteousness, but because of Thy great compassions" (Dan. 9:18). In the spirit of Daniel's prayers, the Rabbis also stressed God's goodness as the sole source of the sinner's hope and help.

A homily by Rabbi Johanan made the frequent recitation of the Thirteen Divine Attributes the core of the *Selihot* prayers. On the verse, "And the Lord passed by before him and proclaimed: 'The Lord, the Lord, God, merciful and gracious'" (Exod. 34:6) Rabbi Johanan made this comment: "Were it not for this verse, we could not [because of its bold anthropomorphism] say this: God wrapped Himself in a *tallit* like one who leads the congregation in prayer, showed Moses this order of prayer [The Thirteen Attributes] and said to him: 'Whenever Israel sins, let them recite this order of prayer and I shall forgive them.' " Even more explicit was Rabbi Judah who said that God established a covenant that a prayer in which The Thirteen Attributes are invoked would never be in vain (R.H. 17b).

For a full discussion of The Thirteen Attributes, see pages 126-27.

Originally the *Selihot* consisted of several groups of biblical verses, each group being climaxed by the recitation of The Thirteen Attributes: "Lord, the Eternal, is a merciful and gracious God, slow to anger and abundant in loving-kindness and truth; keeping mercy for thousands, forgiving iniquity, transgression, and sin, and acquitting the penitent." In Geonic times the *Selihot* prayers were further expanded with *piyyutim*. In the fifth or sixth century the *El Melekh Yoshev* ("God who art loftily enthroned on Thy Throne of Mercy") was composed as the prelude to the recitation of The Thirteen Attributes. The prelude refers to the homily that "God taught us" (*El horeta lanu*) to recite The Thirteen Attributes when we pray for forgiveness. Though there are *Selihot* for all fast days, the term *Selihot* popularly connotes the midnight or early dawn services held before Rosh Hashanah and during the Ten Days of Repentance. In the Sephardic rite, the recitation of *Selihot* begins on the day after the new moon of Elul. In the Ashkenazic rite, *Selihot* are first recited on the Saturday night before Rosh Hashanah, but when Rosh Hashanah falls on a Monday or Tuesday, the *Selihot* services begin a week earlier.

יַעֲלֶה

May our plea ascend before Thee this evening, our cry before Thee in the morning, and do Thou turn to us at evening

This is an inverted alphabetic acrostic in which the *Yaaleh Veyavo* (see p. 108) is a moving avowal of faith in

God's nearness to those who seek Him in truth. The verse
"From evening till evening you shall observe your rest"
(Lev. 23:32) is the source of the refrain *meerev ad erev*
("from even unto even").

שְׁמַע תְּפִלָּה

Thou who hearest prayer, unto Thee all flesh shall come

"Thou who hearest prayer" is a medley of verses culled
from various parts of the Bible. Each verse is linked with
the next through a word which it has in common with it.
Thus *kol basar yavo* ("All flesh will come") leads to
yavo kol basar ("Let all flesh come"). Taken as a whole,
the verses extol the value of prayer, the holiness of the
sanctuary, and the majesty of the Creator. He alone
brought the world into being and He sustains it. To Him
alone we offer song and praise. Before Him we are humbled as we acknowledge that righteousness and judgment
are the foundation of His throne, that our good deeds are
few, that our personal worth is infinitesimal in His sight,
that we can do no other than cast ourselves upon His
mercy and seek His forgiveness. Man, "a withered leaf,
mere dust and ashes," is redeemed from loneliness by the
knowledge of God's love and abundant forgiveness.

Comments on the text

Ismar Elbogen surmised that long before prayer books
were available, such strings of Bible verses were recited
responsively by the reader and the congregation. As
the reader would read the first part of a verse, the congregation would complete it.

There is abundant evidence that a knowledge of the
text of the Bible was widespread among all Jews. In his
polemics against the enemies of the Jews, Josephus (70
C.E.) says with pride: "Among us, every child must know
how to read. We rarely find a Jewish boy who would not
be able to read the Bible, and Jewish fathers deprive
themselves of necessities to give their children an education" (*Contra Apion* II, 15).

There are numerous examples in rabbinic literature justifying Josephus' pride. Rabbi Joshua ben Hananya (Palestine, 2nd century C.E.), when he visited Rome, heard that a Jewish lad was languishing in prison. He stood at the entrance to the cell and tested the child's knowledge of the Bible by quoting the first parts of verses in Isaiah. The child readily completed each verse. Though in later years the child grew to become the sage, Rabbi Ishmael ben Elisha, the questions were by no means intended as more than a normal test offered to an average child (Git. 58a). Similarly, when Elisha ben Abuyah took his teacher, Rabbi Meir (2nd century C.E.), on a tour through thirteen schools, Rabbi Meir asked children in each school to quote the Bible verse they had been studying. The children quoted verses from Isaiah, Jeremiah, and Psalms, evidencing a wide range of biblical knowledge among elementary-school pupils (Hag. 15a). Another tale reflecting the popular knowledge of the Bible is that of a cattle driver who displayed his biblical knowledge before Rabbi Jonathan (Palestine 150 C.E.) as, with the sage's permission, he proved a Samaritan's comment on the flood story to be in contradiction to the plain text of the Bible. The story goes on to say that Rabbi Jonathan was so grateful to the cattle driver and so respectful toward him that, dismounting from the mule on which he rode, he allowed the cattle driver to ride on it, while he followed him on foot for a distance of four miles (*Deut. Rabbah,* ed. Lieberman, p. 79).

We even have an instance where an *am haaretz* (an ignorant man) suggested to a sage a novel interpretation of a verse in the Psalms, and the sage promised to quote in the man's name his interpretation, in a public lecture (*Gen. Rabbah,* 78:12). In a Babylonian synagogue, during the reading of the Torah, a letter in the scroll appeared to be blurred. Rabbi Zeira (*ca.* 350 C.E.) ruled that in such an eventuality, a child who is "neither brilliant nor dull" be called upon to read the blurred word, and that the further use of that scroll for public reading be determined by the ability of that child to read the word at sight (Men. 29b). Jerome (*ca.* 400 C.E.), the translator of the Bible into Latin, observed that the Palestinian Jews of his day were able to recite the text of the Pentateuch and the Prophets by heart.

דַּרְכְּךָ אֱלֹהֵינוּ

Our God, Thou art forbearing toward those
who do evil as well as toward those who do
good

תַּעֲלֶה אֲרוּכָה לְעָלֶה נִדָּף

Bring Thou healing to [man, who is as] a
driven leaf

These two strophes were originally the congregational
responses of an alphabetical acrostic *Amnam Ashamnu*
("Indeed our sins are too numerous to count"). Its
author was Jose ben Jose, the earliest of the *payyetanim*,
who flourished in Palestine about 400 C.E. In contemporary editions of the *Mahzor*, these responses are printed
as if the two constituted an independent composition.

The refrains contain a vigorous refutation of the charge
that Judaism's conception of God is that of a stern and
vindictive Deity. Instead, our entire liturgy is permeated
with the idea that "God is good to all and His tender
mercies are over all His works" (Ps. 145:9).

סְלַח נָא אֲשָׁמוֹת

Forgive the transgressions of Thy people

An alphabetical acrostic by Rabbi Meir of Rothenburg,
based on the prayer of Moses: "Pardon, I pray Thee, the
iniquity of this people according unto the greatness of
Thy loving-kindness" (Num. 14:19). Rabbi Meir's faith
in God's readiness to forgive is matched by his own love
for his people, to whom he refers in such endearing terms
as: "Thy children, Thy banner, Thy dearly beloved, Thy
possession, Thy flock, Thy servants, Thy faithful ones."

But Rabbi Meir's love for his people did not blind him
to their moral shortcomings and derelictions. He asks pardon for their abominations (*giulam*), for the hypocrisy
(*kahash*) of those who make the motions of bowing before
God without genuine love for Him, and for the rebellious
conduct (*meri*) of those whose life should be a witness to

God's unity. He combines candor with compassion as he concludes his prayer with the plea:

> O pardon the folly and infamy of those
> so dear to Thee
> In Thy boundless mercy remove the sins of
> Thy faithful ones.

אָמְנָם כֵּן

True indeed the evil impulse has us in its power

The author, Rabbi Yom Tov ben Isaac of York, expresses remorseful acknowledgment that sin is due to man's surrender to the evil impulse (*yetzer*). Before the Throne of Judgment, the "accuser" stands ready to recount our many misdeeds which testify that we have been unfaithful to God. But God is good and forgiving. He silences the "accuser" and invites the "defender" to plead on our behalf. His plea is that the merit of Abraham may blossom forth into hope and pardon for the people that has been compared to a lily of the valley (Song of Songs 2:1), that the prayers of a contrite people may wipe away sinfulness and sin alike as the divine pardon, "I forgive," is confirmed.

Comments on the text

In one of the stanzas of this alphabetical acrostic, the author pleads: "Look at our humiliation and count it as our sin's expiation." This pathetic plea reflects the torments suffered by the Jews of England during the period of the Third Crusade. From this Crusade, the Jews of France and Germany, who had suffered so much in the earlier Crusades, enjoyed comparative immunity, but its fury descended on the Jews of England. In 1190, mobs being recruited for the crusader army of Richard the Lion-Hearted besieged the Jews of York, who had withdrawn into a castle. The mob offered them a choice between apostasy and death. Among those who died by their own hand was Rabbi Yom Tov, who also inspired sixty others to join him in martyrdom. A contemporary poet, Rabbi Joseph of Chartres, in his elegy on this tragedy, describes Rabbi Yom Tov as a man whose intellectual acumen could "uproot mountains," and who could quote by heart with flawless accuracy from all the classic sources of Judaism.

כִּי הִנֵּה כַּחֹמֶר

**Like the clay in the hand of the potter
So are we in Thy hand**

An alphabetical acrostic of unknown origin, only portions of which are included in the various recensions of the Prayer Book, the basic idea of this prayer is inspired by these verses in the Book of Jeremiah:

The word which came to Jeremiah from the Lord, saying: "Arise, and go down to the potter's house, and there I will cause thee to hear My words." Then I went down to the potter's house, and, behold, he was at his work on the wheels. And whensoever the vessel that he made of the clay was marred in the hand of the potter, he made it again another vessel, as seemed good to the potter to make it.

Then the word of the Lord came to me, saying: "O house of Israel, cannot I do with you as this potter? saith the Lord. Behold, as the clay in the potter's hand, so are ye in My hand, O house of Israel. At one instant I may speak concerning a nation, and concerning a kingdom, to pluck up and to break down and to destroy it; but if that nation turn from their evil, because of which I have spoken against it, I repent of the evil that I thought to do unto it. And at one instant I may speak concerning a nation, and concerning a kingdom, to build and to plant it; but if it do evil in My sight, that it hearken not to My voice, then I repent of the good, wherewith I said I would benefit it." (Jer. 18:1-11)

In his parable of the potter and the clay, Jeremiah boldly declares that though man is but potters' clay in the hands of God, he nevertheless retains his freedom of choice between obedience to God's will and defiance of it. Jeremiah thus implies that God's decision is subject to man's revision, for man's repentance can reverse "an evil decree."

In this acrostic our poet enlarges on the same theme as he refers to various types of craftsmen: the mason, the blacksmith, the mariner, the glass blower, the embroiderer, and the silversmith. As each of them fashions his raw material, he rejects that which does not conform with his will and design. As the "raw material" in God's hands, we pray that we may be willing to be molded in accordance with His will. Man is not a pliant and responsive matter in God's hands. He may choose to resist his Maker, or yield to Him. If man shatters or breaks, if the stuff of his nature withers to the touch of God, he may be rejected. If he is firm and without incorrigible blemish, God may shape him to His will.

Comments on the text

The unknown author of this *piyyut* rhymed the three strophes of each stanza. Thus in the first stanza, *hayotzer* rhymes with *mekatzer* and with *notzer;* in the second stanza, *mesattet* rhymes with *mekhatet* and again with *memotet.*

The author addresses God respectively as: The Keeper of steadfast kindness, the Decreer of life and death, the Sustainer of the poor, God good and forgiving, the Pardoner of all sin, the Champion of justice, and the Healer of the ailing.

"Regard the covenant"

Each stanza culminates in the refrain: "Regard the covenant and not our corruption."

The "covenant" here refers to a phrase in Exodus 34:10: "Behold, I make a covenant." Rabbi Judah interprets this as referring to two earlier verses in which God's Thirteen Attributes are enumerated (*ibid.,* vss. 6-8). God established a "covenant" that whenever the Thirteen Attributes would be invoked in a prayer for forgiveness, such a prayer would not be rejected (R.H. 17b).

זְכֹר רַחֲמֶיךָ

Remember, O Lord, Thy mercies, for they are everlasting

We have said before (p. 207) that originally the *Selihot* consisted of clusters of biblical verses linked by key words. The biblical verses and phrases that follow are linked by these words: *zekhor* ("remember"), *rahem* ("have mercy"), *hashev* ("restore us"), *mehe* ("wipe out our sins"), and *taher* ("cleanse us").

The biblical verses conclude with Isaiah's vision of the

days of restoration: "Even them will I bring to My holy mountain, and make them joyful in My house of prayer; their burnt-offerings and their sacrifices shall be acceptable upon Mine altar; for My house shall be called a house of prayer for all peoples" (Isa. 56:7). In the original context in which it occurs, the passage assures proselytes who join the people and faith of Israel that their worship would be acceptable to God whose restored Temple will be known as "a house of prayer for all peoples."

שְׁמַע קוֹלֵנוּ

Hear our voice and grant our supplication

Since the immediately preceding cluster of biblical verses ended with: "My house shall be called a house of prayer for all peoples" (Isa. 56:7), the word prayer (*tefillah*) is the link with the *Shema Kolenu* ("Hear our voice") which contains the phrase: "And in Thy mercy accept our prayer [*tefillatenu*]."

The order of the *Selihot* follows the rule that the praise of God must be concluded before petitionary prayer is offered (Ber. 32a). After reciting verses depicting God's steadfast mercy, we proceed in *Shema Kolenu* to pray that ours be the will to return to God in wholehearted repentance, that we may be forgiven and reinstated in His good favor, as we return to Him "sincerely and wholeheartedly."

כִּי אָנוּ עַמֶּךְ

We are Thy people and Thou art our God
We are Thy children and Thou art our Father
We are Thy faithful and Thou art our Beloved
We are insolent, but Thou art merciful

These expressions of intimacy between Israel and God are culled from various parts of the Bible. The epithets of endearment reach their climax in a declaration of mutual fealty "We are pledged to Thee and Thou art pledged to us," based on the verse "Thou hast avouched [affirmed] the Lord this day to be thy God. . . . And the

Lord hath avouched [affirmed] thee this day to be His own treasure" (Deut. 26:17-18).

At this point there is a sharp change from a tone of confidence and elation to one of abject contrition. The contrast is now drawn between man's insolence and God's graciousness, between man's obstinacy and God's forbearance, and between man's ephemeral life and God's eternity. Nevertheless, we venture to make entreaty to God because, despite our sinfulness, there is a redeeming quality to our life, in that we confess our sins. "For we are neither so arrogant nor so hardened as to say before Thee, . . . 'We are righteous and have not sinned.' "

THE CONFESSION OF SINS (*VIDDUI*)

1

שֶׁאֵין אֲנַחְנוּ עַזֵּי פָנִים . . . לוֹמַר לְפָנֶיךָ . . .

צַדִּיקִים אֲנַחְנוּ וְלֹא חָטָאנוּ

אֲבָל אֲנַחְנוּ חָטָאנוּ

We are neither so arrogant . . . as to say before Thee, "We are righteous and have not sinned." Verily, we have sinned.

2

אָשַׁמְנוּ. בָּגַדְנוּ. גָּזַלְנוּ. דִּבַּרְנוּ דֹפִי

We have trespassed; we have dealt treacherously; we have robbed; we have spoken slander

3

אַתָּה יוֹדֵעַ רָזֵי עוֹלָם וְתַעֲלוּמוֹת סִתְרֵי כָּל־חָי

Thou knowest the mysteries of the universe and the hidden secrets of all living

4

יְהִי רָצוֹן . . . שֶׁתִּסְלַח לָנוּ עַל כָּל חַטֹּאתֵינוּ וְתִמְחַל

לָנוּ עַל כָּל עֲוֹנוֹתֵינוּ וּתְכַפֶּר לָנוּ עַל כָּל פְּשָׁעֵינוּ

עַל חֵטְא שֶׁחָטָאנוּ לְפָנֶיךָ בְּאֹנֶס וּבְרָצוֹן

וְעַל חֵטְא שֶׁחָטָאנוּ לְפָנֶיךָ בְּאִמּוּץ הַלֵּב.

וְעַל כֻּלָּם אֱלוֹהַ סְלִיחוֹת

סְלַח לָנוּ, מְחַל לָנוּ, כַּפֶּר לָנוּ

**May it be Thy will . . . to forgive us all our
sins, to pardon us for all our iniquities and to
grant us atonement for all our transgressions:
for the sins we have committed before Thee
under compulsion or of our own will. And for
the sins we have committed before Thee by
hardening our hearts. For all these [sins] O
God of forgiveness, forgive us, pardon us, grant
us atonement**

Ten times during the Yom Kippur services the *Ashamnu*
("We have trespassed") and the *Al Het* ("For the sin we
have committed before Thee") are recited. These confessions are prompted by the belief that sin distorts and
diminishes the divine image in which man was created.
Sin is an estrangement of man from God, a breaking of
the link between man and his Maker.

The confession is by no means intended as a mechanical formula of absolution. The prerequisites of God's
forgiveness are reparation, restitution, and reconciliation
with the person who has been wronged. Rabbi Hisda said
that one must ask three times the pardon of the person he
has offended, in the presence of three witnesses (Yoma
87a). A pathetic instance of the need for securing the
forgiveness of one's offended fellow man is this story about
Rabbi Simeon ben Elazar: Once he was returning from a
visit to his teacher. He was riding leisurely along the lake
shore, feeling rather proud of the fact that he had ac-
quired so much learning. While in this mood, he chanced

upon an extremely ugly man. "Wretch," he said to him, "are all the people of your town as ugly as you?" The man replied, "Go to the Artisan who made me and tell him what an ugly vessel he made." Realizing his error, the sage alighted from his animal and asked for forgiveness. The man said, "I will not forgive you till you go to the Artisan who made me and tell him what an ugly vessel He made." Rabbi Simeon followed him and pleaded with him till he reached his home town. On his arrival, hordes of admirers greeted him with the words, "Peace be with you, Master!" The man said, "If this man is a master, may there not be many like him in Israel," and he told them what Rabbi Simeon had done to him. They pleaded with him to forgive the sage, and he finally did so on condition that he should never again act in this manner. Rabbi Simeon then went to the *Bet Hamidrash* (Academy), and when he began his discourse he said: "A man should always be as tender as a reed and not as hard as a cedar tree. Because of its softness, the reed is used for the making of pens with which Torah scrolls, *tefillin* and *mezuzot* are written" (Taan. 20b).

The offended person, on the other hand, was admonished not to bear a grudge and to be forgiving, for he who forgives others is forgiven for his own sins (R.H. 17a).

A rule of conduct in relation to others is strikingly worded in this passage:

If you have done your fellow man a little wrong, let it be a great wrong in your eyes and go and rectify it. If you have done him much good, let it be little in your eyes. If he has done you a little good, let it be great in your eyes. If he has done you a great wrong, let it be little in your eyes (*Abot de Rabbi Nathan, 41*).

Despite the double alphabetical acrostic in which the sins are enumerated, the *Al Het* is not a literary device. The sins it lists are of the stuff of daily life, and point an accusing finger at our repeated moral failures. In *Al Het* we express our contrition for such attitudes as callousness, pride, insolence, and wanton hatred; the abuse of our capacities of speech; the energetic pursuit of evil; being guilty of envy, slander, and gossip; the pursuit of unlawful gain; corrupt business practices; deception, deceit, and false swearing; bribery and the corruption of the courts. Nor is the root of all evil overlooked: the deterioration of respect for parents and teachers.

Because our liturgy is pervaded by the spirit of the Talmud, it reflects an interest in the details of everyday life. It avoids abstract and remote categorizing and concentrates on specifics—on those innumerable nuances of egocentricity which transform occasional lapses of conduct into more violent and persistent vice. Being men of practical affairs rather than theorists, our sages were fully aware of the devices by which men are liable to take advantage of their neighbor. The saintly Rabbi Johanan ben Zakkai (*ca.* 70 C.E.) was rather embarrassed to admit and exhibit his knowledge of the deceptive methods of impostors. After giving a number of examples of fraudulent practices, he expressed his dilemma as follows: "Woe is me if I speak of them and woe is me if I do not speak of them" (Mishnah Kelim 17:16); meaning, thereby, that by speaking of them he might be teaching others such methods of deception, and by not speaking of them, defrauders would be convinced that the lawmakers are unrealistic visionaries, innocent of unrighteous ways.

The *Al Het* does not make specific reference to those sins which entail the violation of the rituals of Judaism. Such infractions as the desecration of Sabbath and Festivals, the ignoring of sacred times and seasons, and the failure to abide by the disciplines that invest our daily life with sacred significance are categorized in the Talmud as "sins between man and God," and can be said to be comprised under the heading *Veal Hataim* ("And for the sins"), which defines transgressions in terms of the "penalties" one incurs in committing them. While opinions differed among the sages of the Talmud as to the propriety or necessity of detailing one's sins when one recites the *Viddui,* it is taken for granted that only sins "between man and man" need be detailed (Yoma 86b). Accordingly, *Al Het* makes specific mention only of those sins by which one commits offenses against one's own person or against other persons. The final series, *Veal Hataim,* is intended to make confession of such offenses as the acrostic might have omitted, as well as of the sins "between man and God." The fifty-four *Al Het*'s of our Prayer Book are an expansion of Saadyah Gaon's six, Amram Gaon's twelve, and Maimonides' twenty-two types of transgressions, listed in their respective versions of the *Al Het*.

When confession is offered in sincerity and with whole-hearted intent, the very words of the confession are said by the Rabbis to have an expiatory effect. The Midrash interprets the verse "Take with you words, and return unto the Lord" (Hosea 14:3) as follows:

The Holy One, blessed is He, said to Israel, "My children, I will accept from you neither burnt-offerings nor meat-offerings, but I expect that you be reconciled to Me by prayer and supplication and by the redirection of your heart through confession, prayers, and tears!" (*Pesikta Rabbati*, ed. Friedman, 198b).

Following the *Al Het* are a series of citations from Scripture, validating the power and efficacy of repentance as a sure means of being restored to God's favor. The verses are in this order: Psalm 19:13, Ezekiel 36:25, Micah 7:18-20, Daniel 9:18-19, Ezra 9:6, Nehemiah 9:17, Jeremiah 15:20, each group of verses from the third section of the Bible (*Ketuvim*) being climaxed by a verse from the Prophets. The recitation of these verses is substantially in the order mentioned in Amram Gaon's *Seder*.

The concluding sections, *Aseh* ("Do so for thine own sake"), *Anenu* ("Answer us, O Lord, answer us"), and *Mi Sheanah* ("He who answered Abraham on Mt. Moriah . . . may He answer us"), are from the older *Selihah* liturgies. *Mi Sheanah* is an expansion of the series mentioned in the Mishnah in connection with the special prayers recited on fast days (Mishnah Taan. 2:4).

Comments on the text

The literal meaning of the word *Viddui* is "declaration." This is evident from a form of confession mentioned in the Palestinian Talmud, which has this wording:

Let it be declared: Whatever I did was because I stood on the road of evil and walked on a road far away from Thee. I shall never do so again. May it be Thy will . . . to pardon me for all my iniquities, forgive me for all my transgressions, and grant me atonement for all my sins (TP Yoma 45c).

Ashamnu and the *Al Het* arose in Geonic times. In early Amoraic times, short formulae of confession were used, and some of them are included in our liturgy. But as early as talmudic times, there must have developed a practice of reciting a lengthy liturgy of confessional prayers on Yom Kippur, since the very extensiveness of these prayers became proverbial. Thus, Rab said that on weekdays one may, after the *Amidah,* freely recite personal petitions, be they "even as long as the order of the *Viddui* of Yom Kippur" (Ber. 31a). Perhaps the inordinate length of the *Viddui* prayers accounts for the statement of Mar Zutra (d. 417 C.E.) that once a person has said *Aval anahnu hatanu* ("Indeed we have sinned"), he need say no more (Yoma 87b). In our liturgy this phrase precedes the recitation of *Ashamnu.* It should be noted that the language of the *Ashamnu* and of *Al Het,* like that of most of the prayers, is cast in the plural. The individual prays as a member of the community when he says: *Ashamnu, we* are blameworthy; *bagadnu, we* have been unfaithful. He affirms the belief that through our sins of omission and our sins of commission, we, as individuals, hold ourselves responsible for the moral state and tenor of the community (Rabbi Max D. Klein).

The full *Viddui* is first recited during the silent *Amidah* at the *Minhah* service of the day before Yom Kippur, and thereafter it is recited eight more times—at the conclusion of each silent *Amidah* and during the fourth blessing (the *Kedushat Hayom*) of the Reader's Repetition of the *Amidah* (*Tosefta Yoma,* 5:14). A shorter form of *Viddui* is recited twice during the *Neilah* service.

The *Tosefta* gives these reasons for the frequent recital of the *Viddui:*

The *mitzvah* of saying the *Viddui* actually begins before dark, on Yom Kippur eve. However, our Sages ruled that one should recite it at *Minhah* on *Erev Yom Kippur* before one eats his meal, lest his mind become unclear through inebriation. And though he has already confessed before his meal, he should confess again after his meal, lest some indiscretion may have been committed after the meal. And though he has confessed after the meal he must do so again during the evening service, and then again in *Shaharit* service and in the *Musaf,* in the *Minhah* and in the *Neilah*—all because of the apprehension that some indiscretion may have been committed (*Tosefta Yoma,* 5:14; cf. Yoma 87b).

In his comprehensive commentary on the *Tosefta,* Saul Lieberman shows how this reference to the second *Viddui* (before the *Maariv*) is the origin of the *Tefillah Zakkah* —a long but deeply moving personal confession recited in the Ashkenazic rite by the individual worshiper before *Kol Nidre.*

The custom of beating one's breast while confessing one's sins is first mentioned in this midrashic passage:

And the living will lay it to his heart (Eccles. 7:2). Rabbi Meir said: "Why do people beat their hearts [in remorse for their sins]? Because the heart is the seat and source of sin" (*Eccl. Rabbah,* Romm edition, p. 36b).

רַחֲמָנָא דְּעָנֵי

O merciful God who answereth the broken of heart, answer us

Written in Geonic times, this closing supplication exhibits the piety which animated our forebears when they recited the *Selihot* prayers. Its spirit is that expressed by the psalmist: "The Lord is nigh unto them that are of a broken heart, and saveth them that are of a contrite spirit (Ps. 34:19).

The broken-hearted, to whom God is near, are not primarily in need of health and sustenance. They are, rather, those depressed by an awareness that in failing to obey their noblest spiritual imperatives, they have also failed God. Because they have become "broken of spirit" by their own remorse, they are again ready and able to experience the nearness of the living God.

For our discussion of Avinu Malkenu *and* Alenu, *which conclude the* Kol Nidre *service, see p. 118 and p. 180. For reference to the* Kaddish, Yigdal, *and* Adon Olam, *see p. 37.*

THE ORDER OF THE *SHAHARIT* (MORNING) SERVICE: YOM KIPPUR

The order of the *Shaharit* service, which precedes the appearance of the first *yotzer* of Yom Kippur, *Az Beyom Kippur*, is the same as that which obtains for the *Shaharit* service for Rosh Hashanah.

For our discussion of the general order of the preliminary service and for the prayers recited before Barekhu, *see pp. 38-50.*

אָז בְּיוֹם כִּפּוּר

Then on Yom Kippur Thou didst teach forgiveness

As a *yotzer* for Yom Kippur, this *piyyut* revolves around the word *or* (light), since it expands on the first blessing: "Creator of light." In this double alphabetical acrostic, "light" alludes to the inner illumination which comes to man when he has unburdened himself before God through confession and repentance. The author recalls the days of old, when the people thronged the Temple courts, and when Yom Kippur was the one day of the year when the High Priest would enter the Holy of Holies to intercede for his people. Like our forefathers, we, too, seek the healing rays of the inner light that come from the fast and prayers of Yom Kippur. We seek purification from our sins as we remove from our hearts the stones of stubbornness to admit the bright light of this day of forgiveness.

Comments on the text

"Then on Yom Kippur"

The day on which God showed mercy to Moses and to His people was the tenth day of Tishri; the day on which Moses was to receive the second Tablets of the Law, Israel spent the day in prayer and fasting, and their ardent prayer moved God to say to them: "My children I swear by My lofty Name that these your tears shall be tears of rejoicing for you, that this day shall be one of pardon, forgiveness, and remission of sins for you, your children and your children's children till the end of time" (*Seder Eliahu Zuta,* pp. 180-81).

"Sin grew stronger while my soul was asleep"

The community of Israel declared before the Holy One, blessed is He: "Sovereign of the universe! I am asleep because of my neglect of *mitzvot*, but my heart is awake for the performance of deeds of kindness. I am asleep in regard to the performance of acts of righteousness, but my heart is awake in the desire to do them. I am asleep in regard to the offering of sacrifices, but my heart is awake for the *Shema* and the *Tefillah*. I am asleep in regard to the Temple, but my heart is awake for synagogues and houses of study. I am asleep in respect to the time of redemption, but my heart is ever awake for it. Even though I am asleep in regard to the redemption, the heart of the Holy One, blessed is He, is awake to redeem me" (*Song of Songs Rabbah*, 5:21).

מַלְכוּתוֹ בִּקְהַל עֲדָתִי

His sovereignty I acknowledge amidst the assembled throng

קָדוֹשׁ אַדִּיר בַּעֲלִיָּתוֹ

The Holy One He is mighty in the heavens

קָדוֹשׁ בִּתְשׁוּבָה שָׁת סְלִיחָתוֹ

The Holy One forgives man upon his repentance

This *piyyut*, like others recited on Yom Kippur, repeatedly refers to God as *Kadosh* ("The Holy One"). In Jewish religion, the idea of God's holiness is often coupled with His goodness and His nearness to man. It is God, the *Kadosh*, who receives the penitents, who rejoices in their atonement, who thinks of the people He loves, and who, with His own cleansing waters, purifies those whom sin has made impure. The latter expression is an allusion to Rabbi Akiba's declaration: "What a fortunate people you are, O Israel. Before whom are you made clean and who cleanses you? It is your Father in heaven" (Mishnah Yoma 8:9).

Why *Barukh Shem* is recited aloud

The refrain of this *piyyut* is: *Barukh shem kevod malkhuto leolam vaed* ("Blessed be His glorious sovereign

name for ever and ever"). Yom Kippur is the only day of
the year when *Barukh Shem* is recited aloud during the
Shema. The reason is that *Barukh Shem* is a singular
reminiscence of the solemn service of atonement that was
held in the Temple on Yom Kippur. In the *Avodah* section of the *Musaf* (see pp. 249-53), we recall that service
with special vividness and repeat the threefold confession
spoken by the High Priest as he recited the Ineffable
Name. As the people heard the Name, they knelt, prostrated themselves, and fell on their faces and said,
"Blessed be his glorious sovereign name for ever and
ever." Indeed, *Barukh Shem* rather than *Amen* was the
response to all blessings uttered in the Temple (*Tosefta
Taan.*, 1:17). The emphasis given to *Barukh Shem* on
Yom Kippur is therefore an added means of reliving and
recalling the atonement rites formerly conducted in the
Temple.

A talmudic legend relates that *Barukh Shem* was taught
by Jacob to his sons as he gave them his parting blessing
(Pes. 56a). Another legend relates that Moses heard
Barukh Shem recited by the angels and he taught it to
Israel. All year we recite it in a whisper, but on Yom
Kippur, when we are cleansed from our sins and are "as
pure as the angels," we recite it aloud (*Deut. Rabbah*,
2:36).

For the discussion of the Shema *and the blessings
which precede and follow it, see pp. 39-40; 63-83.*

READER'S REPETITION OF THE
SHAHARIT AMIDAH: YOM KIPPUR •

אֵימְךָ נָשָׂאתִי

**With trepidation in my heart I offer my sup-
plication••**

This is called a *reshut* ("permission") because in it the
reader begs permission to interpolate *piyyutim* into the

• For the discussion of the standard parts of the *Amidah*, see pp.
85 ff.
•• For a discussion of the reshut *Missod Hakhamim*, which precedes
"With trepidation in my heart," see p. 89.

Amidah. Feeling inadequate as the congregation's pleader and spokesman before God, he prays for the fluency of language and the ardor of feeling which would bring relief and healing to those who have deputed him on their behalf.

Comments on the text

In unabridged editions of the *Mahzor,* this *reshut* is followed by two *piyyutim* composed by the same author, Rabbi Meshullam ben Kalonymos (10th century C.E.), who lived in Italy and moved to Mayence in his old age. The first, *Immatzta Asor* ("Thou didst appoint the tenth day of Tishri"), which is interpolated before the blessing "Shield of Abraham," is an alphabetical acrostic invoking the ancestral merit of Abraham on Israel's behalf. The second, *Taavat nefesh* ("Answer those whose soul longs for Thee"), interpolated before the blessing "He who revives the dead," is an inverted alphabetical acrostic referring to Isaac, who was bound on the altar of the *Akedah* and was "restored to life."

אֱנוֹשׁ מַה יִּזְכֶּה

What is man that he should be deemed pure?

An unknown poet composed this unrhymed alphabetical acrostic. As a summons to repentance, it is more like a homily than a prayer. We are reminded that no man's deeds are wholly free from self-interest, and that our hidden motives are no secret to God, whose searching eyes pierce even the thickest darkness. Before the throne of divine judgment, neither wealth nor pomp nor power can validate a life dominated by egotism.

If man would but meditate on the brevity of human life, on the toil, trouble, and torment which are man's lot until he goes down to his final sleep in the grave! The value of one's life is to be estimated by its moral and intellectual quality. Since toil he must, let man's toil be in the study of the Torah. Since he must be concerned, let his concern be for the welfare of others. Let his aim be to earn a good name through a search for wisdom and through the performance of good deeds. Such strivings will prepare him for old age, and as the day of his death will then mark the consummation of a fulfilled career, it will be more significant than the day of his birth. The "lesson" ends with the declaration that even till the day of a man's death, God awaits his repentance.

Comments on the text

"Let him consider his origin, whence he came, the pit that will mark his grave"

Akabya ben Mahalalel said: "Mark well three things and you will not fall into the clutches of sin: Know whence you came, where you are going and before whom you are destined to give an account and reckoning. Whence you came, from a putrid drop. Where you are going, to a place of dust, worm and maggot. And before whom you are destined to give an account and reckoning, before the King of kings the Holy One Blessed is He" (Ab. 3:1).

"Until the day of man's death Thou dost wait for him to repent"

Rabbi Elazar said: "Repent one day before your death." Said his pupils: "Does man know when he would die?" He answered: "Then he surely must repent today, lest he die tomorrow" (Shab. 153a).

"If he acquireth a good name"

A man is known by three names: The first is the name which his parents give him; the second is the name by which others call him; and the third is the name by which he is identified in the true record of his life, from birth to death, (literally; in the book of the story of his creation) (*Eccl. Rabbah,* 7:1).

"The day of death is better than the day of birth"

The day of death [is better] than the day of birth" (Eccl. 7:1). When a person is born, all his dear ones rejoice. When he dies they all weep. It really should not be so. When a person is born, there is as yet no reason for rejoicing over him, because one knows not what kind of a person he will be by reason of his conduct, whether righteous or wicked, good or evil. When he dies there is cause for rejoicing if he departs with a good name and departs this life in peace (Shab. 153a).

At this juncture in the Shaharit *service, the* piyyut *by Eleazar Kalir,* Attah Hu Elohenu *("Thou art our God"), is recited. See our discussion, p. 94.*

מוֹרֶה חַטָּאִים

Thou who showest sinners the path in which to walk

This *piyyut,* by Meshullam ben Kalonymos, reflects the identification of the deepest spiritual desires of the author with the hopes and the destiny of his people. The poet opens with an expression of gratitude to God for showing him the road to virtue. Every day, morning and evening, it is his privilege to proclaim God's Kingship by reciting the *Shema.* On Yom Kippur the entire people reaffirms its devotion to Him. In its four services, Israel implores His pardon, confident that by evening He would grant His forgiveness. Then the poet proceeds to plead for the restoration of the Temple, where the Levites would again lead in song, and where priests, clad in sacred vestments, would again offer sweet incense. Restored to glory, Israel will assemble to celebrate the restoration of the Sanctuary. They will sing a new song, as victorious in tone as the one sung by the Israelites when they crossed the Red Sea. In the concluding stanzas the poet pleads that the prayers of the congregation be accepted in place of the prescribed sacrifices, and that the weight of sin be lifted from the hearts of all who pray in sincerity and in truth.

Comments on the text

This double acrostic carries the name of the author משולם בירבי קלונימוס חזק Each stanza consists of three strophes, the third strophe consisting of the first part of the verses in Psalm 145, in their regular alphabetical order. The concluding line is an acrostic of משולם the name of the author:

מלך שוכן עד לבדך מלוך עדי עד

אָנָּא אֱלֹהִים חַיִּים

O living God of life, inscribe for life
Those who cleave unto Thee

God is addressed here as the *Mikveh Yisrael*—the purifying pool of Israel. The allusion is to a passage in the
Mishnah which carries a homily on the verse: "Thou
hope (*mikveh*) of Israel, the Lord" (Jer. 17:13). As
the word *mikveh* also means a pool, the Mishnah remarks
that God is for Israel like a pool. As the pool makes the
unclean clean, so does the Holy One blessed is He, cleanse
Israel (Mishnah Yoma 8:9). At the conclusion of *Toharot,*
the last section of the *Mishneh Torah,* Maimonides points
to the psychological difference between a physical cleansing and a "ritual" cleansing. In a physical cleansing, one
can become clean even if one falls into the bath or is
thrown into it against his will. Different, however, is the
case of a priest who is in a state of impurity, and who
must immerse himself in a ritual pool to be permitted
to partake of the priestly sacred portions (*terumah*). He
must undergo the immersion with the proper intent, and
if he merely falls into the pool or is thrown into it, he
does not become purified and cannot partake of *terumah*.
Maimonides proceeds to draw the analogy with Yom
Kippur. Atonement is effective only if the individual celebrates the day with the intent of baring his soul before
God and of ridding himself of moral impurity. A per-
functory observance of Yom Kippur degrades it from a
noble, transforming experience to a magical performance
not worthy of intelligent people.

This acrostic is so arranged that the first letter of the
Hebrew alphabet is followed in the next strophe by the
last letter of the alphabet, so that one half of the alphabet
is in a straight acrostic and the other half is in a reversed
acrostic—called an *atbash* acrostic.

הַיּוֹם יִכָּתֵב בְּסֵפֶר הַזִּכְרוֹנוֹת

On this day, life and death are inscribed in the
Book of Records

The decisive role of Yom Kippur is proclaimed in these
few stirring words. Summoned to supplicate God, Israel is

endearingly referred to as *kanah*, "a choice plant." This is an allusion to the verse "the stock [choice plant] which Thy right hand hath planted" (Ps. 80:16). As well, a plea is addressed to the individual Jew, whose errant life can be redeemed through contrite prayer, as the following tale movingly illustrates:

It was said of Elazar ben Dama that his had been a life of unbridled lust. One of the many lewd women with whom he had consorted told him that a man as deeply mired in sin as was he could not expect the door of repentance ever to be opened for him. In consternation he left her. Stationing himself in a valley between two ranges of mountains and hills, he spoke as follows: "You mountains and hills, invoke God's mercy for me." They answered, "Rather than pray for you we need to pray for ourselves, for Scripture says: 'The mountains may depart and the hills may be removed' " (Isa. 54:10). He then said: "O heaven and earth, pray for mercy in my behalf." They retorted: "Rather than pray for you, we had better pray for ourselves, for Scripture says: 'For the heavens shall vanish away like smoke and the earth shall wax old like a garment' " (Isa. 51:6). He then said, "O sun and moon, pray for me!" Whereupon they said, "We had better pray for ourselves, for Scripture says: 'The moon shall be confounded, and the sun shall be ashamed' " (Isa. 24:23). In desperation he said, "O stars and constellations, will you pray for me?" They answered: "Rather than pray for you we had better pray for ourselves, for Scripture says: 'And all the host of heaven shall moulder away' " (Isa. 34:4). Then Elazar ben Dama said: "I now realize that repentance depends solely on me." Whereupon, with head drooped between his knees, he sobbed with such intensity that he expired. A heavenly voice then proclaimed: "Ben Dama is now eligible to be received in the life of the world to come" (Ab. Zarah 17a).

אָמְרוּ לֵאלֹהִים

Say ye of God: How tremendous are Thy works!

This mosaic of phrases from all parts of the Bible, composed by Meshullam ben Kalonymos, extols the awesome power of the Creator, whose majesty is witnessed to by the universe which He brought into being. God did not, however, abdicate His sovereignty with the creation of his world. The densest darkness cannot hide anything from Him, and from the highest heights He surveys and sees all that transpires among men. He, the solitary Sovereign, nevertheless dwells with him who is of contrite spirit. Though justice is the foundation of His throne, His mercy is extended to all men from whose hearts there emanates an anguished prayer for His forgiveness. His mercy will also be extended to Israel, a people few in numbers, chosen to testify among all mankind to His incomparable power, majesty, and goodness. For as this people continues to proclaim every morning and every evening that God is One, it activates the divine mercy, and thus saves the world from catastrophe.

Comments on the text

The refrain *Imru Lelohim* comes from Psalm 66:3: "Say unto God, how tremendous is Thy work." An acrostic of the name of the author משלם is to be found in these lines of the last stanza:

משיב אף וחרון וקרץ

שוע מחנניו ירץ

לכן יתגאה ה' אדוננו

מה אדיר שמך בכל הארץ

מַעֲשֵׂה אֱלֹהֵינוּ

How great is the work of our God

The limitless majesty of the eternal God is contrasted with the helplessness and the ephemeral life of man. God's glory dazzles even the hosts of heaven, yet He listens attentively to the supplication of the humble and gives them relief in their distress. He extends mercy to those who obey Him and even to those who anger Him. For this reason God is to be exalted above all Creation. But mortal man, whose designs are deceit, whose final home is the grave, of what value are his pomp and pride? It is only when he seeks God's love that man can succeed in his quest for a life of purpose and significance.

This is a full alphabetical acrostic by Meshullam ben Kalonymos, each stanza beginning with a letter of the alphabet. Originally, there was a full parallel acrostic with the heading, *Maase Enosh,* of which only the first stanza has been retained.

תְּנוּ עֹז לֵאלֹהִים עַל יִשְׂרָאֵל גַּאֲוָתוֹ

Ascribe ye strength to God, His majesty is over Israel

As the service approaches the recitation of the *Kedushah,* the hymns speak in more exalted and even in ecstatic language, of the privilege which is Israel's, to proclaim on earth the holiness of God, even as it is proclaimed by the celestial beings on high. This *piyyut* by an unknown author exhausts all the letters of the alphabet in its description of the many ways in which Israel experiences the closeness of God, His holiness, His purity, and His blessing. The hymn enlarges on the theme suggested by Psalm 68:35: "Ascribe ye strength unto God, His majesty is over Israel, and His strength is in the skies."

It is only natural that a people which believes itself to have been appointed to testify to God's unity and to bring the teachings of His Torah to all mankind should express its boundless delight in being the recipient of divine favor. The following passages clearly indicate that the rabbis did not view Israel's special relationship to God as an indication that He is any the less concerned with mankind as a whole:

When Jeremiah referred to God as "King of the Nations" (Jer. 10:7), God remonstrated with the prophet, "You call me King of the Nations. Am I not also King of Israel?" (*Midrash Tehillim,* ed. Buber, p. 43).

"Three times in the year shall thy males appear before the Lord [Master] God [Lord], God of Israel" (Exod. 34:23). Here there are three references to God: Master, Lord, and God of Israel. God said to Israel: "I am the Master (*Adon*) over all mankind, but this does not fully describe my relationship to Israel. I, the Master of all the nations, am also the Lord God of Israel, in that my name is linked with that of Israel" (*Midrash Hagadol on Exod.* ed. M. Margulies, p. 713).

אֵין כָּמוֹךְ בְּאַדִּירֵי מַעְלָה

There is none like unto Thee among the mighty on high

הָאַדֶּרֶת וְהָאֱמוּנָה

Thine are excellence and faithfulness, Thou
who livest forever. Thine are understanding
and blessing, Thou who livest forever

נַאֲמִירָךְ בְּאֵימָה

With awe we acknowledge Thee

רוֹמְמוּ אֵל מֶלֶךְ נֶאֱמָן

Exalt ye God, the faithful King

These four hymns are similar in tone and mood. The
first, "There is none like unto Thee among the mighty,"
by Meshullam ben Kalonymos, is an expansion into a
double alphabetical acrostic of this verse in the Psalms,
which is frequently used in the liturgy, "There is none
like unto Thee among the gods [mighty], O Lord; and
there are no works like Thine" (Ps. 86:8). The second,
"Thine are excellence and faithfulness, Thou who livest
forever," is found, with some variations, in a mystical
work, *Hekhalot Rabbati,* dating from the sixth century.
Medieval commentators called this hymn "the song of
the angels," and Gershom Scholem cites this hymn as "a
classic example of an alphabetical litany which fills the
imagination of the devotee with splendid concepts
clothed in magnificent expression: the particular words
do not matter." • Philip Bloch, cited by Scholem as having described the unique nature of such hymns, shows
how in them "the glorification of God is not that of the
psalm. The psalm either describes the marvels of Creation as proof of the Creator's glory and grandeur, or
stresses the element of divine grace and guidance in the
history of Israel. . . . The mystical hymn is, however,
simply the praise of God. This praise is heaped and
multiplied as if there were a danger that some honorific
word or phrase might be forgotten."
The two acrostics that follow, "With awe we acknowl-

• Gershom Scholem, *Major Trends in Jewish Mysticism* (New York:
Schocken Books, Inc., 1946), p. 59.

edge Thee," and "Exalt ye God, the faithful King," are paraphrases of the preceding *Haaderet Vehaemunah*.

For the discussion of the Kedushah *and the sections of the Reader's Repetition of the* Amidah *which follow the* Kedushah, *see pp. 171-78; then 112-17. For discussion of the* Selihot *and the* Viddui, *see pp. 205-207. For discussion of the* Avinu Malkenu, *see p. 119.*

TORAH READING:
YOM KIPPUR MORNING [*]

"The heritage of the congregation of Jacob"

The Torah reading for Yom Kippur morning was the basis of the impressive ceremonies of the Day of Atonement conducted in the Temple during the period of the Second Jewish Commonwealth. Virtually the entire talmudic Tractate Yoma is devoted to a description and interpretation of these rites, and the *Avodah* section of the Yom Kippur liturgy is a reminiscent re-enactment of them. The destruction of the Temple, which brought about the suspension of the entire sacrificial system, was a catastrophic blow for the Jews of the first century. But with a resilience characteristic of a people so well acquainted with calamity, they recovered from this experience by shifting the emphasis from sacrifices to a service of liturgy. The people came to regard the liturgy as a substitute for the sacrificial system. Thus Rabbi Joshua told his contemporaries that the daily *Amidah* and the prayers recited on Sabbaths, New Moons, and Festivals were instituted as substitutes for the sacrifices (Ber. 26b). Tradition has it that Abraham himself was assured that the reading of the laws of the prescribed sacrifices would, for his descendants in exile, be considered a valid substitute for sacrifices (Meg. 31b). Rabbi Elazar ventured to say that the prayers were even more efficacious than sacrifices (Ber. 32b). Indeed, the inclusion in each *Musaf Amidah* of the biblical verses relating to the prescribed sacrifices of the particular day was prompted by a comforting

[*] For the discussion of the Service of Taking Out the Torah, see pp. 123-28.

234 Justice and Mercy

interpretation of a verse in Hosea, to the effect that with
prayer we fulfill our obligation for the offering of bullocks (Hos. 14:3).

On Yom Kippur the Torah was read in the synagogue
adjoining the Temple of the High Priest himself, and
the chapter he read was the very chapter now under discussion. The Mishnah offers this description of the reading from the Scroll by the High Priest:

> Then the High Priest came in to read. If he was minded to read
> in the linen garments he would do so, otherwise he would read
> in his own white vestments. The sexton would take the scroll
> and give it to the chief of the synagogue, who in turn gave it
> to the High Priest's assistant (*segan*) and the latter would then
> give it to the High Priest. The High Priest would then receive
> it standing and read it standing (Mishnah Yoma 7:1).

The fact that the people heard the High Priest read
the detailed description of the sacrificial order from the
scroll was in marked contrast to the prevailing practice
of other ancient religions, which withheld their sacred
lore from the view or knowledge of the masses. Elias
Bickerman* tells that the sacred books of other religions, from the *Avesta* to the *Commentaru* of the
Roman pontifices, were ritual texts used or recited by
priests only. In Babylonian religious texts, and even in
mathematical texts, the instruction is often repeated that
they are not to be shown to the uninitiated. In Judaism
there were no such "secrets." The contrast is visually ex-
hibited in the difference between a painting found on
the wall of the excavated Mithra temple at Dura and one
of the paintings on a wall of the Dura synagogue. In the
pagan temple, the sacred scroll is held by the Magian
dressed in sacral attire, in his closed hand—since no layman was entitled to view the holy text. In the Dura synagogue, the painting depicts a layman, a man without
sacerdotal attire, reading the open scroll. The reading of
the scroll is central in the synagogue service, and this is
symbolic of the translation into life of the verse: "Moses
commanded us a law [Torah], an inheritance of the congregation of Jacob" (Deut. 33:4).

* Elias J. Bickerman, "The Septuagint As a Translation," *PAAJR*,
XXVIII (1959), p. 39.

Outline of the Torah reading (Leviticus 16)

The consideration of the *Avodah* service in our liturgy will later afford us an opportunity to discuss its symbolism and its contemporary meaning, since the *Avodah* is based on the rites described in the portion read on Yom Kippur from the first scroll. The sequence of the Yom Kippur rites as described in the Torah reading is as follows: As the Divine Presence manifests itself in a cloud over the covering of the ark within the veiled curtain, the High Priest is enjoined not to enter this most sacred area casually (vs.2). He is to enter the Holy of Holies in the manner herewith described: He must take a bullock for his sin-offering and a ram for a burnt offering, and put on white linen garments after bathing in water (vss.3-4). He is to procure from the people two he-goats for their sin-offerings and a ram for a burnt offering (vs.5). With his own sin-offering (cf. vs.3), the High Priest is to make atonement "for himself and for his house" (cf. vs.11) (vs.6). Meanwhile the two he-goats (cf. vs.5) are designated by lot, one "for the Lord" and one "for Azazel" (vss.7-8). The he-goat that has been designated "for the Lord" (cf. vs.15) is to be offered as a sin-offering (vs.9). The other is to be led away alive "to Azazel" into the desert (cf. vs.21) (vs.10).

At this point there begins the actual description of the Atonement rites: After making expiation on it for "himself and his house," the High Priest slaughters the bullock which is to be his sin-offering (vs. 11). He takes from the altar a panful of live coals and two handfuls of thinly beaten incense and brings these behind the veil (*parokhet*) (vs.12). As he puts the incense on the live coals, the cloud of the incense hides from view the cover (*kapporet*) which is on the ark (thus shielding his eyes from the Divine Presence) (vs.13). He sprinkles some of the blood of his bullock seven times over and above the cover (vs.14). After slaughtering the people's he-goat, he brings some of its blood into the most holy area and sprinkles it in the same manner (vs.15). Thus he purges the sanctuary of any pollution caused to the Holy of Holies by virtue of the transgressions and sins of the people. Similar sprinkling is applied to the (outer) Tent of Meeting. It, too, must be cleansed, since it was with the

people in "the midst of their uncleanness" and therefore
needs purification (vs.16). No person is to be in the Tabernacle while the High Priest performs the service of
expiation (vs.17). After he has made expiation for himself
and his household, and for the whole community of Israel
(vs.17), he goes to the altar, and with the blood of the two
sin-offerings, makes expiation for the altar, cleansing it
"from the uncleanness of the children of Israel" (vss.
18-19). Now he brings over the live he-goat (to enact a
symbolic banishment of the sins of the people) (vs.20).
Laying his hands on it, Aaron confesses the sins of the
people and "thus places the sins" on the head of the he-
goat, which is then taken to the wilderness by a designated
person (vs.21). The sins are carried away to the desert
where the he-goat is released in the wilderness (vs.22).
Aaron now leaves the altar, enters the Tabernacle, and
removes the linen garments which he had worn in the
Holy of Holies (vs.23). After bathing, he puts on his
(regular) priestly vestments, goes to the altar, and there
offers his own burnt offering, as well as that of the people.
He burns the fat of the sin-offerings upon the altar (vss.
24-25). Instructions are given for the return to the camp
of the man who had led away the he-goat to Azazel (vs.26).
Since the blood of the two sin-offerings had been brought
into the Holy of Holies, these sacrifices must be burned
outside the camp. Instructions are given for the return
to the camp of the person attending to this burning (vss.
27-28). Yom Kippur is ordained for all time as an annual
day of fasting and of cessation from labor (vss.29-34).

"The Goat . . . for Azazel"

The goat on which the lot fell for Azazel shall be set alive before
the Lord, to make atonement over him, to send him away for
Azazel into the wilderness (Lev. 16:10).

The Talmud makes veiled reference to two primeval
demons, Usa and Azazel (Yoma 67b), the latter of whom
refused to repent of his ways and continued to seduce
human beings into doing evil. It is to them that the
Midrash refers when it tells of the two sacrifices offered
on Yom Kippur: one for God and one for Azazel. The
latter was assumed to be offered in expiation for the sins
of Usa and Azazel (*Yalkut Shimoni, Shemot,* 572). It is

surmised that reference here is being made to a legend about Azazel, a primitive deity. Azazel is said to be the pagan idol Saturn, known among the Arabs, Persians, and Babylonians as Kaiwan. Reference to him is made by Amos, when he says, "So shall ye take up Siccuth [Sukkut] your king and Chiun [Kaiwan] your images, the star of your god, which ye made to yourselves" (Amos 5:26). Many ancient peoples dedicated their New Year Day festivities to a god who was believed to rule over time, and traditionally, the first month of the year bore his name. Among the pre-Israelite Hebrews, the god of time was *Sabtai*, from whose name the word *shabbat* is said to be derived, and the designation *shabbat shabbaton* (Sabbath of Sabbaths) for Yom Kippur (Lev. 16:31). Because this god was the source of evil in the world, the ancients would endeavor to propitiate him and ward him off with sacrifices. This is said to be the earliest origin of "the sacrifice to Azazel." But in the Torah, all traces of these idolatrous origins are obliterated, and both sacrifices are "placed before God." The sending away of the he-goat to Azazel may even have been a means of dramatizing the Torah's admonition: "And they shall no more sacrifice their sacrifices unto the satyrs, after whom they go astray" (Lev. 17:7).*

Rabbinic comments on the text (Leviticus, Chapter 16)

"after the death of the two sons of Aaron" (16:1)

On the eighth day, the climactic day of his consecration as High Priest, and of the consecration of his sons as priests, Aaron was bereaved by the sudden death of two of his sons. What tragic truth we find in the words of Kohelet: "I said of laughter: It is mad" (Eccl. 2:2). When joy is mingled with sorrow, how can one rejoice? The story is told of one of the dignitaries of Kabul who was marrying off his son. He prepared an elaborate feast for the scholars. During the meal he said to his son, "Go to the upper chamber and bring down a barrel of wine." In the upper chamber a serpent bit the bridegroom and he died. Wondering why his son tarried, the father went up to the chamber and found him lying dead. He waited till all the guests had finished their meal and as they were to begin

* Yehezkel Kaufmann, *The Religion of Israel,* translated and abridged by Moshe Greenberg. (Chicago: The University of Chicago Press, 1960), p. 114.

the *Birkat Hamazon* (Grace after meals), he said to them, "My friends, you have come here to recite the prescribed bridegroom's blessings over my son, but instead you must now pronounce over him the mourner's prayers! You have come to bring my son under the canopy, but you are now to carry him to his grave!" At the funeral, Rabbi Zakkai of Kabul concluded his eulogy with the verse, "I said of laughter: it is mad" (*Pesikta de Rav Kahana,* ed. Buber, p. 152).

"Herewith shall Aaron come into the holy place" [*the sanctuary*] (16:3)

"There are six things which the Lord hateth, yea, seven which are an abomination unto Him: haughty eyes, a lying tongue, and hands that shed innocent blood. A heart that deviseth wicked thoughts, feet that are swift in running to do evil, a false witness that breatheth out lies, and he that soweth discord among brethren" (Prov. 6:16-19). On this passage the Midrash makes these observations:

"With wise advice [planning] (*tahbulot*) thou shalt make thy war" (Prov. 24:6). If you have committed bundles (*habilot*) of sins, counteract them by observing corresponding bundles of *Mitzvot:* "Haughty eyes" should be counteracted by putting the *tefillin* between the eyes; "a lying tongue," by teaching God's word to our children; "hands that shed innocent blood," by placing *tefillin* on the hand; "a heart that devises wicked plans" must be counteracted by the rite of circumcision; "a false witness that breatheth out lies" must be counteracted by: "Ye are My witnesses, saith the Lord" (Isa. 43:12), and "he that soweth discord among brethren," by: "Seek peace, and pursue it" (Ps. 34:15). Wherever you go, be like a pilot, ever on the lookout for a meritorious deed (*Lev. Rabbah,* 21:5).

Aaron entered the Holy of Holies with "herewith" (*bezot*), with bundles of meritorious deeds to his credit, for *zot* is associated in Scripture with the observance of Sabbath, with the merit of Jerusalem . . . and with the merit of the love for Israel (*Lev. Rabbah,* 21:6).

The two passages just cited suggest that the battle for the supremacy of the more noble over the base within ourselves can be won only by the conscious acquisition of habits which help us sublimate our "evil" drives and impulses. The "evil impulse" is by no means incurably evil, for it can be directed to worth-while purposes. "Were it not for the evil impulse," say the Rabbis, "no man would build a house, take to himself a wife, beget children or engage in trade" (*Gen. Rabbah,* 9:7).

The Hebrew word for "herewith" בזאת has a numerical value of 410.* This symbolizes the assurance given to Aaron that he would live 410 years. Did he really live 410 years? Does not the Torah tell us that he died at the age of 110? The answer is that the first Temple stood 410 years, and during that entire period Aaron's descendants served faithfully as High Priests and wore the sacred vestments of their ancestors. Hence it is as if he himself had lived through the entire period when his descendants were carrying on the same sacred service (*Pesikta de Rav Kahana,* ed. Buber p. 159).

"The holy linen tunic" (16:4)

At all other times the High Priest wore golden garments, but on Yom Kippur he wore plain linen garments. Rabbi Levi said that this was done to counteract the temptation of pride which a resplendent attire tends to induce. Rabbi Simon said in the name of Rabbi Joshua that the golden garments would have been an accusing reminder of the sin of the golden calf. An accuser cannot serve as a defender (*Pesikta de Rav Kahana,* p. 159).

As the High Priest appeared before God in a simple linen tunic, stripped of all ornamentation, so we need to divest ourselves of all vainglorious pretensions, if we are to experience the purifying effect of the Atonement Day. The *Haftarah* for Yom Kippur expresses this thought in these words:

> For thus saith the High and Lofty One
>   That inhabiteth eternity, whose name is Holy:
> I dwell in the high and holy place,
>   With him also that is of a contrite and humble spirit.
>
> Isaiah 57:15

"for Azazel" (16:8)

Azazel was originally an angel. Once on the Day of Atonement, he accused Israel before God, saying: "Why dost Thou show mercy on them when they provoke Thee? Thou shouldst rather destroy them." God replied to Azazel that if he would be among men he too would sin. Azazel then requested to be

* As in other cultures, every Hebrew letter has a numerical value, *aleph* being one, *bet* two, and so forth.

tested. When, with God's permission, he descended to earth, he was overcome by the evil inclination and fell victim to Naamah, a very beautiful woman. God therefore decreed that since Azazel had sinned and could not return to heaven, he should remain in the desert until the end of time. Thus, he would silence the accusers, for they, seeing his fate, would be warned to be silent. For this reason, the scapegoat is sent to the desert on the Day of Atonement; for the desert is the dwelling place of Azazel, and those who accuse and would mercilessly condemn sinners are warned and silenced (*Imre Noam, Ahare Mot* [end]).

After completion of the reading of the First Scroll, the Second Scroll is then read. Its portion, Numbers 29:7-11, describes the additional communal sacrifices of Yom Kippur. For our discussion of the reading from the Second Scroll, see pp. 133-34.

THE *HAFTARAH:* YOM KIPPUR MORNING

Isaiah 57:14—58:16

This *Haftarah* was designated for Yom Kippur because its main theme is the true purpose of fasting. The prophet declares that by its disobedience, Israel has aroused God's punitive anger. But those whom suffering has humbled will experience the blessedness of God's indwelling spirit, for though His Name is high and exalted and He inhabits eternity, He dwells with the person of lowly and contrite spirit. Healing and wholeness are the reward of those who forsake their evil ways. They will find God because they seek His nearness. But those who persist in their wickedness are like troubled waters, "For it cannot rest and its waters cast up mire and dirt."

At this point, there follows an utterance of singular eloquence and power. It appears to have been spoken by the prophet during a convocation on a fast day when people performed all the proper rituals without the emotions of self-purgation. The prophet warns against reliance on surface religion, the religion of form without feeling. He declares that a fast of self-mortification and prayer is of no avail if it does not induce a just and merciful treatment of our fellow men. A true fast must result in the breaking of the shackles of evil, in the releasing of the oppressed, and in a deeper concern for those in need of help. Only by the removal of evil, and by resolute, righteous conduct, can prayer and fasting bring illumination and hope. The concluding verses of the *Haftarah* are an appeal for a fuller and truer observance of the Sabbath. It is to be a day of delight and of hallowed living, when the ordinary gives way to the extraordinary, and the mundane to the momentous.

Comments on the text (Isaiah 57:14—58:16)

"And he will say, cast ye up, cast ye up" (57:14)

A voice will proclaim that all obstacles must be removed from the road to Zion, which is to be traversed by a repentant and contrite people.

"the iniquity of his covetousness" (57:17)

The sufferings of the people are regarded as consequential chastisements for their greed and their ruthless pursuit of gain.

"I have seen his ways, and will heal him" (57:18)

Man's repentance, followed by God's forgiveness, brings healing to the sinner. Often the Bible speaks of sin as the causes of illness, and of repentance as its cure. The psalmist says, "Bless the Lord O my soul . . . who forgiveth all thine iniquity, who healeth all thy diseases" (Ps. 103:2-3). So deeply is there embedded in the Hebrew language itself the conviction that sin brings suffering in its wake that the word *"avon"* means punishment as well as sin; in rabbinic Hebrew, *puranut* means suffering, but it also means punishment. The Book of Job negates and defies the belief that suffering is always in retribution for sinfulness. But that moral corruption leads to suffering is often validated by experience. Often we are punished not so much *for* our sins as *by* our sins.

"Peace, peace to him that is far off and to him that is near" (57:19)

God, the Creator of speech, will Himself welcome with a greeting of friendship and healing those who return to

Him in sincere repentance. The repentant sinner, who had wandered far away from Him, will be healed even as God's solicitude is extended to the virtuous who are close to Him.

"There is no peace . . . for the wicked" (57:21)

Those who persist in their evil ways will have no surcease from their restlessness.

"Yet they seek Me daily" (58:2)

Ehrlich suggests that this should be rendered as follows: "Raise your voice like a trumpet to speak about the fact that they seek me daily." The prophet is to speak with trumpetlike clarity to a people which is meticulous in its piety, but lax in its morality.

"And exact all your labors" (58:3)

You oppress all who work for you and do not give them fair compensation for their labor.

"So as to make your voice to be heard on high" (58:4)

Ehrlich suggests this interpretation: "Do not fast and make such loud noises (with your insincere wailing) as to reach the very heavens."

Rabbinic comments on the text

"I dwell . . . with him also that is of a contrite and humble spirit" (57:15)

Whenever Scripture makes reference to God's power, it also assures us of His gentleness (Meg. 31a). God who is high and exalted, dwells with the humble man. The Divine Presence descends on the humble man, but it departs when an arrogant man appears, for the Holy One blessed is He, declares, "He and I cannot abide together. For this reason, arrogance, like idolatry, is to be abhorred. God rejected the high mountains and chose lowly Mt. Sinai as the site and scene of the giving of the Torah, even as He chose a mere bush for His appearance to Moses (Sotah 5a).

"Peace, peace, to him that is far off and to him that is near" (57:19)

Rabbi Abbahu said: "From the prior mention of him who has been far off, we learn that a truly repentant sinner is considered even more worthy than a perfectly righteous man." Rabbi Johanan, however, expressed the opinion that in saying this, the prophet was only encouraging repentant sinners. As for him who has never sinned, his reward has not been revealed to anyone (Ber. 34b).

"Declare unto my people their transgressions and to the house of Jacob their sins" (58:1)

Said Rabbi Judah b. Ilai: "My people" refers to the learned whose unwitting sins are regarded as presumptuous ones (since higher standards of moral conduct are to be expected of them); while "the house of Jacob" refers to the untutored, whose deliberate transgressions are regarded as unwitting ones (since their evil conduct stems from ignorance) (B. M. 33b).

"deal thy bread to the hungry" (58:7)

When a person begs for food and clothing, there must be no investigation of his need, for we are told here: "When thou seest the naked . . . cover him" (B. B. 9a).

"And thy righteousness shall go before thee" (58:8)

When a man performs a *mitzvah* in this life, it precedes him and heralds his arrival in the world to come (Sotah 6b).

At the time of a man's departure from this world, there are three who plead for him: his family, his money, and his good deeds. The first two are not deemed to be valid credentials of personal worth, but a man's good deeds precede him and prepare for him the road to eternity (*Pirke de Rav Eliezer,* 34) .

"draw out thy soul to the hungry" (58:10)

If you really have nothing to give to a needy person, at least extend to him your words of comfort and encouragement by saying: "My soul goes out for you that I cannot help you." If you do at least this, your light will shine in the dark (*Lev. Rabbah,* 34:15).

"Thou shalt raise up the foundations of many generations" (58:12)

Rabbi Tarfon gave Rabbi Akiba six hundred silver talents and said to him: "Go and invest it for us in a field, so that we may both have an assured income and then devote ourselves to the study of Torah." Rabbi Akiba took the money and distributed it among the Scripture teachers, among the Mishnah teachers, and among students of Torah. Sometime later, Rabbi Tarfon asked him, "Have you already bought the field that I talked to you about?" He answered: "Yes." "Can you show it to me?" "Yes," he [Akiba] said. He toured the community with him and pointed out the Scripture teachers, Mishnah teachers, and the students. "Does a man make investments for no return?" asked Rabbi Tarfon. "Where is the profit from this investment?" Akiba said, "It is with David, for he said 'He who distributes of his means among the needy, his righteousness endures forever' " (*Lev. Rabbah*, 34:16).

A choice saying of the scholars at the Yavneh Academy was this: "I am God's creature and my fellow man is also God's creature. My work is in the city and his work is in the fields. I rise early to attend to my work (i.e., study of Torah). He too rises early to attend to his work. As he is not arrogant and proud about his work, so must I not be arrogant and proud about my work. Lest you be inclined to say that I am more pious than he, we are taught in the Mishnah that it is all the same whether a man offers much or little, if only he directs his mind towards God" (Ber. 17a).

"repairer of the breach" (58:12)

To him who is mindful of the needy, God says: "This breach was mine to repair and now you have done my work" (Ber. 17a).

A judge who renders a just decision is considered as if he were a partner of God in the work of Creation (Shab. 10a).

"Pursuing thy business on My holy day" (58:13)

Once, on a Sabbath, a pious man walked in his vineyard to ascertain its requirements. He saw a breach in the fence and determined to repair it. After the Sabbath, he decided never to mend that fence, saying: "I shall never mend that fence, inasmuch as this mundane thought entered my mind on the holy Sabbath" (Shab. 150b).

YIZKOR

Memorial prayers for the departed were originally recited only on Yom Kippur, and they were later introduced into the service on the concluding days of the Festivals as well. According to Rabbi Moses Isserles (d. 1572) the reason for the *Yizkor* prayers is that the departed are also in need of forgiveness (*Orah Hayyim*, 621:6).

The concept that the dead are in need of atonement is already found in a rabbinic interpretation of the verse: "Forgive, O Lord, Thy people Israel whom Thou hast redeemed" (Deut. 21:8), these being the opening words of the prayer offered by the elders of a city in whose territory the body of a murdered person had been found, and where the murderer could not be apprehended. On this, the comment is offered: *Forgive Thy people* refers to the living; *whom Thou has redeemed* [from Egypt] refers to the dead. We are thus taught that the dead are also in need of atonement (*Sifre Shofetim,* 209).

It is, however, generally assumed that the practice of reciting *Yizkor* prayers arose after the period of the First Crusade (1096 C.E.), when there was established the practice of reading the names of the martyred dead from the record books of the community. The *Yizkor* prayers are recited only in congregations which follow the Ashkenazic rite, and not in those that follow the Sephardic rite.

On the Service for Returning the Torah to the Ark, see our discussion on pp. 155-58.

STRUCTURE OF THE *MUSAF AMIDAH:* YOM KIPPUR

This *Amidah* consists of these seven blessings:

1. *Avot*
2. *Gevurot*
3. *Kedushat Hashem*
4. *Kedushat Hayom:* This section includes the following:
   a) The three *Uvekhen* prayers
   b) *Attah Behartanu*
   c) *Umipne Hataenu* and the biblical verses relating to the sacrifices offered in antiquity on this day.
   d) *Mehal Laavonotenu* ("Pardon our sins")
5. *Avodah*
6. *Modim*
7. *Berakhah,* which is followed by the *Viddui*

READER'S REPETITION OF THE
MUSAF AMIDAH: YOM KIPPUR •

אֱנוֹשׁ אֵיךְ יִצְדַּק פְּנֵי יוֹצְרוֹ

How can mortal man be considered blameless before his Maker?

This alphabetical acrostic, with some stanzas missing in current editions, is a summons to repentance. It reminds us that no man's deeds are wholly free from self-centeredness and that our hidden motives are no secret to God, whose searching eye pierces even the thick darkness. Before the throne of His judgment neither wealth nor pomp nor power can justify a life marred by selfishness. When a man devotes himself to the joyful performance of deeds of kindness and justice, he wins God's favor and is deserving of God's protection. But no man need despair. God eagerly awaits the sinner's repentance, so that he too may fulfill the purpose for which man was placed on earth: to render praise to God and to live a life dedicated to Him.

Comments on the text

Most extant versions of the High Holy Day Prayer Book incorporate only a few parts of the extensive Kalirian *kerovah* for the *Musaf* service. The entire *kerovah* is known as *Shoshan Emek Uyyamah* ("The frightened Lily of the Valley"), and this *piyyut* by an unknown author is the third of the eleven parts found in the German and Polish rites (cf. Israel Davidson, *Thesaurus*, Vol. III, pp. 439-41).

אֶת לַחַשִׁי עֲנֵה נָא

O answer now my silent supplication

This is the congregational response for the fifth section of the Kalirian *kerovah, Shoshan Emek Uyyamah* ("The

---

• The prayer of the *Sheliah Tzibbur: Hinneni Heani,* which precedes the silent *Amidah,* is discussed on p. 161. As well, discussion of the opening blessings of the Reader's Repetition of the *Amidah,* frightened Lily of the Valley"). The text: *adon lekol amekha* is to be corrected to: *ezon lekol amekha* ("Hearken to the voice of Thy people") as in the Roumanian rite. This response contains acrostics of Kalir's name אלעזר

את לחשי ענה נא זעקי רצה נא

אזון לקול עמך זכר רחמיך

אַל תִּזְכָּר לָנוּ עֲוֹנוֹתֵינוּ

Remember not unto us our iniquities

Israel is in exile. The Temple is in ruins. This is so because we are as yet undeserving of the fulfillment of the covenant God made with our patriarchs. We plead that we may be restored to Zion and thus become again a blessing among the nations, as we rally them to the service of God.

אִמְרוּ לֵאלֹהִים מַה נּוֹרָא מַעֲשֶׂיךָ

Say ye to God, How wondrous are Thy works!

Like its counterpart in the *Shaharit* service (p. 229), this poem is ascribed to Meshullam ben Kalonymos of Rome. It extols God as the Creator of the universe and as its unchallenged Ruler, whose splendor is hymned in the skies, the seat of His majesty. But far from being aloof, He is bound to His people by an indissoluble covenant and will forgive and restore to its former glory the people which proclaims His unity.

Attention is here centered on the theme of God's covenant with Israel, as the author interpolates into the fourth line of each stanza the first half of a verse from the psalm of thanksgiving offered on the day when the ark of the covenant was first brought to Jerusalem (I Chron. 16:8-36). The implication is that as the covenant with Abraham was fulfilled centuries later in the life of his descendants, when Jerusalem was established as

which precedes the first *piyyut* of the *Musaf* service, is found on pp. 85-89.

the seat and symbol of God's presence among His people, so Israel bases its hope for future redemption on the eternity of the covenant.

Only half of this double alphabetical acrostic is found in current editions of the Prayer Book. The full text is found in the Italian *Mahzor*.

וּבְכֵן גְּדוֹלִים מַעֲשֵׂי אֱלֹהֵינוּ

And thus great is the work of our God

This *piyyut* by Rabbi Meshullam ben Kalonymos also has its counterpart in the *Shaharit Amidah* (p. 230). It celebrates the supremacy of God in heaven and on earth. God observes all that transpires in the limitless expanse of the universe. Yet, though His splendor is in the high heavens, He is attentive to the praises and prayers offered by the multitudes on the earth, which is His footstool. God's power is here contrasted with man's vaunted glory, which is ephemeral and undependable. Man's designs are deceit, his habitation is beset by corruption, his breath is fleeting. He should therefore not strut about in arrogant self-sufficiency. He should strive to fulfill his humanity by serving as the terrestrial servant of the Most High.

Comments on the text

Maaseh Enosh ("The work of man"), which contrasts man's impotence with God's omnipotence, appears in the Italian *Mahzor* as a full alphabetical acrostic alternating with *Maaseh Elohenu* ("The work of our God"). In both acrostics each stanza is concluded with a familiar and appropriate biblical phrase.

After Maaseh Elohenu, *the service continues with the following prayers, the discussion of which is to be found as here indicated:* Unetanneh Tokef, *pp. 166-71;* Kedushah, *pp. 171-72;* Vekhol Maaminim, *p. 173;* Uvekhen, *pp. 100-103;* Veyetayu, *p. 174;* Attah Behartanu, *p. 175;* Umipene Hataenu, *pp. 175-78;* Alenu, *pp. 180-81;* Heyeh Im Pifiyot, *p. 179;* Ohilah Lael, *p. 179.*

The *Avodah*

אַמִּיץ כֹּחַ

Thou art powerful beyond comparison (the *Avodah*)

This section comprises a vivid recollection of an unfor-
gotten past. Our version of the *Avodah*, one of several
that are extant, is based on the Mishnah's description of
the prayer and pageantry conducted in the Temple on
Yom Kippur. The *Avodah* begins with the biblical account, richly embroidered with midrashic symbolism, of
how God transformed chaos into Creation. It tells how He
illumined the earth with the light of His garment, prepared it for the miracle of life, and populated its waters
and dry lands with a multitude and variety of creatures.
In the garden of Eden, stately trees bearing luscious fruits
awaited the pleasure of the Creator's important guest.
That guest was man, molded by God out of inert clay
and fashioned in His image. Placed in the garden to
enjoy its earthly delights, man was free from care. His
helpmate, formed out of his own flesh and bone, was to
share with him a life of uninterrupted bliss. But man,
created with a free will, yielded to temptation and disobeyed God's command.

Then there began the recurring tension between man's
willfullness and God's Will. As one generation followed
another, man's corruption increased. Even the punitive
flood in the time of Noah did not result in a new and
chastened humanity. Free to frustrate as well as to fulfill
the moral law, man continued to worship idols. He
even conceived the erection of the tower of Babel,
which would reach to the very heavens and thus challenge the supremacy of the Creator.

A fragmented and scattered humanity, confused by a
chaos of tongues and ridden with fears and hatreds,
needed to be shown the way to righteous living. It
needed to be taught that it is man's paramount duty to
cultivate the godlike capacities of his nature. The task
of serving as exemplars of God's moral law was assigned
to Abraham and to the people that was to issue from
him. A covenant made with Abraham, and reaffirmed
with Isaac and Jacob, defined the role of Israel in the
world: To alert all Creation to man's enormous power

for evil, as well as to his vast capacity for good. Through the Torah entrusted in its care, this people was to make God's will known to mankind. From this people came forth the tribe of Levi, and from that tribe issued the High Priests, who led in the prescribed annual rites for man's purification from sin.

Man needs to take frequent inventory of his conduct. His unconfessed and unforgiven sins threaten to distort and obliterate the divine image within him. The degenerating effects of pride, greed, and stubbornness, the cleansing power of repentance, and the possibility of "returning" to God—whom by sin we banish from our lives—these were the teachings symbolized and enacted in the rites of Yom Kippur.

The *Avodah* continues with a meticulous description, in free verse, of the Yom Kippur service as held in Temple times and as recorded in Tractate Yoma. We follow the prescribed procedure of the High Priest's baths and ablutions, of the selection of the various offerings, of the High Priest's entering the Holy of Holies amidst a cloud of incense to cleanse it of the sins of the people, and of his symbolic purification of the outer altar and the rest of the sanctuary. We read of the sending away of the scapegoat, bearing the sins of the people, to a desert region.

With dramatic impact, the *Avodah* leads up to each of the three confessions uttered by the High Priest. In the first he confessed his own sins, in the second the sins of his fellow priests, and in the third, he offered confession for the entire household of Israel. In each confession he pronounced the Ineffable Name, and in each instance, the priests and the people standing in the Temple court, as they heard the awesome Name, prostrated themselves as they responded: *Barukh shem kevod malkhuto leolam vaed* ("Blessed is the glorious name of His Kingship for ever and ever"). We read the poet's description of the joy that possessed the whole of Israel at the conclusion of the atonement rites. The clouds in the heavens were jubilant, and the rain-soaked fields of the earth rejoiced. Man and nature joined in praise of God, from whom cleansing had come to a people which had been washed of its impurities.

The *Avodah* ends with the High Priest's prayer for

the welfare of the people, a prayer which he uttered as he emerged from the Holy of Holies and before proceeding to his home for a celebration at which his intimate friends joined him.

Comments on the text

The author of this particular *Avodah* is the poet Meshullam ben Kalonymos, who lived in Italy in the tenth century. The rhymeless multiple alphabetical acrostic concludes with an acrostic of the author's name.

The prayer of the High Priest, as found in our *Mahzor*, is an alphabetical acrostic based on various versions found in the Talmud.

In one version of the High Priest's prayer, there are reflected two important concepts of Judaism: the love of Torah, and the love of man as expressed in the practice of charity. This version is as follows:

May it be Thy will O Lord our God and God of our fathers, that no exile shall be decreed for us today or during the coming year. Should, however, exile be decreed for us, may it be an exile to a place of Torah. May it be Thy will O Lord our God and God of our fathers, that no monetary loss be decreed for us during the coming year. Should, however, a monetary loss be decreed for us, may our loss be a "charity loss" (TP Yoma 42c).

The Hebrew expression here for "charity loss" is *hissaron shel mitzvot,* literally, "a loss by reason of *Mitzvot*." This is an example of the frequent use of the word *mitzvah* to denote charity.[*] The High Priest prayed that should it be decreed that the people suffer a financial loss, that decree should be fulfilled through the "financial loss" one sustains in giving charity. The same idea is expressed in this passage:

Just as the financial gains of a person are determined at the beginning of each year (i.e., Rosh Hashanah) so are his financial losses then decreed. If he is meritorious, he suffers "losses" by spending some of his wealth in giving bread to the poor; if he is not meritorious, he suffers losses in being compelled to pay the extortionist levies of the Roman government officials (B. B. 10a).

[*] For other examples of this usage, see *Debarim Rabbah*, ed. Lieberman, p. 71; also, Lieberman, *Greek in Jewish Palestine*, p. 36.

"May their homes not become their tombs"

The houses in the Sharon region in the northeast of Palestine frequently collapsed because of their sandy foundations, and also because their bricks, made of the region's sandy soil, had to be replaced twice in each seven-year period (TP Sotah 23a). Hence the High Priest concluded his blessing with a prayer for the people of Sharon, that their homes should not become their tombs.

The concluding *piyyutim* of the *Avodah*

The *Avodah* continues with *Emet Mah Nehedar,* an alphabetical acrostic, only part of which is found in extant editions, describing the radiant appearance of the High Priest. This is followed by *Kol Elah Biheyot Hahekhal* ("All this happened when the Temple stood"), which is the introduction to a complete alphabetical acrostic, omitted in some current editions, in recollection of the splendors of the ancient Temple. This, in turn, leads into an alphabetical acrostic introduced by *Ashre Ayyin* ("Happy was the eye that beheld all this"), which describes the fortunate lot of those who were privileged to witness the Temple when it was still in existence.

The *Avodah* ends with the prayer that the recollection of the ancient rites and our observance of the privations of Yom Kippur may serve to make the day effective for us as "a day for creating true friendship with our fellow men, a day ending all envy and rancor, a day of full forgiveness for our transgressions."

Mordecai M. Kaplan's Observations on the *Avodah*

The key verse in the Torah's enactment of the Yom Kippur rites is:

And he shall make atonement for the holy place, because of the uncleannesses of the children of Israel, and because of their transgressions, even all their sins; and so shall he do for the tent of meeting, that dwelleth with them in the midst of their uncleannesses (Lev. 16:16).

This verse inspires Mordecai M. Kaplan's* reinterpretation of the symbolism of the *Avodah*. He observes that to be qualified for God's presence, the Sanctuary itself had

* Mordecai M. Kaplan, *The Meaning of God in Modern Jewish Religion* (New York: Bloch Publishing Co. Inc., 1937), pp. 166 ff.

to be cleansed of the impurities caused by the sins of the people. The Sanctuary can be for us symbolic of the home, the synagogue, the school, and other fundamental institutions of the community. These institutions, which should be the abode of God, are often contaminated by people's avarice and self-seeking. Even religious institutions need to be cleansed of corruption. Have not monumental cruelties been practiced in the name of religion? Every one of us should therefore recognize his individual responsibility for the contamination of our social and religious institutions. Institutions are not buildings. They consist of people. Only a wholehearted recognition of our individual responsibility for the quality of our communal institutions will serve to restore the Divine Presence into our community life. Without such an atonement, our "sanctuaries" are in danger of becoming sacrilegious substitutes for authentic religion.

THE *SELIHOT*: *MUSAF* OF YOM KIPPUR

אֵלֶּה אֶזְכְּרָה

These do I remember

The Martyrology

We are taken back eighteen centuries, on an expedition of painful historical reminiscence, as we recall with horrendous realism and vividness the heroic and zealous martyrdom of ten men of learning and piety. Their courage, their saintliness, and their unconditional love of God typified Jewish martyrs through the ages, who died *Al Kiddush Hashem*—for the sanctification of God's Name. In reading of these Ten Martyrs, we of this generation cannot help but direct our thoughts to the six millions of our people, who were slaughtered during World War II. We think of the way they were abandoned to their fate by powerful governments which, aware of the savage plans of the enemy, violated the moral imperative: "Neither shall thou stand idly by the blood of thy neighbor" (Lev. 19:16). They were thus also guilty, for the silent spectator to a crime is as guilty as is the agent of the deed.

But the mood of this martyrology is not one of protest or even indignation. Composed soon after the first Crusade (1096 C.E.), this dirge is a reflection of the utter bewilderment of that generation in their inability to understand the meaning of the martyred death of countless innocents. *Eleh Ezkerah* is an expression of their pathetic search for an explanation of the absence of supernatural intervention in behalf of those done to death by the crusading mobs that invaded the Rhineland. The eleven hundred Jews of Mayence, for instance, who sought refuge in their synagogue, were helpless against the frenzied mobs who would accept only their renunciation of Judaism as a ransom for their lives and the lives of their children. Solomon ben Shimshon, the chief chronicler of this tragedy, tells us how the beleagured Jews expressed in these words their readiness to die for the unity of God's Name: "Happy are we if we fulfill His wish and happy is he who is slain and slaughtered for the unity of His Name. Such a one will be prepared to enter the world to come, to sit in the company of the righteous men, Rabbi Akiba and his fellow sages, who are the foundations of the world and who have died for His Name." After this self-exhortation, they enacted "eleven hundred *Akedot* in Mayence in a single day." What took place was a mass suicide of the entire community, with fathers taking the lives of their children, and husbands slaying their wives. Such unspeakable tragedies had to be explained without impugning the purity and the nobility of the character of the victims, and without accusing God of abandoning His hunted and tormented people. For this reason, they resorted to the tradition of the Ten Martyrs, which told of a previous instance of martyrs suffering death, not for their own sins, but in expiation of the sins of previous generations. The *Midrash of the Ten Martyrs* ascribes the suffering and death of the martyrs to the need for expiating the unrequited sin of the ten brothers of Joseph who had sold him into slavery. The brothers had never paid the penalty prescribed in the Torah: "He that stealeth a man and selleth him . . . shall surely be put to death" (Exod. 21:16). Therefore their guilt had to be expiated by the death of ten illustrious men, known for their piety and learning. Rabbi Joshua ben Levi ventured to say that these ten martyrs of the Hadrianic persecution (135 C.E.) were "seized" for their forebears' sin in selling Joseph. To this strange observation, Rabbi Abun adds the comment that in every generation ten saintly lives are martyred for the same sin, because the sin is still unrequited (*Midrash Hagadol on Gen.*, ed. Margulies, p. 637). In the Midrash *Eleh Ezkerah,* on which this martyrology is based, the still more fantastic statement is made that in heaven there is an altar on which the lives of ten saints are offered every day in expiation for the sin of the ten brothers of Joseph!

These strange concepts collide with the teaching that a person is answerable only for his own conduct, a teaching formulated by Ezekiel in repudiation of the idea of collective and inherited guilt. "The soul that sinneth, it shall die; the son shall not bear the iniquity of his father with him, neither shall the father bear the iniquity of his son with him; the righteousness of the righteous shall be upon him and the wickedness of the wicked shall be upon him" (Ezek. 18:20).

Yet the Rabbis did not hesitate to avow that in times of widespread moral corruption, the righteous are "seized" for the guilt of their generation, and that where there are no righteous men in a particular generation, the children are "seized" for its guilt (Shab. 33b). This conception of the corporate moral solidarity and responsibility of the community is also reflected in an idea, found in the Apocrypha, that martyrs suffer because of the sinfulness of the entire people. Thus Eleazar, when tortured by his heathen persecutors, prays:

Thou knowest O God, that though I might have saved myself, I die in fiery torment for the sake of Thee. Be merciful to Thy people and let my punishment be sufficient for their sake. Make my blood an expiation for them and take my life as a ransom for theirs (IV Macc. 6:27-28).

Eleazar gives voice here to the rabbinic conception that the death of the righteous is an expiation for the sins of all Israel (TP Yoma 38b).

Experience had led our sages to the sad conclusion that sin is contagious in its punitive consequences, that it exacts its toll of innocent victims through the generations. History confirms that seeds of war, hatred, and suspicion, planted in one age, yield their fruits decades later. Moreover, when we fail to live by the ideals for which the martyrs have died, we increase the extent of our own guilt, for then we act as if they had died in vain. Israel Friedlaender, shortly before his own martyr's death while on a mission of mercy in Poland, wrote as follows:

While our hearts are pained for the martyrs who have died, we must not let that for which they died languish and disappear.

In recognition of the spiritual solidarity which binds us to bygone ages, we conclude the Martyrology with the words:

> We have sinned O our God,
> Forgive us O our Creator.

Comments on the text

This poem, an alphabetical acrostic, ends with an acrostic of the name יהודה חזק The story it relates is taken from *Midrash Eleh Ezkerah* (Jellinek, *Bet Hamidrash* II, 64; VI, 19), but an earlier source is *Abot de Rav Nathan*, chapter 38.

The Book of Jubilees records a tradition that Joseph was sold by his brothers on the tenth of Tishre (Jubilees 34:12). This is not, however, the reason for the inclusion of this martyrology in the *Selihot* of Yom Kippur. Similar poems based on the story of the Ten Martyrs are found in rituals of the other Jewish fast days. Thus the well-known dirge *Arze Halevanon*, which is included among the dirges read on the Fast of the Ninth of Ab, also deals with the martyrdom of the ten saints during Hadrian's reign.

In an extensive monograph on the Ten Martyrs, Louis Finkelstein analyzes the historical and literary background of the drama of the Ten Martyrs. "This drama," he says, "was worthy of having Plato as its chronicler and should have taken its place in the history of human civilization with the martyrdom of Socrates himself." After discussing the talmudic account of the death of Akiba, the last of the ten martyrs, Dr. Finkelstein concludes his study with this observation:

By a coincidence, the day of Akiba's death was marked by the birth of the scholar who, more than any other person, was destined to perpetuate his work and memory, Rabbi Judah, the son of Simeon, the Patriarch. After some time the government of Antonius Pius, Hadrian's successor, relaxed the persecution and the Jews were permitted to resume their schools, their studies, and the observance of their laws. The disciples, whom Judah ben Baba [one of the martyrs] ordained, assembled to recall and formulate the traditions they had received from their masters, among whom Akiba had been preeminent. By the time Judah, son of Simeon, had reached his maturity, these disciples had completed their task; and he, using the materials they had gathered, compiled the Mishnah which is the fundamental code of Rabbinic Law, and the core of the Talmud. For seventeen centuries this work has been studied wherever Jews have lived; and to this day its rules are obeyed with utmost scrupulousness by millions of men and women throughout the world. What is less well recognized is the fact that many more millions, who have never heard of either Judah or his masters, are enjoying freedom, happiness, and contentment largely by virtue of the forces which emanated from these Rabbinic academies, and that what Justin said of his fellow Christian martyrs applied with equal force to the contemporary Jews—"they died for the sake of the God of Truth, whose altar was sanctified with their blood." •

For the discussion of the concluding section of the Seliḥot *prayers and the* Viddui, *which follow here, see* *pages 213-21. On the concluding sections of the Reader's Repetition of the* Amidah, *see pages 112-21. On the concluding prayer of the* Musaf, Hayom Teamtzenu, *see p. 187.*

ORDER OF THE *MINHAH* SERVICE: YOM KIPPUR

On all Sabbaths and Holidays, including Rosh Hashanah, the *Minhah* service begins with *Ashre* (Ps. 145) and

• Louis Finkelstein, "The Ten Martyrs," in *Essays and Studies in Memory of Linda R. Miller,* ed. Israel Davidson (New York, 1938), pp. 31, 48-49.

Uva Letziyyon (see p. 62). These are, however, not recited at the *Minhah* service of Yom Kippur, nor is *Avinu
Malkenu* recited after the *Amidah* of this *Minhah* service,
even if Yom Kippur falls on a weekday. The reason for
these omissions is that they are recited in the *Neilah*
service which follows the *Minhah*. For the same reason,
neither at the *Minhah* service nor at *Neilah* service is
Alenu recited, since the worship continues with the *Maariv* service which is concluded with the *Alenu*.

The *Minhah* service for Yom Kippur consists therefore
of the following parts:

1. Service for Taking the Torah out of the Ark
2. Reading of the Torah
3. Service for Returning the Torah to the Ark
4. Reading of the *Haftarah*
5. *Hatzi Kaddish*
6. *Amidah* (consisting of the same sections as the *Amidah* for *Maariv* (see p. 199) and including *Selihot,* and
the *Viddui* prayers, *Ashamnu* and *Al Het* (pp. 215-21)

READING OF THE TORAH:
MINHAH SERVICE OF YOM KIPPUR

Leviticus, Chapter 18

Israel is warned to shun the licentious ways of the heathen peoples with whom they were to come into contact.
Through their practices, the Canaanites polluted the
land, and the land "vomited them out" because of those
abominations. The same fate would meet the people of
Israel, should they be guilty of such behavior. The consequences for civilization of the eradication of such perver-
sions of human dignity are described by W. F. Albright
in these words: "Thus the Canaanites, with their or-
giastic nature-worship, their cult of fertility in the form
of serpent symbols and sensuous nudity, and their gross
mythology were replaced by Israel with its nomadic sim-
plicity and purity of life, its lofty monotheism and its
severe code of ethics." •

• W. F. Albright, *From the Stone Age to Christianity* (Baltimore:
The Johns Hopkins Press, 1940), p. 214.

Through the ages Judaism has been eminently success-
ful in protecting and preserving the sanctity of the family relationship. Many were the false accusations made
against the Jews by their traducers, the most preposterous
of these fabrications being the assertion that Jews use
human blood in their religious rites. But even their most
implacable enemies did not impugn the high standard of
Jewish family life. In his *New Atlantis,* an imaginary
description of a perfect community, Francis Bacon tells
us that only one Jew lived in that utopian community.
When asked what he was doing there, the Jew replied
that he and his family had come there at the invitation
of the inhabitants who wanted him to teach them the
standards of family unity and devotion for which Jews
were known.

Comments on the text

An interesting theory has been proposed to relate some
of the rites associated with Yom Kippur to their pre-
Israelite origins.* In primitive times, the advent of a new
year would be celebrated with riotous hilarity and with
unrestrained abandon and licentiousness. A vestige of an
earlier stage is said to be reflected in the rabbinic observation that he who eats and drinks on the day before Yom
Kippur is considered as if he had fasted two days (Yoma
8b). This advice is said to be an atavism of a time when
the New Year celebration was marked by indulgence in
food and drink. Another atavism is said to be found in
the statement of Rabban Simon ben Gamliel to the effect
that in Temple days there were no more joyful festivals
than the Fifteenth of Ab and Yom Kippur: "On these
days the maidens of Jerusalem would go outdoors in bor-
rowed white dresses, thus avoiding any embarrassment to
maidens who had no dresses of their own. . . . The maidens would dance in the vineyards and say, 'Young man
lift your eyes and see what type of maiden you should
choose for yourself. Have no regard for beauty but rather
for family background. Grace is deceitful, beauty is vain,
only a woman that fears the Lord deserves praise'"
(Mishnah Taan. 4:8).

In accordance with this theory, the practice of reading

* Abraham Epstein, *Mikadmoniyot Hayehudim* (Jerusalem, 1957),
pp. 9-10.

from the Torah, on Yom Kippur, of the biblical laws of
forbidden marriages is said to have been a means of coun-
teracting primitive excesses.

It is, however, more likely that because this chapter
lists the various degrees of forbidden marriages, it may
have been the intention that this portion serve to warn
young men against the selection of their brides from
among prohibited categories.

THE *HAFTARAH: MINHAH* SERVICE
OF YOM KIPPUR

The Book of Jonah

What was the procedure on the last seven days of fasting [in a
prolonged period of public fasting due to unrelieved drought]?
The ark was carried out into the main square of the town and
wood ashes were strewn on it and on the head of the *Nasi* [the
leader of the community], as well as on the head of the *Av Bet
Din* [head of the court]. Everyone present took some of the
ashes and put them on his head. The eldest among them addressed them in words of admonition: "Brethren! Of the people
of Nineveh it is not said: 'And God saw their sackcloth and
their fasting,' but, 'And God saw their works, that they turned
from their evil way' (Jonah 3:10); and in the prophetic books
it is said, 'And rend your heart, and not your garments, and
turn unto the Lord your God, for He is gracious and compassionate, long-suffering, and abundant in mercy' " (Joel 2:13)
(Mishnah Taan. 2:1).

This passage associates the Book of Jonah with public
fast days, and accounts for its selection as the *Haftarah*
for *Minhah* of Yom Kippur. Coming in the afternoon,
the reading of this book can serve us as a reminder not
to underestimate the moral intent of the fast in our concentration upon the observance of its prescribed rites.

The central message of the Book of Jonah is that God's
forgiveness is readily extended to those who abandon
their evil ways. Jonah fled to Tarshish because he knew
that God, who is gracious and compassionate, long-suffering and abundant in mercy, would reverse the evil decree
against the people of Nineveh once they repented, and

that his warnings and admonitory threats would therefore never come to pass.

Yehezkel Kaufmann's analysis and interpretation

Our understanding of the message and purport of the Book of Jonah has been greatly enhanced by Yehezkel Kaufmann, in his monumental work on biblical religion.* Bible critics, prompted by a desire to prove that the Old Testament is for the main part devoid of universalism, had pictured the Book of Jonah as one of the later books included in the biblical canon. Its aim was said to serve as a protest against the chauvinism and isolationism of the earlier books, which depict God as being concerned solely with Israel. According to this theory, Jonah fled because he had yet to learn that the God of Israel cares also for the heathen people of Nineveh. Against this theory Yehezkel Kaufmann marshals formidable internal evidence. He avows that the Book of Jonah was written long before the Babylonian exile, even before Nineveh became the capital of the Assyrian Empire. According to Kaufmann, the book is an allegorical tale about Jonah ben Amitai, a disciple of Elisha (II Kings 14:25), aiming to convey the teaching that God forgives repentant sinners. Here are some considerations which prompt Kaufmann to date the book fully five centuries earlier than the date assigned to it by Bible critics:

1. In the book, Nineveh is not identified as the capital of Assyria, which in 722 destroyed the Northern Kingdom of Israel. Therefore its composition must have predated that event.

2. The book reflects an early biblical conception of God's relationship to heathen peoples. During the earlier biblical stage, it was not considered sinful for heathen peoples to worship idols. The worship of images was originally deemed to have been forbidden only to Israel and to no other people. This is clear from this passage in Deuteronomy:

[Beware] lest ye deal corruptly, and make you a graven image . . . the likeness of any beast that is on the earth . . . any winged fowl . . . of any thing that creepeth on the ground . . . any fish that is in the water; and lest thou lift up thine

* Yehezkel Kaufmann, *The Religion of Israel*, pp. 282-286.

eyes unto heaven, and when thou seest the sun and the moon
and the stars . . . be drawn away and worship them . . . [it is
these] which the Lord thy God hath allotted unto all the peoples under the whole heaven (Deut. 4:16-19).

God demanded of heathen nations obedience to the moral
law, but not the abolition of idolatry. In the prophecies
of Amos (1:3; 2:3) and in those of Isaiah (14:23), the heathen nations are severely condemned for their disregard
of the treaties they made with other nations, but not for
their idolatries. Only in the later prophetic period does
there appear the messianic hope that all nations would
repudiate their idols and worship solely the God of Israel.

3. The Book of Jonah reflects the attitudes of the earlier period: Jonah does not preach against the idolatry of
the Ninevites. The members of the crew on Jonah's ship
pray to their various idols (1:3). The people of Nineveh
are spared, not because they give up idol worship, but because they forsake their evil ways (3:19). The sacrifices
offered to God by the ship's crew (1:16), and the prayer
and fasting of the Ninevites (3:7) are not in repudiation
of their idols, but in grateful recognition of the power of
the God in whose name Jonah had warned them.

Kaufmann proceeds to indicate that what is new and
distinctive in the Book of Jonah is its emphasis on true
repentance as a means of inspiring God's compassion and
of securing His forgiveness. The accent is placed here not
on a ritual of expiation and atonement, but on tangible
acts whereby the sinner removes the evil of his ways. In
fact, no ritual of expiation is even mentioned.

Why Jonah fled from God

The Book of Jonah has a derivative theme, suggested by
some of the rabbinic explanations of Jonah's flight, which
we will discuss later. Jonah preferred to serve as God's
instrument of castigation, as His "angry man," rather
than as the messenger of His mercy and forgiveness. When
a prophet has predicted the disastrous consequences that
later befall the sinner, he has demonstrated and proved
his prophetic foresight, and his prestige is enhanced. But
when he prevents a disaster by persuading a sinful people
to repent, he is at a disadvantage, since what one has pre-
vented from happening is not subject to evidential con-

firmation. To state that a catastrophe might have happened is not as tangible an evidence of one's prophetic power as when a threatened catastrophe actually takes place. Jonah betrayed this attitude when he said after Nineveh was spared: "Was not this my saying when I was yet in my own country? Therefore I fled beforehand unto Tarshish; for I knew that Thou art a gracious God . . . " (4:2).

Quite different was the reaction of Jeremiah under similar circumstances. Jeremiah had been ordered to write on a scroll all the warnings he had uttered "against Israel, against Judah, and against all the nations." The purpose of this is communicated to Jeremiah in these words: "It may be that the house of Judah will hear all the evil which I purpose to do unto them; that they may return every man from his evil way, and I may forgive their iniquity and their sin" (Jer. 36:3).

When the scroll was brought to the King of Judah and his officers and read before him, the king tore it to pieces and burned it (Jer. 36:23). Jeremiah was depressed in fear that, as his warning was being defied, his doleful predictions were to come true. But this was not the case with Jonah. He was disappointed when his warning *did* move the people to repentance and their punishment was averted. He had yet to learn that the people of Nineveh, a city "with more than sixscore thousand persons that cannot discern between their right hand and their left hand, and also much cattle" (Jonah 4:9-11), were the objects of God's concern and abundant love.

Comments on the text

"Tarshish" (1:3)

Said to be in the southwest of Spain. Its mention in this story implies that Jonah was fleeing from God to "the very end of the world." Jonah was to learn later that one cannot flee from God. The psalmist expresses the thought of God's omnipresence in these words:

Whither shall I go from Thy spirit? Or whither shall I flee from Thy presence? If I ascend up into heaven, Thou art there; if I make my bed in the netherworld, behold, Thou art there. If I take the wings of the morning, and dwell in the uttermost parts of the sea, even there would Thy hand lead me, and Thy right hand would hold me (Ps. 139:7-11).

"Joppa" [Jaffa] (1:3)

One of the oldest cities mentioned in the Bible and still known by the same name.

"What meanest thou that thou sleepest?" (1:6)

There is an unconcealed irony in this question. In an hour of danger to so many people of diverse beliefs, Jonah, the messenger of God, is asleep. We are reminded of Isaiah's complaint: "Who is blind, but My servant? Or deaf as My messenger that I sent?" (Isa. 42:19) A heathen shipmaster admonishes the prophet to pray, being apparently more aware of the power and efficacy of prayer than the fleeing prophet.

"What is thine occupation?" (1:8)

Ehrlich suggests that this question really means: "What is the purpose of your journey?"

"I fear the Lord, the God of heaven" (1:9)

Wording the reply in this manner, Jonah may have hinted that he was fleeing from God (Ehrlich). But the sentence really means: I worship the Lord God of heaven.

"What is this that thou hast done?" (1:10)

They are not really asking for details. They are shocked at the thought that their life is imperiled by the presence of a sinful person.

"A great fish" (2:1)

Nowhere are we specifically told that the fish was a whale.

"I called out of mine affliction" (2:3)

The "prayer" is a thanksgiving psalm interpolated here as expressing the confident anticipation of Jonah's deliverance.

"That which I have vowed I will pay" (2:10)

Vows were usually made conditional on deliverance from great peril. This verse is not a boastful announcement of readiness to pay, but a grateful way of saying that one has been delivered from danger (Ehrlich).

"A day's journey" (3:4)

This means that when Jonah was in the very center of the city he started to preach to the people.

"Yet forty days, and Nineveh shall be overthrown" (3:4)

This means that in a short time, a calamity, such as an earthquake, would befall Nineveh. This "sermon" of one sentence had the immediate effect of causing the people to repent, since the consequences of their sinful conduct were acknowledged to be imminent. It requires a greater degree of moral wisdom to foresee and fear the ultimate consequences of corrupt moral conduct. To know that "though the arc of the universe is long yet it bends towards justice" means to avert calamities that might beset future generations. The short-visioned people who taunted the prophet Ezekiel, saying that his predictions would not come to pass during their lifetime, were addressed by him in these words: "And the word of the Lord came unto me, saying 'Son of man, what is that proverb that ye have in the land of Israel, saying: The days are prolonged, and every vision faileth? . . . Thus saith the Lord God: There shall none of My words be delayed any more, but the word which I shall speak shall be performed, saith the Lord God' " (Ezek. 12:21-22; 28).

"And the people of Nineveh believed" (3:5)

Of their own accord, the people of Nineveh undertook to be reconciled with God. They did not wait for orders from their king. It was they who inspired the king to join them in their contrition. A ruler reflects the "public opinion" of his subjects for good or for evil.

"From the violence that is in their hands" (3:8)

Their repentance consisted in their ceasing from the oppression of others.

"Thou hast had pity on the gourd" (4:10)

The argumentation in this verse and in the concluding verse may be paraphrased as follows: "That gourd was not of your growing and it required no toil on your part.

It is a plant that springs in a night and that must whither in a night. Yet you deemed it to be so valuable as to wish to have it spared. Shall then not I (the Creator) consider the vast population of Nineveh and its large number of cattle to be valuable enough to be the objects of My compassion?"

Rabbinic comments on the text*

Why Jonah was afraid to go to Nineveh

Jonah was a disciple of Elisha. He had previously been charged with the task of proclaiming the destruction of Jerusalem. The people repented and, as his prediction was not fulfilled, he became known as a "false prophet." He was therefore afraid to go to Nineveh because, he said, "I am certain that the heathen will repent and as the punishment with which I shall threaten them will not be executed, I shall become known as a false prophet also among the heathen."

"Jonah rose up to flee unto Tarshish" (1:3)

Jonah fled to the sea, where he thought God's rule and glory did not prevail. There was no vessel at Jaffa, but God caused a storm to arise and it carried a vessel back to Jaffa after it had already been at a distance of two days' journey from the harbor. Jonah was so anxious to get away that, contrary to the then current practice of paying for passage on arrival at one's destination, he paid in advance and even paid the whole amount for the entire vessel.

The merciful heathen crew of the vessel

People of all the seventy nations were among the passengers on this ship, each with his idol. They wanted Jonah to pray to his God who had performed for Israel the deliverance at the Red Sea.

The heathen passengers were loath to throw Jonah into the sea, though the lot had decided against him.

---

* The main sources of the following rabbinic comments are *Pirke R. Eliezer*, Chap. 10, and *Midrash Jonah*. The translations are adapted here from Louis Ginzberg, *The Legends of the Jews* (Philadelphia: The Jewish Publication Society of America, 1954), IV, 246-53.

They first tried to save the vessel by throwing the cargo overboard. When this did not avail, they tried to return to shore, but they could not. Then they placed Jonah by the side of the vessel and said, "O Lord of the universe, do not consider that we have shed innocent blood, for we do not know the case of this man. It is he himself who bids us throw him into the sea." Even then, they only lowered him into the water up to his knees. The storm ceased. Then they pulled him back in the vessel, and the storm raged again in great fury. They then lowered him up to his navel, and a second time up to his neck. Each time the storm subsided, but raged again when they pulled him into the vessel. Finally, they had to abandon him to his fate and then the waters grew calm.

"The Lord prepared a great fish" (2:1)

The fish which swallowed Jonah was created during the six days of Creation solely for this purpose, for *vayeman* "and he sent" (2:1) means that the fish was *memunneh* "prepared" from the time of Creation.

"A great fish" (2:1)

The interior of this fish was as large as a vast synagogue. The eyes of the fish, like two windows, admitted the light from the outside. Besides, there was a diamond inside the fish which shone as brilliantly as the midday sun. The fish even took Jonah on a tour of all the world's waterways and showed him mysterious and wonderful places. When the fish showed Jonah the solid rock which was in the deep below the holy Temple at Jerusalem, Jonah prayed for his release. His prayer was answered only when he vowed to make of this fish a repast for the righteous at the time of the redemption of Israel. Then the fish spewed him out. This miracle inspired the ship's crew to abandon idolatry, to return to Jaffa, and become true proselytes in Jerusalem.

How Nineveh repented

Jonah went directly to Nineveh and immediately proclaimed the destruction of the city. His voice boomed forth so loudly that it was heard over the vast area of the city. People and king alike fasted and repented. The mercy of God was invoked when the people held up their infants toward heaven and tearfully prayed, "For the sake of these innocent babes, answer our prayers."

But they did not limit their repentance to fasting and praying. By their deeds they proved that they were true penitents. A man who had stolen another's property willingly tore down his house in order to restore a stolen brick to its rightful owner. People confessed before courts of justice crimes known to none besides themselves, and stood ready to submit to any prescribed punishment, be it even death.

One case can serve to illustrate the complete moral transformation of the people of Nineveh. A man found a treasure in a parcel of land he had bought from his neighbor. Both buyer and seller disclaimed ownership of the treasure. The buyer claimed that he had bought land, not a treasure. The seller claimed that the buyer of the land was entitled to all that it contained. They were both overjoyed when the judge succeeded in finding out the name of the man who had hidden the treasure there and in locating his heirs, for they then could return the treasure to its legitimate owners.

Jonah extols God's mercy

Jonah's sufferings were intense when the gourd withered as it was smitten by the sun, since he was attacked by swarms of insects. He wished for death to release him from his misery. From this experience of Jonah, we derive the teaching that he who fails to pray for the welfare of his fellow man is punished with great suffering. When God remonstrated with him, Jonah realized that it was wrong of him to desire that God should deal harshly with the Ninevites, just for the sake of his reputation as a prophet. He therefore prayed for forgiveness. In this prayer he said, "I did not realize that Thy power manifests itself in Thine abundant mercy. Thou hast indeed done right in showing mercy to Nineveh, tearing up the evil decree intended for them. Thou art indeed a merciful God, forgiving sin and pardoning transgressions. Do Thou O God, guide the world according to Thy goodness."

READER'S REPETITION OF THE
MINHAH AMIDAH: YOM KIPPUR

אֵיתָן הִכִּיר אֱמוּנָתֶךָ

The patriarch who proclaimed his trust in Thee

Comments on the text

This *kerovah* by Rabbi Elijah ben Mordecai (11th century) invokes the merit of the patriarchs as it supplicates God that He heed the prayers of their descendants. The following midrashic and talmudic passages are among the sources on which the author drew:

"Ethan believed in Thee [in an age of unbelief]"

Scripture informs us that Solomon was wiser than Ethan the Ezrahite (I Kings 5:11). Ethan is none other than Abraham (B. B. 15a).

"In an age of unbelief"

Abraham began to worship God when he was three years old (Ned. 32a).

Once, when Abraham was very young, he observed the sun as it was setting. As he saw the stars appearing he said: "These are the gods." But when dawn came, and the stars could no longer be seen, he said: "I will not worship the stars, for they are no gods." Then the sun rose and he said, "This is my god and him will I extol." Toward evening the sun set again and he saw the moon. He thought he would pay homage to her, but then the moon was obscured. He then exclaimed "This too is no god! There is One who set them all in motion" (Jellinek, *Bet Ha-Midrash, I, 26*).

Abraham's discovery of God is comparable to the case of a wayfarer who saw a castle in flames. Said the stranger, "Is it possible that this castle has no master?" Whereupon the owner of the castle looked out at him and said, "I am the owner of this castle." Similarly, when Abraham saw the world in conflagration he said: "Is it possible that this world has no master?" Whereupon the Holy One blessed is He, looked out and said "I am the Master of the universe and I have made the conflagration because of the vice and corruption of mankind" (*Gen. Rabbah,* 39:1).

In ancient times when mankind was corrupt, there were five great leaders: Noah, Shem, Eber, Asshur, and Abraham. Noah was not concerned with spreading faith in God; he planted his vineyard and engaged in material pleasures. Shem and Eber went into hiding. Asshur said: "I cannot live among such sinners," and he left the country. The only one who remained constant was Abraham. He said: "I will never forsake God." Therefore, God did not forsake him (*Midrash Tehillim,* ed. Buber, p. 484).

For our discussion of the opening blessings of the Reader's Repetition of the Amidah *which precedes this* piyyut, *see pp. 85-91.*

מָאֲהָב וְיָחִיד לְאִמּוֹ

The only beloved son of his mother was a willing sacrifice

Comments on the text

In the second part of his *kerovah* the author expands on the merits of Isaac. As Abraham is associated with the first blessing *Magen Avraham,* so is Isaac associated with the blessing *Mehayyeh Hametim,* since, according to tradition, he was virtually revived from the dead when he was spared at the *Akedah.* Among the midrashic allusions in the second half of the *kerovah* are the following:

"Isaac surrendered himself for a sacrifice"

Abraham and Isaac walked together in the same spirit—one with the intent to sacrifice his son at the command of God, and the other with the intent of being sacrificed (*Gen. Rabbah,* 56:3).

When told by his father that, by divine command, he was to be offered as a sacrifice, Isaac said: "There is nothing in my heart to make me deviate from the word God has spoken to you . . . I am joyful and cheerful in this matter and I say: 'Blessed is the Lord who has this day chosen me as a burnt offering before Him' " (*Midrash Yashar Vayyera,* 45b).

"The seraphim from their heights cried aloud"

When Abraham was about to apply the knife to his son, the angels burst into weeping and said, "The highways lie waste, the wayfarer has ceased. Where is Abraham's reward for his hospitality to strangers? What of Thy covenant with Abraham that by Isaac his seed shall be established?" (*Gen. Rabbah, 56:5*).

"May the remembrance of him be before Thee now, as the ashes of offering in Thy Temple court"

On fast days the ark is placed in the public square of the city and ashes are strewn on the ark (Mishnah Taan. 2:1). The purpose of the ashes was symbolic. They were to be regarded as if Isaac had actually been sacrificed and as if his ashes had actually been strewn on the altar (TP Taan. 65a).

The Minhah *service continues with the following prayers, the discussion of which is to be found as here indicated:* Mehayyeh Hametim, *p. 92;* Kedushah, *pp. 171ff.;* Uvekhen, *pp. 100ff.;* Yaaleh Veyavo, *p. 108;* El Melekh Yoshev *and* Selihot, *pp. 213ff.;* Viddui, *pp. 219ff.;* Kedushat Hayom, *p. 199; Concluding Blessings of the* Amidah, *pp. 12ff.*

THE *NEILAH* SERVICE

Introduction

The realism with which the liturgy recalls the rites held in the Temple on Yom Kippur is again demonstrated by the name of the fourth service: *Neilah. Neilah* (closing) preserves the name of the concluding ceremony in the Temple when, at the end of the day, before closing the gates of the Temple, the priests dismissed the people. The Mishnah refers to *Neilah* as *Neilat Shearim*—"The closing of the gates" (Mishnah Taan. 4:1). The Palestinian Talmud speaks of it as *Neilat Shaare Shamayim*, "The closing of the gates of heaven," rather than as *Neilat Shaare Hekhal*, "The closing of the gates of the Temple." This distinction is made because the usual time for the *Neilah* service on Yom Kippur is at sunset when "the gates of heaven close"—which is an hour later than the closing of the gates of the Temple. We are informed in the Palestinian Talmud that it was Rab's practice to ask that his cloak be fetched "when the sun is seen over the top of the trees" so that he might then begin to recite the *Neilah* prayers and prolong his prayers till "the closing of the gates of heaven" (TP Taan. 67c).

The image of the "closing gates" is the theme of a number of *piyyutim* in the *Neilah* liturgy. They allegorize the "gates of heaven" in the light of a homily by Rabbi Elazar, to the effect that, although the gates of prayer have been closed since the Temple was destroyed, the "gates of tears" (i.e., fervent prayer) are never closed (Ber. 32b). The most impressive of these "closing of the gates" hymns is *Petah Lanu Shaar:*

> Open for us the gate
> At the time of the gate's closing.
> The day is done,
> The sun is setting, soon to be gone,
> Let us enter Thy gates.

The *Neilah* service thus takes on the aspect of a final appeal that the twenty-four hour day of self-deprivation and prayer now coming to a close should have its atoning effect. At *Neilah* the fervor of worship is heightened. In many synagogues the ark is kept open and the congregation stands during the entire service. In the *Amidah* and in its repetition by the reader, only the *Ashamnu* is recited in the *Viddui*. Instead of *Al Het,* two new prayers are introduced: *Attah Noten Yad Laposheim* ("Thou stretchest out a helping hand to sinners") and *Attah Hivdaltah Enosh Merosh* ("Thou didst distinguish man from the beginning"). These prayers emphasize the eagerness of God to accept the prayer of the penitent sinner and to forgive him.

As in the previous *Amidah* prayers, the recitation of the confession is in accordance with the rule that *Viddui* be recited by the individual at the very end of the silent *Amidah* and by the entire congregation at the blessing of *Kedushat Hayom* during the Reader's Repetition of the *Amidah* (see page 220). In place of the prayer, "Inscribe us [*katvenu*] in the Book of Life," the corresponding prayer in the *Neilah* is: "Seal us [*hatmenu*] in the Book of Life."

After the recitation of *Avinu Malkenu,* the congregation recites the *Shema* once; *Barukh Shem* ("Blessed be His glorious Kingship for ever and ever"), three times;

and *Adonai Hu Haelohim* ("The Lord alone is God"), seven times.

The sounding of the *shofar* at the end of *Kol Nidre* was said by Rabbi Hai Gaon (11th century C.E.) to be reminiscent of the sounding of the jubilee trumpet in the Temple on the tenth of Tishre as ordained in this passage: "Then shalt thou make proclamation with the blast of the horn on the tenth day of the seventh month; in the day of atonement shall ye make proclamation with the horn throughout the land" (Lev. 25:9-10).

This explanation was called into question because the jubilee year was celebrated only once in fifty years, while the *shofar* was sounded every year at the conclusion of the Yom Kippur day. A *Tosefot* comment (Shab. 114b on *veammai, ad locum*), rejecting the jubilee year explanation, suggests that the purpose of the sounding of the *shofar* at the close of Yom Kippur is to inform the mothers that they may then begin to cook the meal for their children. Louis Ginzberg saw in this practice another instance of the tendency to retain on Yom Kippur vivid associations of the practices before the destruction of the Second Temple. As it was the practice in Temple times to sound the *shofar* at the close of every Yom Kippur as well as at the close of every Sabbath, this practice was continued on Yom Kippur even after the destruction of the Temple.•

ORDER OF THE *NEILAH* SERVICE

The *Neilah* service consists of the following parts:

I. *Ashre* and *Uva Letziyyon*, followed by *Hatzi Kaddish*.

II. The silent *Amidah*, consisting of the following seven blessings:

    1. *Avot*

    2. *Gevurot*

    3. *Kedushat Hashem*, in which are included the three *Uvekhen* prayers

• Louis Ginzberg, *A Commentary on the Palestinian Talmud*, II, 22.

4. *Kedushat Hayom,* including *Attah Behartanu* and *Yaaleh Veyavo,* and closing with "Pardon our iniquities on this Atonement Day."

5. *Avodah*

6. *Hodaah*

7. *Berakhah*

III. The *Viddui,* consisting of *Ashamnu* (p. 215), *Attah Noten Yad* and *Attah Hivdalta* (p. 278)

IV. *Netzor Leshoni Mera* ("Guard my tongue from evil") (p. 33)

READER'S REPETITION OF THE *NEILAH AMIDAH* •

אָב יְדָעֲךָ מִנֹּעַר

The patriarch acknowledged Thee from childhood

The alphabetical acrostic interpolated into this *Amidah* is by Rabbi Simon ben Isaac ben Abun of Mayence (11th century). The acrostic reaches only to the letter ל and ends with this acrostic of the author's name שמעון

שמע נא סלח נא עבור כי פנה יום
ונהללך נורא ואיום

Rabbinic sources

Like most interpolations into the first three blessings of the *Amidah,* the *piyyutim* elaborate the merits of Abraham, Isaac, and Jacob. They contain the following talmudic allusions:

• For discussion of the opening blessings of the *Amidah* which precede the first *piyyut,* see pp. 85-89.

"The patriarch acknowledged Thee from childhood"

Rabbi Levi said in the name of Rabbi Simon ben Levi: When Abraham was only three years old, he arrived at his belief in God (*Gen. Rabbah*, 61:1).

"Thou didst test him with ten trials"

Abraham our father was subjected to ten tests and he withstood all of them (Ab. 5:3).

By the merit of him who sat "in the heat of the day"

On the third day after his circumcision, when Abraham was suffering and in pain, the day was exceedingly hot, for God had caused the sun to come out with a blazing heat so that no wayfarer would venture out in the highways, and Abraham would not be disturbed by guests. But the absence of guests caused Abraham great vexation and he sent his servant Eliezer out to look for them. When Eliezer reported that his search was fruitless, Abraham, himself, in spite of his illness and the scorching heat, prepared to go forth on the highway and see whether he could not find some tired and famished wayfarer (B. M. 86b).

When God and the angels visited Abraham, he was sitting. He wanted to rise out of respect for the Divine Presence. But God said to him: "Remain seated. You are a prototype of your descendants. They too will have the Divine Presence standing by them when they sit in the synagogues and houses of study and recite *Shema* while they are seated" (*Gen. Rabbah*, 48:7).

When Abraham's guests would rise to thank him for his kindness, he would say: "You owe thanks not to me, but to the King of the universe of whose bounty you have partaken" (Sotah 10b).

The Holy One, blessed is He, brought Abraham from Babylon to the land of Israel. There Abraham built an inn, gave food to wayfarers and brought men beneath the wings of the Divine Presence (*Num. Rabbah*, 2:12).

טֶבַע זִיו תָּאֳרָה

The form of Jacob's beautiful countenance hath the Lord engraven on his glorious throne

Rabbinic sources

"Jacob's beautiful countenance"

The angels were assembled on high and saw Jacob's features engraven above the heavenly Throne. They came down, saw him asleep and mocked him saying: "Are you the same one whose image is engraved above?" (*Gen. Rabbah*, 68:12)

In his notes on *The Legends of the Jews*,[*] Louis Ginzberg points out that the idea that Jacob's countenance is engraved on the Throne of God is frequently mentioned in rabbinic literature. Jacob is taken as the prototype of the ideal man, and his countenance represents the human race at its best. This is clearly implied in a midrash pregnant with rich symbolism, which tells that from the very beginning of creation the angels praised God with the words "Blessed be the Lord, the God of Israel." They did not, however, know who Israel was. When Adam was created they asked: "Is this the man whose God we daily proclaim Thee to be?" God replied, "No, he is a thief; he partook of the forbidden fruit." When Noah was born they repeated this question and were told that it was not Noah, for "he is a drunkard." At the birth of Abraham they again addressed the question and were told that Abraham, being a proselyte, was not born into the faith. Isaac was ruled out because he loved Esau whom God had rejected. When Jacob was born and the angels asked the same question, God said, "Yes, he is the one" (*Tanhuma Kedoshim*, 2).

"When the faithful one [Jacob] saw how awe-inspiring was the place"

This is an allusion to these verses:

Jacob awaked out of his sleep, and he said: "Surely the Lord is in this place and I knew it not! . . . How full of awe is this place! This is none other than the house of God and this is the gate of heaven" (Gen. 28:16-17).

The service continues with the following prayers, the discussion of which can be found as here indicated: Kedushah, *p. 171;* Hamol Al Maasekha and Uvekhen, *pp. 100ff.;* Attah Behartanu, *p. 103;* Yaaleh Veyavo, *p. 108.*

[*] Louis Ginzberg, *Legends of the Jews, III,* 290-91.

THE *SELIHOT* OF THE
NEILAH SERVICE

With *Petah Lanu Shaar* ("Open for us the gate"), the *Selihot* prayers and *piyyutim* begin. The *El Melekh Yoshev* and the Thirteen Attributes are recited at the end of each *Selihot* section (see pp. 205ff.).

Among the *piyyutim* included here are:

1. *Petah Lanu Shaar* ("Open for us the gate"). A deeply moving twilight hour appeal. As the gate is about to close, we ask that it be opened wide, so that, cleansed of our sins, we may be reinstated in the divine favor.

2. *Umi Yaamod Het Im Tishmor* ("Who could live on, if Thou wouldst record our sins?"). This is a conflation of two *piyyutim* by two different authors. The first half was composed by Solomon ben Judah ha-Bavli (10th century), whose name שלמה הקטן is the acrostic 'formed by the first letters of the last two stanzas. The second half of the *piyyut,* beginning with *Merubim Tzorkhe Ammekha* ("Thy people's needs are large"), is by Rabbi Joseph ben Isaac of Orleans, France (12th century). The full text is a complete alphabetical acrostic concluding with an acrostic of the author's name יוסף בר יצחק In the first half the author takes his cue from the verse: "If Thou, Lord, shouldest mark iniquities, O Lord, who could stand? For with Thee there is forgiveness, that Thou mayest be feared [worshiped]" (Ps. 130:3-4). The psalmist asserts here that were God to hold man fully accountable for his sins, no one would deserve to survive. However, God needs to forgive man; otherwise, none would remain on earth to render Him homage were He to withhold His forgiveness.*

In the second half of the *piyyut,* the poet says that while our needs are many, our power of expression is limited, since we lack leaders of requisite piety and learning to plead our cause. The author, therefore, pleads that his prayer, inadequate as it may be, should find favor in God's eyes so that it might elicit the sealing of a heavenly decree of life and joy for His people.

* This interpretation was given to me orally by Professor H. L. Ginsberg, of The Jewish Theological Seminary of America.

3. *Zekhor Berit Avraham* ("Remember the covenant of Abraham"). This is an alphabetical acrostic by Rabbenu Gershom (11th century), who was called *Meor Hagolah* ("The Light of the Exile"). Only part of the full alphabetical acrostic is preserved in printed editions of the *Mahzor*.

4. *Enkat Mesaldekha* ("May the cry of those who praise Thee"). This and the succeeding stanzas are of the composite authorship of poets from Italy and France, who lived during the ninth, eleventh, and thirteenth centuries.

5. *Ezkerah Elohim* ("I remember, O God, and I am deeply vexed [troubled]"). The author, Rabbi Amittai ben Shefatiah, whose name אֲמִתַּי is the acrostic formed by the first letters of the four stanzas, lived in Italy in the beginning of the tenth century. Sorely depressed, he compares the devastated city of Jerusalem and its abandoned ruins with the cities of other lands and other peoples which had been rebuilt after being devastated. But as he invokes the Thirteen Attributes and the Merit of the Patriarchs, he is fortified by the belief that God will treat His people with tender mercy.

At this point the service continues with *Ki Anu Ammekha* and *Ashamnu* (see page 214). The *Viddui* for *Neilah* then continues with the two prayers which follow.

אַתָּה נוֹתֵן יָד לְפוֹשְׁעִים

Thou stretchest out Thy hand to transgressors. What is our life? What is our piety? What is our strength?

אַתָּה הִבְדַּלְתָּ אֱנוֹשׁ מֵרֹאשׁ

Thou hast distinguished man from the very beginning

Judaism is distinctive not only in what it teaches about God, but also in what it teaches about man. These two prayers, which in the *Neilah* service replace the *Al Het*, reflect Judaism's conception of God and of man's relation to Him. God is kind and compassionate, and not vindictive: "Thou stretchest out Thy hand to transgressors and

Thy right hand is stretched out to receive the repentant."

But with a realism as sobering as it is sublime, the prayer proceeds to state that the magnanimity of God's forgiveness is necessitated by man's creatureliness and moral fragility. Even men of renown and of power are woefully defective in spiritual constancy, moral courage, and wisdom:

What are we? What is our life?
What our piety? What our righteousness? What our help?
Are not all the mighty ones as naught before Thee?
Are not wise men as though without knowledge and men of
    understanding as though without discernment?

This derogation of man aims to humble, but not humiliate us. It is balanced by the next prayer: "Thou hast distinguished man from the beginning," which depicts man as God's most favored creation, singled out and set apart from other creatures.

Judaism's affirmation of man's uniqueness is to be contrasted with the debasing pessimism which would reduce the barrier between man and animal life to one of degree and not of kind. In such a view, man's actions are deemed to be conditioned by the "struggle for existence," and his moral values to be solely derived from biological, environmental, and historical factors.

In the face of this reduction of man to a helpless creature of impulse and circumstance, Judaism reaffirms its belief that man is "made in the image of God," and that every human being is of incalculable worth. Man's distinctiveness lies in the fact that he contemplates the universe with wonder. He is potentially greater than his own limited understanding of himself. His is the capacity to transcend himself and to reach out for the Reality behind reality and to establish *what ought to be* as the measuring scale of *what is*. He alone must come to terms with death which, of all creatures, he alone knows to be inescapable. An irresponsible, "scientific" determinism tends to focus man's attention on his animal heritage, as if directing him to look back to his lowly origin. Judaism also reminds man that he comes from a putrid drop (Ab. 3:1), but the purpose of this is not to equate him with other living things, but to remind him that his moral accountability is the differential that sets him apart from other creatures.

In effect, Judaism says to man: "Look back and ponder your creatureliness, and then look up and realize the divine image in which you are fashioned. By doing so, your life will be one of service as God's collaborator in the continuing process of transforming chaos into creation." These are the considerations that will enable us to recite with conviction the words of the second prayer:

Thou hast distinguished man from the beginning . . . and filled him with the desire to seek Thy Presence.

Comments on the text

The two prayers are composites of various prayers of confession mentioned in the Talmud (Yoma 87b). The part beginning with "What are we? What is our life?" is said to have been added to the confessional by Samuel (Babylonia, third century). This, together with Rabbi Johanan's introduction, "Master of the universe, it is not because of our virtues that we address our plea to Thee but because of Thine abundant mercies" (Yoma 87b), is incorporated into the preliminary service of the daily prayers.

The closing words of *Attah Hivdalta* ("Thou didst distinguish man") consist of this biblical passage: "Have I any pleasure at all that the wicked should die? saith the Lord God; and not rather that he should return from his ways, and live?" (Ezek. 18:23). The Hebrew for "that anyone die" is *bemot hamet,* literally: "That the dead should die." A similar phrase in the Torah, "By two witnesses, shall a man be executed (*yummat hamet*)" (literally: "Shall the dead be executed"), occasions the comment that while the wicked are considered to be dead even when they are alive, the virtuous are considered to be alive even after their death (Ber. 18b).

As already noted, the *Viddui* precedes the *Kedushat Hayom* in the reader's repetition of the *Amidah*. As during each *Amidah* on Yom Kippur, the *Kedushat Hayom* closes with the words: "Blessed art Thou O Lord our King who pardonest and foregivest our iniquities and the iniquities of the house of Israel, who makest our trespasses to pass away year by year, Thou King over all the earth, who sanctifiest [the Sabbath], Israel and the Day of Atonement."

The *Neilah* service continues with the *Kedushat Hayom* ("Pardon our iniquities on this Atonement Day") and the concluding blessings of the *Amidah: Avodah, Hodaah* and *Berakhah.* These are in turn followed by *Avinu Malkenu.*

שְׁמַע יִשְׂרָאֵל

Hear O Israel

בָּרוּךְ שֵׁם כְּבוֹד

Blessed be the name of His glorious Kingdom [Kingship] forever and ever

ה' הוּא הָאֱלֹהִים

The Lord, He is God

As has been said earlier, the fast of Yom Kippur is climaxed by the recitation of: *Shema Yisrael* once, *Barukh Shem Kevod* three times, and *Adonai Hu Haelohim* ("The Lord, He is God") seven times.

The declaration "The Lord, He is God" is associated with a profoundly stirring incident described in the First Book of Kings (Chapter 18). Under the influence of Jezebel, wife of the Israelitish king Ahab, the cult of Baal had been introduced into the land. Elijah denounced the people's vacillation between the worship of Baal and that of the God of Israel. At Mt. Carmel he summoned the people to cease "halting between two opinions" and to choose between God and Baal. Impressed by a spectacular demonstration of the power of God and of the impotence of Baal, the people "fell on their faces and they said, 'The Lord, He is God; the Lord, He is God' " (I Kings 18:39).

Fierce objection to the worship of alien gods is the burden of Moses' admonitions to his people, recorded in the Book of Deuteronomy. The God of Israel, he taught, is a God who demands from His people exclusive and undivided loyalty, for on this basis He established His covenant with them. Should they revert to the worship of alien gods, severe punishments would be their recompense (Deut. 29:15-23). Similar warnings were re-iterated by Joshua in his farewell message shortly before his death. Addressing the people whom he had sum-moned to Shechem, Joshua began with a review of their early history from patriarchal times until the Exodus. He recalled the long pilgrimage through the wilderness and the manner in which they received divine help in the conquest of Canaan. He expressed concern lest the people revert to the idolatrous practices of prepatriar-chal times and to the cultic practices they might have learned from the Egyptians. He admonished them as follows: "Now therefore fear the Lord, and serve Him in sincerity and in truth; and put away the gods which your fathers served beyond the River [Euphrates], and in Egypt, and serve ye the Lord. And if it seem evil unto you to serve the Lord, choose you this day whom ye will serve . . . " (Josh. 24:14-15).

To a man, the people expressed their determination to serve only God, who had redeemed them from slavery. "Therefore we also [like our forebears] will serve the Lord, for He is our God. But Joshua needed an even more unequivocal avowal of fealty. He warned them of the divine wrath that would descend on them should they lapse into idol worship: Joshua said unto the peo-ple, "Ye cannot serve the Lord; for He is a holy God; He is a jealous God; He will not forgive your transgres-sions nor your sins. If ye forsake the Lord and serve strange gods, then he will turn and do you evil, after that He hath done you good" (Josh. 24:19-20).

It is this exclusive nature of Israel's relationship to God that is conveyed in the declaration: "The Lord, He [alone] is God." To us, the affirmation that the Lord alone is God can serve to express the truth that our re-ligious convictions must permeate every facet of our life and being. Too often our religion is ambivalent. We mouth pious phrases as we perform impious deeds. "Thou shalt be wholehearted with the Lord thy God" (Deut. 18.13) is the sentence in which Moses summarizes his plea to his people that they should not engage in the idolatrous and superstitious practices of the nations around them. The willingness to be alone in one's faith amid the diverting fashions of the time is the conclusive relevance of this summation of the liturgy.

Adonai and *Elohim*

Adonai and *Elohim* occur together in the prayers recited on all occasions, be they in the liturgy of the synagogue service, or in the blessings of thanksgiving recited
on various occasions. In the Bible and even more so in
the Talmud, *Elohim* connotes the concept of God as
Creator whose ultimate purposes and ways are beyond
man's ken, while *Adonai* connotes the personal experience of God as the Source and Sanction of man's spiritual
life. Already in the Torah, *Adonai* is associated with the
divine qualities of love and compassion. "I am the Lord
[*Adonai*] and I appeared to Abraham, and unto Isaac
and unto Jacob as God Almighty [*El Shaddai*], but by
my name *Adonai* I made Me not known to them . . .
Wherefore say unto the children of Israel: I am the
Lord [*Adonai*] and I will bring you out from under the
burdens of the Egyptians and I will deliver you from their
bondage" (Exod. 6:3-6).

In the preceding passage, we are told that it was as
El Shaddai ("God Almighty") that God appeared to the
patriarchs, but that it was as *Adonai* that He manifested
His concern for His tormented people. Likewise, in our
prayers we address God as *Adonai* as we seek His nearness, as we experience Him as our Stay and our Shield
in times of trouble, as the Source of our blessings and
the answer to our quest for life's meaning.

But in addition, the Rabbis associated the name
Adonai with moral practices which man is expected to
perform. On the verse "Whosoever shall call on the
name of the Lord shall be delivered" (Joel 3:5) the
Midrash comments that by this is meant that as God
is compassionate and gracious, slow to anger and abounding in kindness (Exod. 34:7), so must man strive to cultivate the same qualities (*Sifre Ekev*, 49). The meaning of
the "Imitation of God" is even more explicitly given in
this passage:

Said Rabbi Hanna ben Hanina: "What does Scripture mean
when it says, 'After the Lord your God shall ye walk?' (Deut.
13:5) Is it possible to walk after the Divine Presence? Is it not
said, 'For the Lord thy God is a devouring fire?' (*ibid.*, 4:24)
This means rather that one should follow the attributes of the
Holy One. As He visits the sick (Gen. 18:1), so thou visit the

sick. As He comforts the bereaved (Gen. 25:11), do thou likewise . . ." (Sotah 14a).

The same concept is reflected in a midrash which relates that when Abraham practiced charity and loving-
kindness, God said to him, "You have chosen My profession, therefore you shall also become like Me, an ancient of days" (*Gen. Rabbah,* 58:9).

The association of *Adonai* with the duty to be just
and compassionate is already established in the Torah's
"Holiness Code" (Lev. 19:1-37):

When ye reap the harvest of your land, thou shalt not wholly
reap the corner of thy field . . . [or] glean thy vineyard . . .
[or] gather the fallen fruit of the vineyard . . . leave them for
the poor and the stranger: I am the Lord your God [*Adonai*]
(Lev. 19:9-10).

Ye shall not steal; neither shall ye deal falsely, nor lie one to
another. Ye shall not swear by My name falsely . . . I am the
Lord [*Adonai*] (Lev. 19:11).

Thou shalt not oppress thy neighbor, nor rob him; the wages
of a hired servant shall not abide with thee [overnight]. Thou
shalt not curse the deaf, nor put a stumbling-block before the
blind, but thou shalt fear thy God: I am the Lord [*Adonai*]
(Lev. 19:13-15).

Ye shall do no unrighteousness in judgment; thou shalt not
respect the person of the poor [be partial to the poor] nor
favor the person of the mighty; but in righteousness shalt thou
judge thy neighbor. Thou shalt not go up and down as a tale-
bearer [slanderer] among the people; neither shalt thou stand
idly by the blood of thy neighbor [when your neighbor's life
is threatened]: I am the Lord [*Adonai*] (Lev. 19:15-17).

Thou shalt not hate thy brother in thy heart; thou shalt surely
rebuke thy neighbor and not [lest you] bear sin because of him.
Thou shalt not take vengeance nor bear any grudge against
the children of thy people, but thou shalt love thy neighbor as
thyself: I am the Lord [*Adonai*] (Lev. 19:17-19).

Bible and Talmud alike teach that when we emulate
God's love we serve as the witnesses to His reality and
that when we so fail to act, we lead others to doubt and
even deny His reality. This is rather boldly stated in the
following rabbinic comment:

The Day of Atonement (Yom Kippur)   285

"Ye are My witnesses," says the Lord, "and I am God" (Isa. 43:12). When you are My witnesses, I am God, but when you are not My witnesses, I am not God (*Sifre, 346*).

Comments on the text

The Talmud forbids the recitation of "Hear O Israel the Lord is our God the Lord is One" more than once at a time, since repetition might seem to avow belief in "two deities" (Ber. 33b). There being no interdiction against the repetition of the two other declarations, they are recited three times and seven times respectively, because each of these numbers bears with it sacred associations in Jewish tradition. Here are some examples of the symbolism attributed to the number "three":

The third month was chosen for the revelation because everything that is closely connected with the Torah and with Israel is triple in number. The Torah consists of three parts: The Pentateuch, The Prophets, and the Writings. The oral law consists of *Midrash, Halakhah,* and *Haggadah.* The communications between God and Israel were carried out by three: Moses, Aaron, and Miriam. Israel itself consist of three divisions; priest, Levite, and layman. The patriarchs are three in number: Abraham, Isaac, and Jacob (*Pesikta de Rav Kahana,* ed. Buber pp. 186-187).

Already in the Torah, the number "seven" is an index of emphasis and importance: The seventh day of the week is the Sabbath, each seventh year is a sabbath of complete rest for the land to lie fallow (Lev. 25:4) and for the remission of debts (Deut. 15:1-2). The year of jubilee occurs after each seventh period of seven years (Lev. 25:8-9). Finally, the solemn Holy Days of Rosh Hashanah and Yom Kippur are observed during the seventh month of the Hebrew calendar.*

A symbolism attributed in post-talmudic times to the threefold recitation of the *Barukh Shem* is that it is meant to correspond with the threefold liturgical declaration: "The Lord is King, the Lord was King, the Lord shall be King forever and ever" (*Levush,* 623). The sevenfold exclamation of "The Lord, He is God" has been interpreted as symbolizing the idea of God's universal sovereignty, since His abode is "beyond the seven

* See also *Pesikta de Rav Kahana,* ed. B. Mandelbaum, pp. 343-44.

heavens" (*Tosefot* on *amar pesuka pesuka vekafleh*, Ber. 33a).

IN CONCLUSION

Judaism exhibits the way of living life in holiness. The holiness which Judaism defines is not that which the hermit seeks, in isolation from society. Probably warning his contemporaries against separatist sects, who abandoned life's normal routine in anticipation of the imminent end of the world, Hillel said, "Do not withdraw from the community" (Ab. 2:5). Even more explicit was his younger contemporary, Hanina ben Dosa, who taught: "He in whom his fellowmen find pleasure, God finds pleasure in him, and he in whom his fellowmen find no pleasure, God finds no pleasure in him" (*ibid.*, 3:11). Judaism's deeply rooted belief in *Olam Haba* ("The World to Come") did not lead to the derogation of this life. Rather, the attainment of *Olam Haba* was conceived of as the result of an earthly life of moral, intellectual, and spiritual attainment. The Rabbis taught that by living a life of *Kedushah* (holiness) man has indeed a foretaste of the world to come, but that his gaze must ever be directed to the supreme goal of this life: to live, as it were, in the constant companionship of God. George Foote Moore, in his monumental study of rabbinic Judaism, writes:

Judaism was the public as well as the personal religion of the Jewish people. A Jew did not embrace it nor adhere to it to escape the perils of the soul beyond the tomb, much less the retributive justice of God. Religion, in the higher conception of Judaism, was not a means to that or any other end; it was the divinely appointed *end*.

Wholehearted and whole-souled love to God was its essence; its duties to God and man were truly done only when done for God's sake, or for their own sake, not for any self-regarding motive.*

The long blast of the *shofar* is followed by the recital of the *Maariv* service. But the return to the normal rou-

* George Foote Moore, *Judaism in the First Centuries of the Christian Era* (Cambridge:Harvard University Press, 1927), II, 320-21.

tine was further delayed for a little while by the *medak-dekim*—those endowed with an extra measure of piety. Of them, the Maharil (Germany, 1365-1427) relates as follows:

Immediately after *Maariv,* those who are *medakdekim* take the first step in the construction of the *sukkah* and thus proceed from one *mitzvah* (i.e., the observance of Yom Kippur) to the other (that of the *sukkah*) (Rama, in *Orah Hayyim,* 624:5).

During the Ten Days of Awe, Judaism calls on its adherents to contemplate the meaning and purpose of life with a view to redirecting their life along the paths that lead to God and godly conduct. Five days after Yom Kippur comes Sukkot, and a full transition is made from the awesome consideration of our failures and shortcomings to a sharing of joy with "the stranger, and the fatherless, and the widow, that are within thy gates" (Deut. 16:14). That joy is *Simhah Shel Mitzvah*—the joy of performing the will of God.

ת' ו' ש' ל' ב' ע'•

GLOSSARY

Adonai (*lit.* "Lord"). The name which the Rabbis interpret as connoting God's quality of mercy.

Akedah (*lit.* "binding"). The biblical account of how Abraham met the test of loyalty when asked by God to offer Isaac as a sacrifice (Gen. 22).

Al Het (*lit.* "for the sin"). A series of confessions alphabetically arranged, specifying sins of thought or deed, for which God's forgiveness is asked on Yom Kippur.

Aliyah, pl. *aliyot* (*lit.* "going up"). An honor bestowed on a person who is "called up" to the Torah.

Amidah (*lit.* "standing"). The prayers silently recited by the congregation in a standing position.

Aron (*lit.* "closet"). The ark containing the scrolls of the Torah.

Arvit, or **Maariv.** The evening service.

Aseret Hadibrot, or **Aseret Hadevarim.** The Ten Commandments.

Ashkenazic (*lit.* "German"). The liturgical rites of the Jews in Central and Eastern Europe.

Avinu Malkenu (*lit.* "Our Father, Our King"). A litany of brief supplications, each of which begins with the words: "Our Father, Our King."

Avodah (*lit.* "service"). The service of the prescribed sacrificial offerings brought into the Temple. In the Yom Kippur liturgy the word designates that part of the service which recalls the rites anciently conducted in the Temple on the Day of Atonement. The word also denotes the first of the last three blessings of the *Amidah*.

Avot (*lit.* "fathers"). The first blessing of the *Amidah,* so called because it refers to God as the God of the patriarchs.

Baal Kore (*lit.* "the man who reads"). A popularly used connotation for a person who reads the Torah at a synagogue service.

Barukh (*lit.* "praised," or "blessed"). The opening word of a *Berakhah*.

Berakhah (*lit.* "blessing"). A prayer of praise or gratitude.

Bet Din (*lit.* "court"). A term designating the High Court at Jerusalem and later at Jamnia, which made decisions and proclamations regarding the calendar.

Bimah (*lit.* "platform"). The raised place of the lectern from which the service is conducted and the Torah is read.

Birkat Hagomel (*lit.* "blessing of thanksgiving"). A set prayer of gratitude to be recited by one who has recovered from a severe illness, or who has had a narrow escape from danger.

Birkhot Hanehenin (*lit.* "blessings on things enjoyed"). Prescribed blessings recited before partaking of food or drink.

Elohim (*lit.* "God"). The name which the Rabbis interpret as connoting God's quality of justice.

Gaon (*lit.* "eminence"). The title of the heads of the Babylonian academies, from the sixth to the eleventh centuries.

Gemara (*lit.* "study"). The discussions and deliberations on the text of the Mishnah conducted in the talmudical academies of Babylonia and Palestine. The Talmud comprises the Mishnah and the Gemara.

Geulah (*lit.* "redemption"). A blessing in the morning service, and a similar one in the evening service.

Haftarah (*lit.* "conclusion"). A selection from the Books of the Prophets read at the conclusion of the Torah reading on Sabbaths, holidays, and fast days.

Halakhah (*lit.* "rule"). An accepted decision in rabbinic law.

Hallel (*lit.* "praise"). Psalms 113-118 recited on the Festivals, New Moons, and Hanukkah. *Hallel* is not recited on Rosh Hashanah or Yom Kippur.

Hatzi Kaddish (*lit.* "half *Kaddish*"). The first part of the *Kaddish* doxology. The full *Kaddish* is called *Kaddish Shalem*.

Havdalah (*lit.* "division," or "distinction"). A prayer and ritual which mark the end of a Sabbath or Festival day and the entering of an ordinary day or weekday.

Hazarat Hashatz (*lit.* "repetition by the *Sheliah Tzibbur* [reader]"). The reader's repetition of the *Amidah*.

Hodaah (*lit.* "thanksgiving"). The second of the last three blessings of the *Amidah*.

Kaddish (*lit.* "sanctification"). The prayer which marks the end of a unit of a service and which is also recited as a mourner's prayer.

Kaddish Titkabbal. A text of the *Kaddish* which includes the petition beginning with *titkabbel:* "May the prayers of the house of Israel be accepted."

Kavanah (*lit.* "intention"). Sincere devotion in prayer.

Kedushah (*lit.* "sanctification"). A doxology, recited during the repetition of the *Amidah,* which includes the "Thrice Holy" (*Kadosh, Kadosh, Kadosh*) response.

Kedushat Hayom (*lit.* "the sanctification of the day"). The fourth blessing of an *Amidah* read on Sabbaths, New Moons, and holidays. Such a blessing makes reference to the sanctity of the specific day.

Kerovah, pl. *kerovot* (*lit.* "prayer"). A schematic series of poems interpolated into the blessings of the *Amidah*.

Ketuvim (*lit.* "writings"). "Hagiographa," the Hebrew designation of the third division of the Holy Scriptures.

Kiddush (*lit.* "sanctification"). A prayer over wine, recited on Sabbath eve and on the eve of a holiday.

Kiddush Hashem (*lit.* "The Sanctification of the Name"). The term is most often applied to the act of martyrdom, but is applicable to any noble deed or *mitzvah* whereby "the name of God is sanctified."

Kittel. The white cotton garment worn on the High Holy Days, to symbolize the confidence that God forgives the truly repentant sinner.

Kol Nidre (*lit.* "all vows"). A formula for the absolution of vows, recited at the opening of the Yom Kippur evening service.

Maariv, or **Arvit.** The evening service.

Mahzor (*lit.* "cycle"). A prayer book containing the liturgy for the High Holy Days or Festivals.

Maftir (*lit.* "he who concludes"). The person called to the concluding section of the Torah reading. He is so designated because he reads the *Haftarah.*

Malkhut Shamayim. The Kingship of God.

Malkhuyot (*lit.* "kingship verses"). A section of the Rosh Hashanah *Musaf* service which contains ten biblical verses referring to the universal Kingship of God.

Meturgamon (*lit.* "translator"). The person who reads the Aramaic translation (Targum) that anciently accompanied the Torah reading.

Mezuzah (*lit.* "doorpost"). An encased piece of parchment containing the *Shema,* affixed on the doorpost of a Jewish home.

Middat Hadin. The attribute of Divine Justice.

Middat Harahamim. The attribute of Divine Mercy.

Midrash (*lit.* "interpretation"). An interpretation, or homily, based on a rabbinic exposition of a biblical verse. The plural, *Midrashim,* is applied to texts or collections of such homilies. The singular also designates any citation from a midrashic source.

Minhag (*lit.* "custom"). In liturgical terminology, one of the various rites of liturgical usage.

Minhah (*lit.* "meal offering"). The afternoon service.

Minyan (*lit.* "number"). Quorum of ten males over the age of thirteen, needed for a congregational service and for certain other religious rites.

Mishnah (*lit.* "repetition," or "teaching"). The fundamental code of rabbinic law edited by Judah the Prince toward the end of the second century C.E.

Mitzvah, pl. *mitzvot* (*lit.* "commandment"). A moral or ritual deed motivated by a spirit of obedience to the will of God.

Musaf (*lit.* "addition"). The additional *Amidah* read on Sabbaths, holidays, and New Moons.

Nasi (*lit.* "president"). The head of the Sanhedrin.

Neilah (*lit.* "closing"). The closing service on the Day of Atonement.

Ner Tamid (*lit.* "regular light" and, popularly, "eternal light"). A designation derived from Leviticus 24:2, for the light suspended above the ark.

Neviim (*lit.* "prophets"). The Hebrew name for the second division of the Holy Scriptures.

Parokhet (*lit.* "curtain"). The curtain of the holy ark.

Pesuke de-Zimra (*lit.* "verses of praise"). Psalms and other biblical passages in praise and appreciation of God and His goodness, which are contained in the preliminary part of the daily morning service.

Petihah, pl. *petihot* (*lit.* "opening"). A point in the service where the ark is opened. A *petihah* also denotes an honor given to a person who is designated to open the ark.

Payyetan (*lit.* "poet"). A composer of *piyyutim*.

Piyyut, pl. *piyyutim*. A liturgical poem.

Reshut (*lit.* "permission"). A prelude in which the reader requests the permission of the congregation, and invokes divine aid in his intended interpolation of *piyyutim* into the *Amidah*.

Rimmon, pl. *rimmonim* (*lit.* "pomegranate"). Because the pomegranate was a symbol of fertility and life, the *rimmon* is one of the silver ornaments adorning the headpiece of the Scroll of the Torah, which is a "tree of life."

Sanhedrin. Supreme council and tribunal consisting of seventy-one members. It had jurisdiction over religious matters and more important civil and criminal cases. It met daily, except on the Sabbath and on Festivals.

Selihot, sing. *selihah*. A series of penitential prayers, in which divine forgiveness is implored.

Sephardic (*lit.* "Spanish"). The liturgical rites of the Spanish–Portuguese and the Oriental Jews.

Shaharit. The morning service.

Sheheheyanu (*lit.* "Who has kept us in life"). A prayer of gratitude and celebration, recited on the eve of a holiday and on other special occasions.

Sheliah Tzibbur (*lit.* "emissary of the congregation"). A person who is designated to lead the congregation in the prescribed prayers.

Shem Hameforash (*lit.* "the explicit Name"). The Ineffable Name of God, pronounced only by the High Priest at the Temple.

Shema (*lit.* "hear"). The biblical passages (Deut. 6:4-9, 11:13-21; Num. 15:37,41) recited mornings and evenings. The opening verse is, "Hear (*Shema*) O Israel the Lord is our God, the Lord is One."

Shemoneh Esreh (*lit.* "eighteen"). The *Amidah* for weekdays, which originally contained eighteen blessings.

Shevarim (*lit.* "broken sounds"). One of the *shofar* notes, consisting of three "broken" sounds.

Shofarot (*lit.* "*shofar* verses"). A section of the Rosh Hashanah Musaf service, which includes ten biblical verses referring to the *shofar*.

Siddur (*lit.* "order"). The Prayer Book in use at other than High Holy Day or Festival services.

Sidrah (*lit.* "portion"). The portion of the Torah read on the Sabbath.

Tallit (*lit.* "garment"). A four-cornered prayer shawl with fringes on each corner, as prescribed in Numbers 15:37-41.

Tashlikh (*lit.* "Thou wilt cast"). A custom observed on the first day of Rosh Hashanah, or on the second day, when the first falls on the Sabbath. Prayers are recited near a body of water, and crumbs of bread are thrown in, as an action-symbol of the possibility of man's ability to make a fresh beginning. The prayers include the verses in Micah 7:18-20, "Thou wilt cast their sins into the sea" being one of the verses.

Tefillah (*lit.* "prayer"). In rabbinic literature this word connotes the *Amidah*.

Tefillin (*lit.* "prayer appurtenances"). Two small leather cases, in which are contained parchment slips with the text of the *Shema*. One is fastened with leather thongs to the left arm, and the other to the forehead, in compliance with Deuteronomy 11:18.

Tekiah. An unbroken *shofar* sound ending abruptly.

Teruah. A wavering *shofar* sound consisting of nine staccato notes.

Torah (*lit.* "teaching"). In its limited meaning, the word connotes the Five Books of Moses. In its wider meaning, it connotes any insight or instruction derived from the study of the Bible, the Talmud, and the other classic literature of Judaism. Torah also designates the scroll which contains the Hebrew text of the Penta-teuch.

Tzitzit (*lit.* "fringes"). The fringes on each of the four corners of a *tallit*.

Viddui (*lit.* "confession"). The liturgy of confession in-cluded in each *Amidah* on Yom Kippur.

Yaaleh Veyavo (*lit.* "may our hopes and prayers go up [before God]"). A prayer inserted on holidays and New Moons in the *Amidah,* and in the grace after meals.

Yamim Noraim (*lit.* "Days of Awe"). The ten days of the High Holy Day period, which begins on Rosh Ha-shanah and ends on Yom Kippur.

Yetzer Hara. The evil inclination in human nature.

Yetzer Tov. The good inclination in human nature.

Yizkor (*lit.* "may He remember"). Memorial prayers re-cited in the synagogue on Yom Kippur and on the three Festivals.

Yom Hadin (*lit.* "the Day of Judgment"). One of the designations of Rosh Hashanah.

Yom Hazikkaron (*lit.* "the Day of Remembrance"). One of the designations of Rosh Hashanah used in the liturgy.

Yom Teruah (*lit.* "a day of sounding [the *shofar*]"). One of the designations of Rosh Hashanah used in the liturgy.

Yotzer, pl. *yotzrot* (*lit.* "creation [poems]"). Poems inter-polated into the *Yotzer* ("Who createst light") sec-tion of the morning service.

Zekhut Avot (*lit.* "merit of the patriarchs"). The rabbinic teaching that the good deeds of the patriarchs win favor for their descendants in judgment before God.

Zikhronot (*lit.* "remembrance verses"). A section of the Rosh Hashanah *Musaf* service which contains ten bib-lical verses referring to God's merciful remembrance of mankind and of Israel.

SELECTED BIBLIOGRAPHY

Agnon, Samuel J. *Days of Awe*. New York: Schocken Books, Inc., 1948.

Barish, Louis. *High Holiday Liturgy*. New York: The Jonathan David Co., 1959.

Baron, Salo W. "Worship: Unity Amidst Diversity," *A Social and Religious History of the Jews,* Vol. VII, pp. 62-134. Philadelphia: The Jewish Publication Society of America, 1958.

Davidson, Israel. *Mahzor Yannai*. New York: The Jewish Theological Society of America, 1919.

———. *Thesaurus of Mediaeval Hebrew Poetry*. New York: The Jewish Theological Seminary of America, 1929.

Finesinger, Sol B. "The Shofar," *Hebrew Union College Annual,* Vols. VIII-IX, 1931-32.

Finkelstein, Louis. "The Development of the Amidah." *Jewish Quarterly Review,* XVI, pp. 11 ff.

———. "Jewish Religion: Its Beliefs and Practices," *The Jews, Their History, Culture and Religion,* ed. by Louis Finkelstein, pp. 1739-1799. New York: Harper & Row, Publishers, 1960.

———. "The Ten Martyrs," *Essays and Studies in Memory of Linda R. Miller*. New York, 1938. Privately printed.

Freehof, Solomon B. *The Small Sanctuary*. Cincinnati: Union of American Hebrew Congregations, 1942.

Garfiel, Evelyn. *The Service of the Heart*. New York: National Academy for Adult Jewish Studies, 1958.

Ginzberg, Louis. *Legends of the Jews*. 7 vols. Philadelphia: The Jewish Publication Society of America, 1928.

———. "The Religion of the Jews in the Time of Jesus," *Hebrew Union College Annual,* Vol. I, 1924.

Gordis, Robert. *The Ladder of Prayer*. New York: National Academy for Adult Jewish Studies, 1956.

———. *A Faith For Moderns*. New York: Bloch Publishing Co., Inc., 1960.

Greenberg, Simon. *The Jewish Prayer Book: Its Ideals and Values*. New York: National Academy for Adult Jewish Studies, 1957.

Hertz, Joseph H. *The Authorized Daily Prayer Book*. New York: Bloch Publishing Co., Inc., 1952.

Heschel, Abraham Joshua. *God in Search of Man*. New York: Farrar, Straus & Company, Inc., 1955.

———. *Man's Quest for God*. New York: Charles Scribner's Sons, 1954.

Idelsohn, A. Z. "The Kol Nidre Tune," *Hebrew Union College Annual*, Vols. VIII-IX, 1931-32, pp. 493-509.

———. *Jewish Liturgy and Its Development*. New York: Holt, Rinehart and Winston, Inc., 1932.

Italiener, Bruno. "The Mussaf-Kedushah," *Hebrew Union College Annual*, Vol. XXVI, 1955.

Kadushin, Max. *Organic Judaism*. New York: The Jewish Theological Seminary of America, 1938.

———. *The Rabbinic Mind*. New York: The Jewish Theological Seminary of America, 1952.

Kaplan, Mordecai M. *The Meaning of God in Modern Jewish Religion*. New York: Behrman House, Inc., 1937.

Kaufman, Yehezkel. *The Religion of Israel*. Chicago: The University of Chicago Press, 1960. Translated and abridged by Moshe Greenberg.

Kieval, Herman. *The High Holy Days*. New York: Burning Bush Press, 1959.

Liebreich, Leon J. "The *Pesuke de-Zimra* Benedictions," *Jewish Quarterly Review*, Vol. XLI, pp. 255-67.

———. "Aspects of the New Year Liturgy," *Hebrew Union College Annual*, Vol. XXXIV, pp. 125-175, 1963.

Moore, George Foot. *Judaism in the First Centuries of the Christian Era*. Cambridge: Harvard University Press, 1930.

Schechter, Solomon. *Aspects of Rabbinic Theology*. New York: Schocken Books, Inc., 1961.

Scholem, Gershom G. *Major Trends in Jewish Mysticism*. New York: Schocken Books, Inc., 1946.

Spiegel, Shalom. "On Mediaeval Hebrew Poetry," *The Jews, Their History, Culture and Religion*, ed. by Louis Finkelstein. New York: Harper & Row, Publishers, 1949, pp. 884-892.

Wieder, Naphtali. *Islamic Influences on the Jewish Worship*. Oxford: Oxford University Press, 1957.

Werner, Eric. *Sacred Bridge*. New York: Columbia University Press, 1959.

Zimmels, Hirsch Jacob. *Askenazim and Sephardim*. New York: Oxford University Press, Inc., 1958.

About the Author

Rabbi Max Arzt, Vice-Chancellor of The Jewish Theological Seminary of America and its Israel Goldstein Professor of Practical Theology, was born in Stanislaw, Poland, and came to the United States with his parents at the age of four. In 1918 he received the degree of Bachelor of Science from the College of the City of New York; in 1921, the degree of Master of Arts from Columbia University; and in 1934, the degree of Doctor of Hebrew Literature from The Jewish Theological Seminary, which awarded him the honorary degree of Doctor of Divinity in 1950.

Rabbi Arzt is the author of talmudic researches which appeared in the Jubilee Volumes published in honor of Professor Alexander Marx and Professor Mordecai M. Kaplan. He is a contributing editor of *Judaism,* and is one of seven scholars presently engaged in translating the Hebrew Scriptures into English for The Jewish Publication Society of America.

For nearly twenty years Rabbi Arzt served actively in the rabbinate: from 1921 to 1924 as rabbi of Temple Beth El, Stamford, Connecticut; and for fifteen years as rabbi of Temple Israel, Scranton, Pennsylvania. During his service as rabbi in Scranton, Doctor Arzt was a member of Governor Earle's Commission on Public Relief and Assistance, for the Commonwealth of Pennsylvania, which abolished the Poor Boards and established the State Department of Public Assistance and Relief. In 1959 Dr. Arzt was a United States delegate to the Atlantic (NATO) Congress in London. He was a Charter Member of the Advisory Council of the International Movement for Atlantic Union, Inc.

Doctor Arzt lives in New York City with his wife, Esther. They have three children: Miriam, who is married to Rabbi Saul I. Teplitz, and two sons, Rabbi A. David Arzt and Rabbi Raphael B. Arzt.